Doing early childhood research

International perspectives on theory and practice

Glenda Mac Naughton
Sharne A. Rolfe
Iram Siraj-Blatchford

OPEN UNIVERSITY PRESS

Open University Press
McGraw-Hill Education
McGraw-Hill House
Shoppenhangers Road
Maidenhead
Berkshire
United Kingdom
SL6 2QL

email:enquiries@openup.co.uk
world wide web: www.openup.co.uk

and
Two Penn Plaza
New York, NY 10121-2289, USA

First published in 2001
Reprinted 2004

A catalogue record of this book is available from the British Library

ISBN 0 335 20902 5

Typeset in 10.5/12pt Sabon by Midland Typesetters, Maryborough, Victoria
Printed and bound by Bell & Bain Ltd., Glasgow

10 9 8 7 6 5 4 3

Contents

List of tables   v
List of contributors   vi

Introduction—*Glenda Mac Naughton, Sharne A. Rolfe,
Iram Siraj-Blatchford*   x

Part I: The nature of research
  1 Research as a tool—*Sharne A. Rolfe and
      Glenda Mac Naughton*   3
  2 The research process—*Glenda Mac Naughton and
      Sharne A. Rolfe*   12
  3 Paradigms, methods and knowledge—*Patrick Hughes*   31
  4 Doing research for the first time—*Sharon Ryan and
      Sheralyn Campbell*   56
  5 Ethics in early childhood research—*Margaret M.Coady*   64

Part II: Analysis and design
  6 Design issues—*Alan Hayes*   75
  7 Quantitative designs and statistical analysis—
      Linda Harrison   93
  8 Qualitative designs and analysis—*Anne Edwards*   117
  9 Equity issues in research design—*Susan Grieshaber*   136

Part III: The research process in action

10   Surveys and questionnaires: an evaluative case study
        —*Iram Siraj-Blatchford and John Siraj-Blatchford*   149
11   Interviewing children—*Liz Brooker*   162
12   Interviewing adults—*Leslie Cannold*   178
13   An ethnographic approach to researching young
        children's learning—*Iram Siraj-Blatchford and
        John Siraj-Blatchford*   193
14   Action research—*Glenda Mac Naughton*   208
15   Direct observation—*Sharne A. Rolfe*   224
16   Policy research—*Ann Farrell*   240
17   Developing reciprocity in a multi-method small-scale
        research study—*Mindy Blaise Ochsner*   254

Appendix: Getting the terms right   264
Glossary   268
References   275
Index   300

List of tables

7.1 Means, standard deviations and bivariate-correlations
between relevant maternal, child and family variables   103

7.2 Proportion of mothers nominating reasons for choice of
care by child-care type   105

7.3 Descriptive statistics for independent and relevant variables
by infant–mother attachment (A, B, C, D) classification   106

7.4 Logistic regression analysis for predictors of secure versus
insecure attachment classification   111

List of contributors

Liz Brooker is currently researching and teaching Early Childhood Education at the London University, Institute of Education. She was an Early Years teacher in London for twenty years, and developed particular interests in the learning of bilingual and minority ethnic children. She is additionally interested in parental involvement in their children's learning; in the effects of pedagogic discourses on the learning of different class and cultural groups; and in the explanations offered by social theorists for children's educational outcomes.

Sheralyn Campbell is a doctoral student at the University of Melbourne, in the Department of Learning and Educational Development. She has worked in a range of child-care services within the Australian context and has been involved in training early childhood students. Currently, Sheralyn is a member of an action research team working at the Swanston Children's Centre, Melbourne, Australia. Her research interests are materialised in questions about how early childhood theory and practice can be reconceptualised to improve the way social justice and equity operates for staff, students, families, and children in child-care services.

Leslie Cannold is an honorary fellow at the Centre for Applied Philosophy and Public Ethics, and has just submitted her doctoral thesis in the Department of Learning and Educational Development at the University of Melbourne. She has worked for over ten years in the community, academic and business sectors as a qualitative researcher. She is a regular columnist for the *Age* newspaper in Melbourne and the author of *The Abortion Myth: Feminism, morality and the hard choices women make* (Cannold, 1998 and 2000).

Margaret M. Coady is Program Manager in Professional Ethics for the Australian Research Council Special Research Centre for Applied Philosophy and Public Ethics, and a Senior Lecturer in the Early Childhood Studies Unit at the University of Melbourne. She has published widely in professional ethics and children's and families' rights. She has held Research Fellowships at the Center for Human Values at Princeton University, the Rockefeller Center at Bellagio, Italy, and the Kennedy Institute for Ethics at Georgetown University.

Anne Edwards has been undertaking qualitative research in early childhood services and schools for the last twenty years. Her background is in both history and psychology and she works within sociocultural frameworks to explore how adults support children as learners. Her most recent book (Anning and Edwards, 1999) tells the story of a research partnership between the two researchers and twenty early childhood staff as they developed pedagogical strategies for helping children from birth to five become confident learners. She is currently Professor of Pedagogy at the School of Education, University of Birmingham in the United Kingdom.

Ann Farrell is a researcher in the Centre for Applied Studies in Early Childhood, Queensland University of Technology. Her research interests include policy research, family studies and early childhood curriculum. She has researched children and families in the criminal justice system in Australia and the United Kingdom and has an ongoing advisory role with government and community bodies in social, family and education policy. Her experience is as both practitioner and academic, having taught in Australia, Canada and the United Kingdom.

Susan Grieshaber is a Principal Researcher at the Centre for Applied Studies in Early Childhood and a Senior Lecturer in the School of Early Childhood, Queensland University of Technology. She has wide experience as an early childhood teacher in urban and rural communities and has worked with children and families from diverse contexts, including Aboriginal children, children from non-English speaking families, children with disabilities, and children and families from all socioeconomic backgrounds. Her research interests include early childhood curriculum, families and gender. She has also written about policy in early childhood education.

Linda Harrison is Senior Lecturer in Early Childhood Education at Charles Sturt University, Bathurst, New South Wales, having recently returned to work in regional Australia after a number of years at metropolitan universities in Sydney and Melbourne. Her research experience includes ten years of collaborative work with the Sydney Family Development Project, a longitudinal study of 150 children and their families, based at the Department of Psychology, Macquarie University, Sydney. Linda's research interests lie in the broad area of child-care and family influences on children's development, centred specifically on the nature of children's relationships with important adults and the ways these relationships impact on children's socio-emotional and cognitive adjustment at key periods in development.

Alan Hayes is Professor of Early Childhood Studies and Foundation Dean and Head of the Australian Centre for Educational Studies, a Division of Macquarie University, Sydney. With 25 years' experience as a researcher in the area of applied developmental psychology, his particular focus has been on issues related to risk, resilience and individual differences. Currently, he is researching the relationships among child development, family functioning and community networks and supports. The work particularly explores the contribution of early childhood services to community development, the prevention of educational and social problems and the provision of better contexts for the development of children.

Patrick Hughes is a Lecturer in Communications at Deakin University, Victoria, having taught Media and Cultural Studies at London University and at the Open University. His research interests are: how multinational corporations affect the entertainment industry; how science centres popularise science; and staff–parent relationships in early childhood services. His work has been published as books, book chapters and articles in Australia, the United Kingdom and the United States.

Glenda Mac Naughton is an Associate Professor in the Department of Learning and Educational Development at the University of Melbourne. She has worked in the early childhood field for nearly 30 years, as a practitioner and a manager and as a senior policy advisor to government in the United Kingdom and Australia. Glenda's early childhood research has focused on social justice and equity issues and she has published widely from her research. She is currently researching how gender, class and race intersect and construct young children's learning, and facilitating several practitioner action research groups.

Mindy Blaise Ochsner currently works in the Department of Elementary Education at Rhode Island College, Providence, in the United States. Her research experiences have been qualitative in nature, including small studies conducted in her preschool classroom as a teacher researcher, large-scale projects documenting how standards-based education impacts on classroom instruction, and her dissertation, which documented and analysed the social construction of gender in a preschool classroom. Her research interests include exploring gender in early childhood classrooms and using feminist theoretical frameworks to inform research designs, methods and data analysis.

Sharne A. Rolfe is a Psychologist and Senior Lecturer in early childhood development at the University of Melbourne. She has been researching child development for over twenty years, with a primary focus on observation of interactions and relationships between infants and parents, infants and caregivers and between preschool-aged peers. She provides clinical observational assessments of child development and family relationships for child-care and protection agencies and is a consultant to the Victorian Government in regard to high-risk infants.

Sharon Ryan is assistant professor of early childhood education in the Graduate School of Education at Rutgers University in the United States. She began her work as a researcher by conducting qualitative evaluation studies of a special education programme and a teacher research project in South Australia, and several children's arts programmes in New York City. Since completing the poststructural case study of student choice in a kindergarten classroom reported in Chapter 4 she has begun work on a qualitative and quantitative study of how a group of teachers and their students enact and experience a statewide early childhood policy.

Iram Siraj-Blatchford is Professor of Early Childhood Education and the Head of the Child Development and Learning Group at the University of London's postgraduate Institute of Education. She has researched on early childhood policy, curriculum quality and pedagogy and social justice. She is committed to research which informs the demise of cycles of disadvantage. Iram has conducted funded research in several countries for organisations such as UNESCO, the Aga Khan Foundation, the Leverhulme Trust and the British government. She is currently co-director of a five-year longitudinal study, the Effective Provision of Pre-school Education, funded by the Department for Education and Employment in the United Kingdom, and an evaluator of the Early Excellence Centres.

John Siraj-Blatchford is a Senior Lecturer at Homerton College, Cambridge. He has taught in infant, primary and secondary schools. In the past ten years he has conducted a number of research projects and his publications have included more than a dozen papers in refereed journals. *Educating the Whole Child*, a book jointly edited with Iram Siraj-Blatchford, was published by the Open University Press in 1995; his *Learning Technology, Science and Social Justice* was published by Education Now in 1996. *Researching into Student Learning and Support* (with Margaret Jones and Kate Ashcroft) was published by Kogan Page in 1997 and *Design, Technology and Science in the Early Years* (with Iain MacLeod Brundenell) was published by the Open University Press in 1999.

Introduction

**Glenda Mac Naughton   Sharne A. Rolfe
Iram Siraj-Blatchford**

This book is about how to conduct research in and about the early childhood years. It is written specifically for novice and early career researchers and their mentors. The book shows the many different ways in which research in early childhood can be approached and emphasises that there is no one right way to conduct research in early childhood. However, we do believe that all research needs to be theoretically grounded, well designed, rigorously analysed, feasible and ethically fair and just. The book attempts to show how to do this from within diverse theoretical traditions and paradigms.

To accomplish this task we have drawn on a team of international early childhood researchers who represent the multi-disciplinary nature of much early childhood research. They bring an authority, breadth and depth to the discussion of research in early childhood that we believe would not be possible in a sole-authored text.

We see two main reasons for publishing a book on the research process written specifically for the novice early childhood researcher. First, as early childhood studies are multi-disciplinary, standard texts written for students of the social sciences or the humanities are often not sufficiently broad for the needs of the early childhood field. Second, general education research texts often focus specifically on research in classrooms and thus often do not meet the needs of the early childhood researcher, who must be familiar with methods and techniques relevant to research in the multitude of contexts experienced by the child from birth through to the early years of school.

In Chapters 1 and 2 Rolfe and Mac Naughton attempt to 'demystify' research by emphasising that the research process is simply a tool by which we can answer important questions about early childhood. Readers are shown how to:

- Select a topic
- Review literature
- Formulate a research issue/question
- Design research
- Collect data
- Sample populations
- Explore questions of validity
- Process/analyse data
- Draw research conclusions
- Write research reports.

Chapter 3 introduces readers to four major research paradigms that underpin early childhood research—positivism, interpretivism, structuralism and poststructuralism. Hughes uses case studies of research on children and the media to explain these paradigms and show how they influence the researchers' choice of method and their results. Chapter 4 draws on the experiences of Campbell and Ryan to highlight the practical and theoretical issues faced when beginning research. They use a conversation with each other to capture the highlights, challenges and pitfalls in different phases of the research process. Chapter 5 discusses key ethical issues in research, with a focus on those that arise in early childhood research. In particular, it canvasses the ethics of researching with children and how to manage informed consent in research with children, using international comparisons to highlight how the early childhood field addresses ethical dilemmas.

Part II introduces the reader to key issues in research design and analysis. In Chapter 6 Hayes uses examples of recently published early childhood research to provide a foundation understanding of design. He discusses design options (experimental, quasi-experimental and non-experimental), the dimension of time (in retrospective, prospective, cross-sectional and longitudinal designs) and sampling issues to do with both the selection of participants and the settings of research. Harrison in Chapter 7 provides an overview of the information needed by researchers to undertake simple quantitative research in early childhood. She brings this discussion to life using her own research to work through the meaning of statistical analysis, to discuss probability levels and explore what 'statistical significance' means. Her discussion explains statistical concepts and procedures, descriptive statistics, inferential statistics and computer analyses. Edwards (Chapter 8) provides an overview of the information needed by researchers to undertake simple qualitative research in early childhood. In the final chapter in Part II, Grieshaber introduces the reader to a series of design principles for ensuring equity in research for those researching in multicultural settings, researching with indigenous peoples and researching with women.

Part III presents case studies illustrating some of the most commonly used early childhood research methods—including surveys and questionnaires, interviewing, ethnography, action research, direct observation, policy research and multi-method small-scale research.

In each chapter a published early childhood researcher has written a narrative about how they conducted a specific research project, or commented on a number of published research projects. To ensure that the novice researcher is able to readily compare and contrast methods, each writer explores questions that include: 'How did you arrive at this research question?', 'How did you answer it and why did you do it this way?' and 'How did you interpret what you found?

We use several devices throughout the book to ensure that it will act as a readily accessible, practical and user-friendly *aide-mémoire* for the novice and early career researcher:

- closure summary in each chapter of the key ideas covered;
- boxed summaries, checklists and/or explanations of key concepts, processes and themes in all chapters;
- post-text questions in each chapter to help readers review their learning and extend their thinking about the issues/methods raised in the chapter;
- further reading lists, annotated to show how they might best be used to further understanding of the material covered in the chapter; and
- a glossary of key terms is supplied at the end of the book.

Part I

The nature of research

1

Research as a tool

Sharne A. Rolfe and Glenda Mac Naughton

Have you ever done research? If you have not, or if you are very new to it, you may be feeling daunted by the thought of becoming a researcher. When we approach anything new we generally feel a combination of emotions, both positive and negative. But with growing experience and knowledge comes confidence. Sometimes the hardest part is taking the first step!

Our aim is to demystify research and the research process. We want this book to build students' confidence so they are able to take that first step. There is nothing like experience, under the guidance of those more skilled, to promote optimal learning. In this book you will have the opportunity to hear from many experienced researchers working on a diverse range of topics, using a wide range of methods and approaching research from different philosophical perspectives or **paradigms**.

If you are already an experienced researcher, we hope this book will facilitate your attempts to demystify research for your students. In this chapter we emphasise that research is simply a tool that helps us answer important questions about early childhood, questions that would remain unanswered were it not for the willingness of practitioners and academics alike to engage in the research process. Research is about discovery. Research creates knowledge. The best research will always involve close, ongoing collaboration between those who plan the research, those who carry it out, those who participate in it and those for whom the results have impact. Research is hard work, but it should also be fun.

WHY BOTHER WITH RESEARCH?

Given the skill it requires, the resources (both financial and human) it consumes and the time it takes, an important question to be answered is: 'Why do research at all?'. Research can have negative, as well as positive outcomes. In her discussion of research **ethics**, Coady (Chapter 5) describes the case of 'Genie', who was isolated in a bedroom of her parents' home for most of her childhood. After she was discovered, she became the focus of intensive research directed to understanding how these early experiences had influenced her development (see Curtiss, 1977). Many have questioned the impact of this research on 'Genie' and her subsequent life course. The case highlights tensions that may exist between benefits to the participants in research and benefits to the researcher. A clear implication is that researchers must understand and address ethical issues that arise in research, including the need to protect the interests and ongoing welfare of research participants. Such concerns lie at the heart of our choice of research methods and how we go about doing research. This is discussed further by Grieshaber in Chapter 9.

With careful attention to such concerns, can research make positive differences in the lives of children? The answer is a resounding yes! In this book you will find many examples of research that has made, or has the potential to make, such a contribution. Some studies have at their core the quest to describe or to understand. To do this, researchers often favour **qualitative approaches** that encourage complexity and diversity in the research data. For example, Ochsner (Chapter 17) explored how children's understandings of femininity, masculinity and gender norms both resist and maintain the gendered social order of the classroom. To do this, she conducted a detailed case study of one urban preschool classroom, observing the children and developing a relationship with the teacher that enabled her to uncover complexities of gender within that setting that would likely have been inaccessible via other research approaches. Farrell (Chapter 16) used document analysis, questionnaires, interviews and observation to develop an understanding of the lived experiences of incarcerated mothers and their young children. Understandings such as these enable practitioners to rethink what they do, how they do it and how this effects children and their families in a variety of settings. They have the potential to impact on policy directions and how governments respond to emerging social issues.

For other research studies, the aim is explanation, rather than, or in addition to, understanding. This approach lends itself to **quantitative approaches**, in which careful experimental control is essential to conclusions about cause and effect. An example of this approach is found in research on the effects of non-parental child-care on children's development and mother–child relationships (see Harrison, Chapter 7).

Harrison's study, part of the Sydney Family Development Project, involved data collection over time and included assessment of the participant children at ages 1 year, 2.5 years and 6 years. **Longitudinal research** of this kind allows examination of how certain events or experiences impact on children's well-being and development, both currently and at later stages. Another example of this kind of research began in 1955 on the Hawaiian island of Kauai. Extending over more than three decades, the research followed the development and life course of nearly 700 infants who experienced various risk factors pre- and peri-natally (see Werner, 1993). An important outcome of this research has been identification of 'protective factors' that enable some at-risk infants to be resilient to early disadvantage and trauma.

Longitudinal research need not involve such long time frames. One study, a classic in the field of developmental psychology, involving shorter time frames of several months, examined how maternal responsiveness impacts on infant crying over the first year (Bell and Ainsworth, 1972). The study found that infants who were responded to quickly cried less after a period of months than infants whose mothers delayed responding. This finding challenged the prevailing view that responding to infant cries simply reinforces crying behaviour, thus encouraging even more of it. Bell and Ainsworth's research, and similar studies, have helped parents and early childhood practitioners alike gain insights into how adult behaviours impact on children and, more generally, to understand the kinds of experiences that promote optimal outcomes.

Research is also beginning to enlighten us about how different cultures understand development, and what early childhood practitioners can learn from these cultures about care and education of young children (see Grieshaber, Chapter 9). Research thus challenges habitual ways of doing things, and provides reasons to modify, refocus or change. Throughout this book you will have the opportunity to learn from various researchers whose own research has contributed, sometimes in major ways, to just these sorts of outcomes.

WHO CAN DO RESEARCH?

We are all 'amateur' researchers. As humans, we have an inbuilt propensity to want to understand and explain what we experience, to make sense of it. Many developmentalists (for example Jean Piaget) have outlined theories about how we do this. We develop **hypotheses** and then we test them out, usually in haphazard ways with limited data. Sometimes we become inappropriately confident about our amateur research outcomes, reaching hasty and premature conclusions. Racist categorisation of individuals, or groups of people, is an example of this sort of 'research' gone wrong. Sometimes we rely on the opinions or knowledge of others. This is also problematic, as opinions may be based on stereotypes, sometimes passed down through generations. These informal ways of gathering knowledge often lead to faulty or incorrect assumptions and conclusions. Generating research outcomes that have significance, add to our understanding, provide reliable and valid measures and/or explanations requires a different approach altogether. The characteristics of research that can achieve these outcomes are well known. We summarise them later under the rubric of high quality research.

While most research, including early childhood research, is undertaken by people working in or associated with universities or educational institutions, quality research is not the sole province of university-based academics with doctoral degrees. Many people are able to do research that can make a valuable contribution to practice, provided that they have access to sufficient financial and human resources. The questions thus become, 'Who can do high quality research?' and 'Who should do research?'

Wadsworth (1984) argued strongly that those affected by research can and should do research: 'Research is a process legitimated in our society as producing knowledge and therefore ought to be in the hands of those who want to use and benefit from it—particularly when it is information about our own lives' (p. iii).

Applying these ideas to researching early childhood, research can and should be done by parents, children and practitioners. Doing or being part of research can improve professional practice (Wiersma, 2000). Following what is known as the 'Teacher as Researcher' movement (see Elliot, 1991), many practitioners are increasingly involved in researching early childhood. There are good reasons to encourage practitioners to research. It is often more meaningful to other practitioners than university research (for example, Flake et al., 1995) and consequently it is more likely to change practice. Recognising this, an increasing number of early childhood courses include research training as part of their syllabus so that graduates can be researchers as well as informed consumers of the results of research undertaken by others.

LEARNING TO RESEARCH

When you first think about questions to research, you might consult experts, read about different opinions and even talk to your colleagues and friends about their views. This may help you to clarify what it is that you really want to know. But this is not enough to generate high quality research results. Neither is intuition. Irrespective of who is researching, quality research requires knowledge, skill and experience, which can be gained in numerous ways. Reading this book is a great place to start. It is also helpful as you begin to learn about research to have the right sort of attitude to research—that you see it as a tool.

Seeing research as a tool

It is important to understand that research is just a tool we can learn to use. Thinking about research in this way is helpful particularly if the research process seems unduly complex and therefore inaccessible. Thinking about research as a tool means that you as the researcher control the research process, not vice versa. You begin the process by your interest in an early childhood topic or question. Not content to accept what is already known and written about this topic, you want to know more. You want to answer previously ignored questions, or you want to approach old questions from a different angle. Sometimes nobody has previously asked the question you want answered. Research can satisfy your fascination and others can evaluate and benefit from your work.

Some research topics and questions come from our personal or professional experiences. Others arise from careful reading of the literature. When we are just beginning to research, our topic may be given to us so we can focus our attention on planning, designing and executing the research, then evaluating our results, drawing conclusions and writing them up. Regardless of how we come to our topic, it is by learning to use research as a tool that we can achieve an answer to the question or questions with which we set out. We can then inform others of what we have found. The next chapter explores these processes in more detail.

Learning to be sceptical

It is important to note here that research studies rarely stand alone. An important part of research is **replication**. That is, different researchers study the same phenomenon, using the same or similar methods, in order to determine whether the same results will pertain. This helps to establish the **generalisability** of the results and the conclusions based on them. Clearly if one study reports a particular result, but seven further similar studies cannot replicate it, the first study's findings are thrown into question. Certainly one would want to look carefully at the details of how the study was done to establish reasons for the discrepant results. The point is that it is good to be sceptical of research outcomes, just as it is good to be critical in our evaluation of whatever we read or are told. The case of maternal responsiveness to infant crying discussed above illustrates this point well. Although recent research has confirmed Bell and Ainsworth's original findings (for example, Hubbard and van IJzendoorn, 1991), the results have been very actively scrutinised, especially by those espousing theories thrown into doubt (for example Gewirtz and Boyd, 1977).

Some research, however, such as action research (see Chapter 10) or case study research (Chapter 17) is about creating change or understanding in a specific setting rather than producing generalisable results. In this research validity arises through the way the research is conducted and analysed rather than through its replicability and generalisability.

Becoming apprentices

Recognising the challenge involved in learning about the research process, many institutes of higher education provide the opportunity for students to learn about research via an 'apprenticeship' model. That is, the student works closely with an experienced researcher, either on the researcher's own project or on a project that they develop together that is appropriate to the level of skill and resources available to the student. This is one of the best ways to learn about doing research. Early in their course undergraduates can, with guidance, plan and carry out small research projects, often pooling the data they collect with others who have (ideally) conducted the research in the same way.

Preparing for surprises

When we set out to discover things about our social world we are often surprised along the way. By their nature, surprises can't be anticipated. So, no matter how well planned your research endeavour is, expect surprises. Theories, events, well-tested methods, children and adults may each surprise you when you begin research. Achenbach (1978) pointed to some of the common practical surprises that can confront you: 'Sometimes known as Murphy's Law, this hallowed principle states: If anything can go wrong, it will. Equipment failure, experimenter illness, subjects who fail to show up, computer errors, and misunderstandings among coworkers are but a few common examples of Murphy's Law' (p. 189).

Surprises are not always negative, or practical in nature. Theories can surprise you by unsettling your taken-for-granted assumptions about how the world works, and children and adults can surprise you with their responses to your research. These surprises can be exciting, fun, enlightening and reviving. They can motivate you to explore more and challenge you to think differently. Surprises are what good research is all about and what make research meaningful and enjoyable.

We started this chapter by saying that research is about discovery. As you begin your research endeavour, prepare for discovery. Expect the unexpected and ask of it, 'What can I learn from this?' and 'How does this help my research?' After all, if we knew all we needed to know about something then there would be no point researching it! Realise that sometimes the question we start off with isn't the question we end up researching, and that is okay.

'GOOD' RESEARCH AND 'BAD' RESEARCH?

'Good' research does not rely on one particular method or paradigm. However, researchers' views on what is a good research method will be determined by the research paradigm they espouse. There is lively debate among early childhood researchers about the different ways of approaching and doing research involving, among other things, discussion of research agendas, research assumptions, methods and objectives (for example, Cannella and Bailey, 1999).

One example of differing views concerns the optimal relationship between researchers and researched. Dallape (1996) clearly believes that good research rests on a close involvement between them: 'The poor have always been the object of research, they are only rarely the subjects and controllers of knowledge. They have been asked to give information about their way of life, they have seldom been asked to interpret this information . . . people who will be affected by the research must be involved in the whole process' (p. 283).

Other researchers argue that good research maintains an objective distance between researchers and researched. You will find a detailed discussion of how choice of research paradigm influences views of good research in Chapter 3.

Irrespective of the research paradigm you choose, there are some basic principles that underpin all quality research. For us, quality research is always ethical, purposeful, well-designed, transparent, contextualised, credible, careful, imaginative and equitable.

Principles for high quality research
- ethical
- purposeful
- well-designed
- transparent
- contextualised
- credible
- careful
- imaginative
- equitable.

IN OVERVIEW:

- *Ethical research* is based on informed consent, does not harm participants, attempts to benefit them and it makes a positive contribution to knowledge and to the broader social good. (Chapters 5 and 9 offer a more detailed discussion of these issues).
- *Purposeful research* has clear aims and justifiable strategies for working towards these aims. We talk more about this in Chapter 2.
- *Well-designed research* is systematic and designed in a way that is consistent with its topic, theoretical underpinnings, aims, research strategies and methods. Chapters 6, 7 and 8 introduce you to processes for developing well-designed research.
- *Transparent research* allows other people to follow your research trail and the decisions you take at different points in the process. You should be scrupulous about recording what you did and why and how you reached your research decisions, findings and conclusions, so that others can evaluate your conclusions.
- *Contextualised research* acknowledges its own philosophical, theoretical, policy and social contexts. This means that you must be able to show how your research developed in and from a specific theoretical context, and how specific policy and social contexts influenced how you conducted your research and what was found. Chapters 16 and 17 provide examples of strongly contextualised research.
- *Credible research* follows accepted principles for framing research questions, investigating them, analysing the findings and drawing conclusions from them. Chapter 2 details broadly accepted principles for engaging in credible research.
- *Careful research* acknowledges its limited scope and its design limitations. You need to identify these limitations and be careful not to draw conclusions or inferences that ignore these limitations.
- *Imaginative research* is innovative and original. It captures the imagination of the researcher and those that hear about the research. It is unreasonable and inappropriate to expect that every research study will be entirely original. This is particularly the case for beginning researchers. Even experienced researchers, as we have already discussed, may choose to closely follow the design of an earlier study with the aim of establishing whether the results can be replicated. Most research will nonetheless benefit from you bringing your creative skills to the fore when you design and analyse it.
- *Equitable research* acknowledges the biases, interests and concerns of the researcher. You need to think carefully about how your own biases and background might impact on your research. Learning to do equitable research, as outlined in Chapter 9, is central to doing high quality research.

Whether or not research is 'good' hinges on how well the researcher has worked through the various steps that constitute the research process. We begin to discuss these steps in Chapter 2, where we look at how you can bring the principles of quality research to life throughout each phase of your research endeavour. You will find these principles illustrated and amplified many times in the case examples presented throughout this book.

QUESTIONS FOR REFLECTION

- Do you think specific research has influenced your views about young children? Can you provide an example or two?
- Where else have your views come from and how trustworthy do you now feel these sources are?
- Do you know anyone who has done research? What have they told you about their experiences?
- What do you see as the main challenges you face in learning to research?
- What aspects of learning to research excite you?

FURTHER READING

Charles, M. 1998, *Introduction to Educational Research* (3rd. edn), Addison Wesley Longman, New York. Chapter 1: 'Educational Research—its nature and rules of operation' provides a very clear and detailed discussion of what constitutes good scientific educational research that can be readily adapted to research in early childhood.

Goodwin, W. L. and Goodwin, L. D. 1996, *Understanding Quantitative and Qualitative Research in Early Childhood Education*, Teachers College Press, New York. As the name implies this book looks broadly at the nature of the research process as it applies to early childhood education. Chapter 1 includes a discussion of the value of research and some early childhood topics that are the focus of much current research.

Kagan, S. L. and Wechsler, S. 1999, 'Changing realities—changing research', in S. Reifel (ed.), *Advances in Early Education and Day Care Volume 10: Foundations, Adult Dynamics, Teacher Education and Play*, JAI Press, Stamford, Conn. Focusing on the changing nature of human services in the United States, this chapter explores the challenges that researchers now face in evaluating social policy and discusses new research tools, including how the integration of qualitative and quantitative methods offers promise as an alternative to conventional approaches.

2

The research process

Glenda Mac Naughton and Sharne A. Rolfe

Research means finding out about things. To this extent, the job of the researcher is like that of a detective. Both search for clues to advance theories about how and why things happen and start their work with questions about something intriguing, mysterious or puzzling. They then use well-tested methods to gather the clues and information need-ed to help them 'solve', understand or explain their intrigue, mystery or puzzle. This chapter introduces you to the well-tested processes that researchers use to give shape and direction to these efforts.

Like detectives, researchers have different ideas about the best way to do their work. Some researchers pursue their research in a linear, logical and step-by-step way. In more technical terms, this is referred to as a **deductive research methodology**. It is associated with **positivist** paradigms and often uses quantitative approaches to data. Researchers who approach their work this way generally wait until all their data are in before beginning to analyse and draw conclusions. They usually set out to test hypotheses based on theory and research already completed and carefully design their studies with this intention. Examples of this sort of research approach can be seen in Chapter 15. Other researchers have a more fluid and intuitive approach. In technical terms, they engage in what is referred to as an **inductive research methodology** often associated with **interpretivist** and **postmodern** paradigms, often using qualitative approaches to data. The researcher generally tries to avoid too many preconceptions about what will be discovered and is keen to stay close to and analyse the data, emerging theory

12

from it and perhaps even modifying the line of inquiry in response to developing understandings. Examples of this approach can be seen in Chapters 12, 14 and 17.

Both approaches offer important, albeit different, insights into the phenomena of interest. The approach chosen will usually reflect the particular way of looking at the world that the researcher brings to the task. Different sorts of questions also lend themselves to different sorts of approaches—which are not mutually exclusive, however. Many researchers use a combination to gain a more complete picture of what they are interested in. The use of different methods within the same study—**triangulation**—is discussed in Chapter 8.

Regardless of the approach taken, at some point in the research process most researchers find that they need to complete the following steps if they want to generate research that is informative, ethical, meaningful, persuasive and significant:

- selecting a topic
- searching and reviewing the literature
- formulating a specific research issue/question
- designing the research
- collecting data/information
- processing/analysing data
- drawing conclusions
- writing research reports.

In this chapter we summarise what is involved in each of these steps. The remaining chapters show you in more detail how these steps work and how the specific approach that you take influences the role that each of these steps has.

SELECT A TOPIC

Providing and operating services for young children is complex. It requires good information about questions as diverse as:

- How do young children learn, grow and develop?
- How can we best use this knowledge to optimise children's learning, growth and development?
- How is it best to organise, fund and regulate services for young children?
- What curriculum is best suited to young children? Who should decide this?
- How can we ensure services are relevant to the diverse and complex needs of different families and children?
- How is it best to train staff to work with young children?
- What is the best way to staff services for young children?

- How should parents and the wider community be involved in decisions about the operation and provision of services for young children?

This diversity of issues and the complexity within each means that early childhood researchers are rarely short of possible research topics. The issue that many beginning researchers face is not so much finding a topic as selecting one from all their ideas. For instance, in just ten minutes in a workshop on early childhood research, one group of Australian early childhood practitioners identified 22 research questions that they believed needed further exploration. The topics ranged from communication between different sectors within the field to approaches to staff training and job satisfaction through to equity issues of gender and disability. Even if you are not yet an experienced practitioner, your practicum experiences have probably left you wondering about children, their development and how best to care for and educate them. As we explored in Chapter 1, many research topics emerge from our own experiences. Another source of ideas is what we read in books and journals, especially as part of a course of study.

In the face of such diversity, how do you decide? The simple steps that follow can help you to settle on a research topic.

First, choose a topic that interests you personally. Are you interested in any of the following?

- Children's learning, growth and development. What aspect of this interests you?
- The organisation and management of services for young children. What aspect of this interests you?
- Early childhood curriculum, teaching and learning. What aspect of this interests you?
- Community and parent involvement. What aspect of this interests you?
- Policies for young children and their services. What aspect of this interests you?
- Social justice issues for young children. What aspect of this interests you?
- Other issues. What are they?

Second, choose a topic that will be of interest and significance to other people. Research is about exploring relationships between events, seeking explanations about why things happen, comparing approaches to practice, predicting events and building new understandings about policy and practice. It may highlight the complexities, shortcomings, possibilities, challenges and applicability of what we know and do for and with young children. As you explore the research case studies in this book, you will see that each of the researchers, in different ways, has set out to research something that matters to them and to others.

If your research matters to others, it has some chance of making a difference to how we understand and practice our work with young children.

Choosing a topic—questions to help

- Is it novel for you? Or is it something you have pondered for some time?
- Either way, will you be able to maintain your interest in it over time?
- Are the sorts of questions that may emerge from this topic area manageable with the time and resources you have?
- Do you have the relevant expertise or knowledge?
- Can you get the information you need in your daily work?
- Is it ethical?

SEARCH THE LITERATURE

Once you settle on the general topic of your research, it's important to find out what is currently known about it and how this knowledge has been gained. To do this you undertake a search of the literature that has been published on your topic. This has three broad aims: to acquaint you with what other people know and have said about your chosen topic, to inform the way you formulate your research question and guide your choice of design for your own study. Within these broad aims, a literature search and review involves several specific tasks. You need to first find the literature that is most relevant to your own research topic.

Finding the relevant literature

Finding literature on a research topic has been made faster and easier with the availability of on-line databases that index and abstract research. These databases vary in the amount of detail accessed on-line. For instance, the Educational Resources Information Collection (ERIC) database often used by researchers in early childhood indexes two types of materials—education journals and ERIC documents. ERIC documents include unpublished items that would otherwise be difficult to access such as theses, conference papers and government reports.

Most university libraries have staff to advise you on how best to search the on-line databases to which their library subscribes. The libraries will generally have access to powerful electronic search engines that can quickly and effectively search through on-line databases for information about published research on your topic. For the beginning researcher, using on-line database searching with an experienced guide is a most effective way to begin your literature review.

However, before you approach your librarian for assistance with such a search, do some preparatory work. Identify the key words or concepts in your research topic first. Most databases have a thesaurus of key terms that they use for indexing and abstracting purposes. Guidance from your library staff on how to use the thesaurus can save you lots of wasted search time.

From on-line database searching you can find:

- Summaries (abstracts) of research articles on your topic and details about how to access the full-text documents
- Some full-text journal articles, reports and research summaries
- Abstracts of books and book chapters related to your research
- Conference paper abstracts.

While on-line database searching is an efficient and effective way to access material it is not the only way, and it has its limits. To improve the scope and currency of your search use the following strategies:

- Talk to the information services librarian about the pros and cons of using the particular on-line databases to which your library subscribes. Some databases focus on specific geographic regions (for example, ERIC is dominated by North American research) and some only index journals and not conference papers. It is important to be clear what you are accessing.
- Search the hardcopy indexes of key early childhood journals to get a feel for what the journal publishes and to access material not abstracted in the major on-line databases.
- Learn where books related to your topic are kept in the library and scan the shelves occasionally.
- Keep an eye on the new arrivals shelf.
- Subscribe to the on-line contents pages notification for key journals in your area.
- Get into a routine of browsing the academic bookshops near you for recent arrivals.
- Participate in conferences related to your topic. It can take many months and sometimes years for a conference presentation to appear as a journal article. Conferences are one way of learning about who is doing what, now.
- If you can't participate yourself, talk to people who have been to recent conferences (for example, academic staff, research students, early childhood practitioners). They may also help you find out what conferences are planned and where they will be. The newsletters of professional organisations sometimes provide lists of upcoming events, including conferences. Conference organisers produce programmes that provide at least the titles of papers and

symposia being presented. You could then ask someone who is attending to request a copy of a paper of interest for you, or write to the author and request a copy yourself. Most conference programmes provide author contact details, such as e-mail addresses, to facilitate this. Finally, many conferences produce a book of abstracts of proceedings that usually can be purchased even if you did not attend.

Useful research databases for early childhood researchers

- AskERIC provides abstracts and full text documents related to education and has a specialist early childhood collection (USA)
- Australian Education Index (AUS)
- BIDS ISI Data Service provides bibliographic data and full text services for higher education and research (UK)
- British Education Index is an electronic and printed guide to the contents of British educational periodical literature (UK)
- Canadian Education Index (CAN)
- Child Development Abstracts and Bibliography
- Current Contents
- DESIRE is the Development of a European Service for Information on Research and Education. (Netherlands)
- Education Abstracts
- Educational Research Abstracts on-line
- Exceptional Child Education Abstracts
- Expanded Academic (with full-text component)
- FAMILY—for Australian material (AUS)
- Mental Measurements Yearbook. This has full text information about and reviews of all English-language standardised tests covering educational skills, personality, vocational aptitude, psychology and related areas.
- Proquest Education Complete has a full-text component
- PsycINFO
- QUALIDATA ESRC Qualitative Data Archival Resource Centre (UK)
- Qualitative Research Web Sites at the School of Social and Systemic Studies at the Nova Southeastern University, Florida (CAN)
- QualPage provides resources for qualitative researchers (CAN)
- REGARD is a new database service containing a wide range of information on social science research (UK)
- Social Science Citation Index
- Social Science Plus (with full-text component)
- Sociological Abstracts

The extent of your literature search

As you can see, there are many ways to access the research literature and—depending on your general topic area—you may find there is a lot of literature to consider! How extensive your literature search becomes should be guided by practical considerations, particularly the nature of the research task at hand. Some research projects are very small, perhaps undertaken as a minor assessment requirement for one subject. Your lecturer may have provided you with the key references and ask you to locate just one or two more that are relevant. For a year-long research project, a more detailed, extensive search may be warranted; and, of course, if you are undertaking higher-degree research, or funded research, it is your responsibility to 'know' the literature very well indeed.

FORMULATE A RESEARCH ISSUE OR QUESTION

In addition to familiarising you with your general topic area, the literature review should be seen as the vehicle by which you begin to refine the broad topic area of interest to you into a researchable question or questions. Wadsworth (1991) wrote 'research begins with the conscious asking of questions' (p. 3). We would add that it also continues, and often ends, with asking questions. In any event, finally deciding on your initial research question(s) is often the most challenging part of research. In our experience, it is certainly the first part of the research process that students may really struggle with. How much of a struggle it is depends on the topic area chosen. Some areas are very broad and students find it difficult to narrow the topic down to one or a small number of workable (researchable) questions. An example of this is the student who wishes to research a topic like 'preschoolers' play'. There are a myriad of different questions, probably thousands, that have been already investigated and probably thousands more that have yet to be researched. Other areas are quite narrow, with little written about the topic because little research has yet been done. One example of this would be the student who is interested in the topic of 'paternal separation anxiety', that is, how fathers feel about being separated from their infant children, for example in the context of leaving them in child care. In this case, the topic may need little refining to bring it down to a workable question. Either way, there will be challenges. This section aims to provide some ideas to help avoid common pitfalls at this stage of the research process.

The first step to formulating your research question involves a thorough review of the literature generated by your literature search. Reviewing the literature involves:

- Identifying what other researchers know about the topic;
- Identifying the key arguments, themes and issues that have emerged to date from other research and theoretical writing on the topic;
- Identifying the key theoretical perspectives that have been used to frame research on and to analyse the topic;
- Identifying gaps in knowledge and identifying contradictions and disagreements about what is known about the topic; and
- Identifying areas of uncertainty, puzzlement or confusion in what is known.

These steps help you to refine, limit and refocus your own research by:

- Reviewing how other research has been conducted on the topic;
- Reflecting on the difficulties and successes other researchers have noted in their own research;
- Noting the implications for your own research for any critiques of specific research approaches or theories;
- Identifying how your own research could add to the topic through discovering new information, refining or clarifying current understandings;
- Identifying the similarities and differences in context, method and questions between existing research and your proposed project;
- Ensuring that your own research is in some way(s) original and is not unknowingly replicating other people's research; and
- Seeking support from within the literature for the specific approach or theoretical framework you want to use.

When your initial literature review is complete, you should be familiar with key writings and research on your topic. You should know about the quantity and the quality of this work. You should be able to reflect on how this knowledge will inform your own research question. You should now be ready to refine your initial research questions and to formulate a research question or issue that is original and justifiable given the current state of knowledge about your topic.

If your research is using a deductive approach your research problem and question will be precisely defined at this point. This precision should involve clear **operational definitions** of the key terms and variables that you intend to investigate. For further discussion on this point refer to Chapter 7. Researchers using an inductive approach need to ensure that they have developed a research issue or question that enables them to describe and analyse people's social realities (see Chapter 8). Questions developed at this stage of a qualitative study may be less precise than those in a quantitative study, but it is still important to be clear about what you mean by each of your key terms and what it is that you are going to measure in your research.

Refining the topic—some steps to help

- Identify your broad topic
- Break your large topic into sub-areas
- Eliminate those sub-areas that interest you least
- Choose one sub-area
- Generate questions about that sub-area using how, why, what, when and where questions
- Reflect on the questions that are most likely to generate new and improved understandings
- Consider the resources—financial, human and time—available to you
- Decide on a question that is workable within your resourcing constraints and that interests you most (based on Charles, 1998; Berg, 1995; Kumar, 1996).

Your research question(s) should be meaningful, workable and relatively precise.

Refining the questions

- Are you clear about what you mean by the key terms?
- Will your question/topic require you to describe what exists, explore relationships between events or people, explain relationships or change them?
- Does your question enable you to focus on a combination of at least two of the following: people, problems, programmes or phenomena?
- State your main objective and then check that the question enables you to meet it (based on Charles, 1998; Berg, 1995; Kumar, 1996).

In many studies, this part of the research process also involves developing the hypothesis or hypotheses of the study. This is the expectation of what your study will find, usually based on the outcomes of previous research.

The practicalities of deciding what is a workable research question

The resources available and the time period in which the research study must be completed are important practical considerations in refining your final research question. Some researchers have the financial resources to employ a research assistant or have very few competing demands. The question(s) they select may be different to those chosen by a researcher who will be doing all the work herself, completing course work, part-time paid work and maybe caring for a family as well. Research projects that must be completed in a few weeks will research different questions to those that will extend over months or even years. Whichever is the case, it is absolutely essential that you take the time (ideally in discussion with an experienced researcher) to make good decisions at this point. There is nothing more devastating for a student than to find halfway through her research time that the question she set out to answer is too complex or too broad.

Many beginning researchers are far too ambitious about their research questions, usually because they want their research to make a major impact in terms of its conclusions. Simplifying questions may make them appear trivial, and therefore not worthwhile or less worthwhile. Two considerations may be helpful here. One is to realise that very few research studies, in and of themselves, provide major answers to major questions. Research is not like that. Even well-funded research projects are usually made up of a series of smaller studies planned in a programmatic way so that the results of one inform the next and so on. Knowledge is thus slowly and systematically built up, and it is the sum total of all the studies, and usually the studies of many others as well, that eventually lead to major breakthroughs. As a researcher, one learns to be content with making small but meaningful contributions to the ongoing quest for understanding or explanation.

Breaking up a complex area into a series of smaller areas and questions is good discipline for any researcher. The advantage of this is that the student may feel more content knowing that if progress is very good, it may be possible to include a further question or study if time and resources permit. Far better to find that this is not possible and have sound data on one relatively simple question, than to run out of time or resources while trying to tackle a large, complex question.

We cannot stress enough that it is worth spending time finding workable, appropriate questions, for they drive the remainder of the research process. Your research question will influence what you research, how you research it and what you find out from your research efforts.

Organising and summarising the literature review

As you proceed through the literature search and review stages, it is essential that you organise the literature you access. When preparing a literature review as part of a thesis or research report you need to demonstrate that you are familiar with previous thinking on your chosen topic and that you have critically engaged with it. This does not mean that you include a summary of every article or book that you have read on your topic. Instead, you organise your readings into the key themes and issues that you feel capture current and past thinking on your topic. Then you can write a summary of this literature based on examples that help you to illustrate these themes and issues. Your illustrative material should be indicative of the relative quality and quantity of material on each theme or issue you identify. The following questions can help you organise and summarise your literature and to select appropriate examples to illustrate your discussion:

- What are the key arguments, themes and issues?
- How have these changed over time?
- How many writers have explored each of these themes and issues?
- What seem the main points of agreement and disagreement between different writers?
- How representative of the theme or issue is the material you intend to include?

Continuing to learn from the literature

As your research continues, it is important to keep up to date with emerging ideas and new research on your topic. You can do this by setting aside a regular time every month or so to update your on-line searches. The time needed to do this will be reduced if you keep a logbook in which you note the terms used to search each database and when you did the search. Then you can do a quick update rather than re-run your whole initial literature search. It is also useful to get into the habit of regularly browsing the new arrivals on the library shelves and in bookshops nearby.

As you continue to learn from the literature, your reading is likely to become more specialised and increasingly focused on the specific issues you are exploring in your research. It is at this point that you begin to become an 'expert' on your chosen topic and can begin to speak with authority about it.

Keeping track of literature

There is nothing worse at the end of a long research process, when you are preparing your report, than trying to find the details of a reference used in your literature review some months previously. To avoid looking for the 'red book with a nice cover' be determined from the start of your research to keep good records of the literature that you have read and that is informing your project. There are many ways to do this. You can use index cards, a logbook or computer software packages such as ENDNOTE to manage your bibliography. Whatever system you use, always note down the full details of each piece of literature so that it can be readily retrieved when you prepare a report of your research for others. Time spent on this early in the research process is time well spent.

DESIGN THE RESEARCH

Careful design of research takes time, and it is again time well spent. Good design will ensure that your research provides you with data that enable you to achieve what you set out to achieve—whether it is to describe, understand or explain what interests you. In other words, it is primarily your research question (as well as practical considerations like the financial and time resources available to you) that will guide your research design. Your research design should be a well-laid-out plan of action that you will follow throughout the conduct of your research.

For those following a deductive research process, this plan once formulated will be rarely deviated from. This is because the plan has been prepared to address particular questions with expected outcomes (hypotheses) and to rule out possible alternative explanations of the results obtained. To change the plan halfway would risk serious breaches of the control needed in this sort of research. Let us assume, for example, that a researcher is interested in how different early childhood curricula impact on children's peer relationships. Searching and reviewing the literature has led the researcher to the expectation (hypothesis) that Curriculum A is likely to facilitate positive peer relationships more than Curriculum B. Luckily for the researcher, there are two preschools in her area that use Curriculum A exclusively and two that use Curriculum B exclusively. She designs a study involving observations of equal numbers of children at all four preschools in terms of their peer relationships. She decides to use videotaping to collect her observations. So far so good. If she sticks with this design, and she observes more positive peer relationships among the children in preschools using Curriculum A, her hypothesis is supported.

But let us say this is not what happens—that at some point in the study, when she has almost completed data collection at the two A preschools and still has lots of observations to complete at the two B preschools, our researcher decides that using videotaping is a waste of time. She decides to change her plan. She decides from now on to just sit amongst the children and write in longhand what she sees. After all, that's what she was doing back in the lab when she looked at her videotapes. Or she may decide to let someone else do the observations, for example asking the teachers to rate the children yet to be observed using some rating scale of peer interaction. If her data end up showing more positive peer interaction at the A preschools, can she still confidently assert that her hypothesis is supported? If you think about it carefully you will see that she cannot. She cannot reach such a conclusion because her method changed during the study. As a result most of the data collected on children at the A preschools was collected in a different way to data on children at the B preschools. We are left with the possibility that it was the different data collection method that accounted for the different results. As we cannot rule this out, our researcher has at best learned a very valuable lesson in research design and at worst wasted her own and the research participants' time.

Researchers following an inductive approach also need to think about and plan their research strategies, but because they constantly engage with their emerging data, they often choose to make alterations to their research plan in the light of their new insights and understandings. Remember that in this approach it is unlikely that the researcher starts with a clear hypothesis but remains open to a range of possibilities and discoveries as the study unfolds. Cannold provides one example of this in Chapter 12 in her description of her Women Without Children study. She talks about how her literature search and review had led her to expect that women aged in their late 30s and early 40s would be appropriate participants in her study which aimed, among other things, to understand fertile women's experiences of decision-making about motherhood or childlessness. However, after several interviews, it became clear to her that many women of this age had already made their decisions, worked through the issues and possibly reached resolution of them. It was quite legitimate for her then to change this part of her research plan, as she did, and interview participants of a younger age. Data from all participants, both younger and older, were still important and usable for the purposes of understanding her research questions.

Generally speaking, the design stage of research involves making decisions about how the study will be executed. Decisions need to be made about how the phenomena of interest will be measured, how data will be collected, how many participants will be included and what characteristics they will have. In more technical terms, considerations of **sampling**, measurement, **validity** and **reliability** must be addressed. Getting these decisions right is of such importance that Part II of this book is dedicated to these various topics. Quantitative and qualitative design issues are both considered in depth. It is important to remember that no matter what kind of research you conduct, whether it is quantitative or qualitative, principles of good design still apply. The new researcher will gain enormously from the help of more experienced researchers as she develops her research design.

Sampling populations

No matter how well funded your research, it is usually impossible to include in your study all the individuals of interest to you. This might not apply if your study is very small scale—if you are only interested in studying the children in one classroom, for example. But if this is the only group you study, you cannot generalise your results to children beyond this group, even to those that come into that classroom next year, regardless of whether [the] same or not. The reason you cannot generalise [in] this way is because to generalise from one gro[up the] group you study (your so-called sample) must b[e] similar to (representative of) the larger group [you want] to generalise (the so-called population). This [is] commonsense. Taking a simple example: if you wanted to know what outside play activities 4-year-old children in preschools (the population of interest) enjoyed most, it would make little sense to observe and/or talk to only 4-year-old preschool girls. By excluding boys from the sample, you have effectively prevented any generalisations to 4-year-old preschoolers in general. By now you would also realise that you have also limited your study because you could not compare the preferences of girls and boys, which may be important and interesting data to consider.

Selecting representative samples is quite complex and entails decision-making around not only the characteristics of the participants, but also how many of them should be included (the so-called sample size). This is also a sticking point for new students of research. The simple answer is usually to include as many participants as possible, based on pragmatic factors like how much time you have for data collection, how readily accessible are members of the population of interest and how many resources are available to help you both collect and analyse the data. Generally speaking, more data means more time in the collection phase and more time analysing results. This is less of an issue if you are using structured assessments like questionnaires or checklists and are able to use computer programmes.

Sample size and sampling plans will also vary according to whether you have chosen a quantitative or qualitative method. Qualitative data, such as that based on interviews, may involve fewer participants, because each participant generates a large amount of data that must be transcribed (usually from audiotape) and then analysed in some way. Even using computer programmes for qualitative data relies on transcribed data. If you are doing the transcription yourself, it can take up to eight hours to transcribe each hour of audiotape. Qualitative researchers are also less likely to use sampling plans focused on achieving a so-called representative sample because representativeness is not their primary goal, or may not be a goal at all. They are more focused on understanding than generalising and 'they select persons or a site that will yield important data on the topic of interest' (Goodwin and Goodwin, 1996, p. 115).

Whichever approach you use, it is critically important that you accurately describe the sample that you use, its size and

25

acteristics when reporting your research (see below). You can
en draw your readers' attention to any concerns you have
with these aspects of the study and any limitations associated with
them. Other researchers are then able if they wish to replicate your
study.

Ethical considerations

Essential to the design phase of the research process is a sound appre-
ciation of the ethical considerations associated with doing research.
Ensuring that the study conforms to ethical standards is of paramount
importance. This will include the development of appropriate plain
language statements (PLS) about your research and consent forms
to be signed by participants or, in the case of children, their parents or
guardians. How to do this is discussed in depth in Chapter 5.

COLLECT DATA

Once your design has been worked out, and you have obtained
approval to proceed with your research from your institution's research
ethics committee, it is time to collect your data. This phase of the
research process is often the one where students begin to feel they are
at long last researchers. The nature of your research question and the
design chosen to address it will determine where you find yourself
during the data collection phase. Assuming you are the person doing
the data collection, you may spend many hours in preschools or other
early childhood services. While there you may be observing children,
interviewing them, observing teachers or parents or maybe interviewing them. You may visit many preschools or other services, or you may
concentrate your efforts in only one. You may spend time studying
policy documents or historical texts as part of your research. Another
possibility is to collect your data using mail-out questionnaires or
rating scales completed by teachers or parents. This may save a lot
of time, but the nature of your data will be very different from that
collected through interview or observation. You may find yourself
collecting data in family homes or in other settings such as parks and
shopping centres, or in university laboratories.

Before any of this can occur, however, you need to gain the permission of the person or people responsible for the setting as well as the
consent of the participants themselves. For example, if your research
involves observing children in a preschool, you will need to approach
the director of the service and the management committee first. They
will usually require a clear statement from you about the nature,
purpose and design of the study and evidence that the relevant institutional ethics committee has approved it.

It is important to remember that all of these approvals take time, and even more time if you are using multiple sites. You should factor this into your overall research plan, especially if you have a tight time-line for completion of your study, which is often the case. You also need to be prepared for delays if child or adult participants become ill or go on holidays. Equipment breakdown, postal delays, inclement weather and so on are all possible and, depending on your method, may act to further delay and frustrate your data collection plans.

PROCESS/ANALYSE DATA

Once data collection is complete, the phase of data processing and analysis can begin. How this will proceed will depend mainly on whether you have used a quantitative or qualitative approach. Quantitative data involves numbers, which must be collated and then analysed using statistical procedures. Some statistical procedures are relatively simple and straightforward. These include so-called descriptive statistics, such as measures of central tendency including means (averages) and measures of variability, like the range and standard deviation. Inferential statistics, which enable the researcher to test whether their hypothesis is supported or not, may also be used. Statistical tests of this kind are more complex, and usually a computer software package would be used. Statistical analyses are discussed in Chapter 7.

Qualitative data is usually text (for example, words in an interview transcript). Data in this form can be analysed in a number of ways. Some qualitative data can be recoded into numbers, and then statistical tests used, as the data is now in a quantitative form. The researcher may wish to retain the complexity and diversity inherent in the text and use analysis techniques, such as content analysis, that retain these aspects. If this is chosen, computer software packages that can be used to assist in the process are also available. Qualitative data analysis is discussed in Chapter 8.

It is important to draw on your literature review to develop a conceptual/theoretical framework for analysing the data. This is another area that students struggle with. This framework is made up of concepts, built from the literature, that you will apply to organisation and selection of data as well the analysis. There are some good examples of this in Chapter 14, 16 and 17.

As Wiersma (2000) warns, it is important not be discouraged if your data are not perfect from your point of view, perhaps because they have not turned out the way you expected or wanted. Your hypotheses may not have been confirmed. Your outcomes may differ from other studies in the area. Sometimes the beginning researcher sees this as a flaw—but there may be many reasons why your data has turned out the way it has. Perhaps you have made a design error, perhaps there were other mistakes along the way. Learning from these errors and accepting the constructive criticisms of others are important for all researchers, both novice and experienced. That is why it is so important to document how you did your study so that its limitations can be seen by you and others and your interpretations of the data developed accordingly. However, it may also be that you have made a new and important discovery, and uncovered one of those surprises we talked about in Chapter 1. This may offer the promise of new insights of great significance for early childhood practice.

DRAW RESEARCH CONCLUSIONS

We said in Chapter 1 that research is a tool that can be used to improve the lives of young children and their families. To do this, we need to be able to draw lessons or conclusions from our research and share them with others.

Here are some simple steps and questions to guide you through the process of drawing conclusions:

- Look at your research question.
- Identify what you have learnt. What does your data tell you about this question?
- Summarise what you have learnt into key themes and issues.
- Identify the contextual, methodological, practical and theoretical limits and influences on what you have learnt. How has your method, sample size, context and conceptual or analytical framework influenced your findings?
- Note the effects of these limits and influences on your findings.
- What implications do your findings have for theory, practice and policy around your chosen topic?

WRITE RESEARCH REPORTS

The final phase of the research process is sharing your results with others. The research report is how most people do this. Your report may take the form of a seminar, a project report, a thesis, a journal article or a conference paper, or it may be a combination of these. Irrespective of its form, your report as a beginning researcher should follow accepted conventions. These cover content, style of presentation and approaches to referencing.

Conventions differ from journal to journal, university to university and conference to conference. Always check the particular conventions associated with the form and context in which you will publish your results. If you do not follow the conventions for your particular institution or the journal to which you submit an article, your work can be rejected!

In most instances the content of your report will include:

- Title—the title of your research project.
- Your name, qualifications and institutional affiliation.
- Acknowledgments—sources of support and funding you have received.
- Abstract—a summary of the research question, methods and findings.
- Introduction—this sets the contexts and issues of your study, summarises key theories and findings from earlier research and may state your hypotheses or expected outcomes.
- Method—usually includes a description of the participants in the study, your measuring instruments (such as questionnaires, checklists, behavioural codes) if any, and the procedures you used to collect the data. It may also include a description of your design and in some cases the limits to your research.
- Results—summarises the data you collected and the themes and issues in your findings.
- Summary, conclusion and recommendations—discussion of your findings and their implications. Here you can interpret your findings, speculate about their implications, raise questions for further research and identify the limitations of your own work.
- References—an alphabetical list of all sources you have used in your work. There are conventions about how these should be presented that you need to check for your specific context.
- Appendices—include material that is too bulky for the main body of the report but is important for your readers to have access to (this may include raw or uncollated data, copies of questionnaires or interview questions or transcripts).

The accepted styles of presentation for research reports are often very specific and detailed. They will often detail things such as:

- type style and size
- page layout including margin sizes, placement of page numbers, etc.
- heading styles
- reference style
- presentation of tables.

Learning to prepare a research report that follows accepted presentation conventions becomes easier over time. If you can get the format right, people will focus on the content of what you have presented and its implications more readily.

QUESTIONS FOR REFLECTION

- What areas do you think we need to know more about in early childhood?
- What research questions would you like investigate?
- What sort of research design would you use to investigate this question?
- Which step(s) of the research process do you think you would find the most difficult? Why?
- Which step(s) would you enjoy the most?

FURTHER READING

Cryer, P. 1996, *The Research Student's Guide To Success*, Open University Press, Buckingham. A useful how-to book for those undertaking research as part of a higher degree or via the 'apprenticeship' model that discusses preparing for and settling in to the life of the research student, developing positive relationships with colleagues and supervisors, time management, creative thinking and coping with 'flagging'. Although some of the book (such as registering for a research degree) is specific to the UK, other parts will be helpful to research students in general. These include discussion of record keeping, planning, recognising good research and issues of originality. There is a select bibliography on relevant titles at the end.

Jipson, J. 2000, 'The stealing of wonderful ideas: The politics of imposition and representation in research on early childhood', in L. Diaz Soto (ed.), *The Politics of Early Childhood Education*, (pp. 167–177). Peter Lang Publishers, New York. This chapter raises some important questions about what counts as useful research in early childhood and how we can do research that is inclusive and respectful.

3

Paradigms, methods and knowledge

Patrick Hughes

This chapter examines some major paradigms found in the early child-hood field. It shows that a researcher's view of the world influences their choice of paradigm, and that their choice of paradigm effectively determines their methods and the type of knowledge they produce. The relationships between paradigm, methods and knowledge are illustrated by examples of research into relationships between children and the media. At a broader level, these relationships are applicable to any area of research into early childhood—indeed, to any area of research in general.

PARADIGMS AS FRAMES

Different people can mean different things when they use the term 'paradigm'. Much of its current usage derives from Thomas Kuhn's (1970) use in his book, *The Structure of Scientific Revolutions,* and it is his sense of the term that I will use. Kuhn's book concerns the role of paradigms in the history of the natural sciences or physical sciences, but his arguments about paradigms also apply to research in the social sciences and humanities.

In very simple terms, a paradigm is a way to 'see' the world and organise it into a coherent whole. Just as a picture frame 'frames' a picture, a paradigm frames a research topic; and just as our choice of picture frame influences how we see the picture within it, so our choice

31

of paradigm influences how we see our research topic. For example, if we frame a portrait within a large, ornate, gold frame of the type used to frame old masters in art galleries, we see it very differently to the way we see it if we use the simple chromium frame commonly used to frame family photos. Similarly, if we frame a research topic within one paradigm, we see it very differently to the way we see it if we frame it within another. This chapter illustrates how that framing happens by showing how researchers have framed children's relationships with the media within various paradigms, each one giving us a different view of those relationships.

A paradigm is more than a theory. Each paradigm is a specific collection of beliefs about knowledge and about our relationships with knowledge, together with practices based upon those beliefs. Any particular paradigm has three elements:

- A belief about the nature of knowledge—what it means to say that we know something.
- A methodology—what to investigate, how to investigate it, what to measure or assess and how to do so.
- Criteria of validity—how to judge someone's claim to know something.

We never see the world 'outside' a paradigm (frame). Each of us (not just researchers), always and inevitably, frames the world in the process of seeing it. Consequently, what we learn about the world will depend on how we see it; and how we see it depends on our choice of paradigm. Different paradigms give us different perspectives on the world, and so we should try to keep an open mind about the paradigm we favour as researchers and be prepared to try different ones.

To see how Kuhn's idea of paradigms can help researchers into early childhood, I will examine four major paradigms—positivism, interpretivism, structuralism and poststructuralism. I will describe each paradigm in terms of the three elements just mentioned, then show how it has been used in research on children and media.

POSITIVISM

Positivists believe that the world consists of two levels—a continuously changing surface of events and appearances, and an unchanging foundation of order, expressed in universal laws.

Positivist knowledge

Positivists try to explain and predict their surroundings in terms of cause-and-effect relationships between apparently random events and appearances and an underlying order of universal laws. Those universal laws are hidden from our immediate gaze, like a building's foundations, but we can discover them by observing and recording events and appearances and then deducing the law or laws that caused them. Some positivists claim that experimental research can *prove* the existence of such universal order. Other positivists maintain that we can only disprove the existence of such underlying laws—we can't prove that they exist because they are, after all, invisible. In very general terms, scientists are positivists and vice versa. Traditionally, scientists have claimed that scientific (positivist) knowledge is the only form of knowledge that can be proven true (or false). Other forms of knowledge (for example, myths, dreams or intuition) may be very interesting, they say, but we can neither prove nor disprove them.

Positivist methodology

Positivists have argued that strict adherence to the stringent, technical and impersonal rules of scientific investigation, such as rigorously conducted experiments in strictly controlled circumstances, produces results that simply and straightforwardly reflect the world, unmediated or undistorted by the researcher's personal interests, prejudices, involvement and idiosyncrasies. From this perspective, knowledge that is produced according to the rules of scientific (positivist) investigation is objective knowledge, untainted by the researcher's own **subjectivity**; it concerns an objective world that exists independently of a particular researcher's perceptions of it.

Positivist validity

Positivists validate knowledge by seeking to replicate it. The impersonal rules governing positivist (scientific) research render the particular researcher who uses them irrelevant to the results. If the results of a specific positivist research project are valid, they will be replicated whenever, wherever and by whomever the project is repeated.

The following example of positivist research on children and the media can serve as a case study of positivism in practice. I will summarise the study, then explain what makes it positivist.

CASE STUDY

Positivism in research on children and media

Szarkjowicz, D. L. 1998, ' "Are you thinking what I'm thinking?":
Bananas in Pyjamas as a medium for exploring young children's understanding of mind.' *Australian Journal of Early Childhood*, 23(2), pp. 1–5.

Background

The focus of this study was 'Magic Carpet', a story from the Australian Broadcasting Corporation (ABC) television series for children, *Bananas in Pyjamas*. A character in the story (Morgan) believes that he is flying on a magic carpet. However, his belief is false—the Bananas in Pyjamas have blindfolded him, sat him on the carpet and then moved it around to make him believe that he is flying.

Aim

To discover whether context influenced young children's ability to hold a false belief, that is, a belief that is incorrect.

Methods

Szarkjowicz randomly assigned 47 children between 3 and 6 years old to one of two groups. Group 1 (23 children) watched the 'Magic Carpet' video twice; group 2 (24 children) had the 'Magic Carpet' book read to it twice. The first watching/reading was uninterrupted; Szarkjowicz interrupted the second at appropriate points with questions designed to discover the extent to which the children understood false beliefs. These included: 'What does Morgan think he is doing? What do you know is really happening?'; 'What does the Rat in the Hat think the carpet is? What do you really know about the carpet?' Szarkjowicz also sought to discover whether the children held second order beliefs (beliefs about beliefs) by asking questions such as: 'What do the Bananas think the Rat thinks he is doing? What do the Bananas know the Rat is really doing?'

Results

- Seventy-four per cent of the children from the video group answered all the questions correctly, compared with 21 per cent of the book group. Szarkjowicz (p. 3) showed that this comparison between the two groups was statistically significant: '$t(45) = 3.71$, $p < .05$'.
- Of the children in the video group who answered all the questions correctly, 59 per cent were less than 54 months old. This showed that under-5s can—in particular circumstances—understand false beliefs, contradicting previous research evidence.
- The two groups showed no difference in understanding second order beliefs. Only 13 per cent of each group answered these questions correctly, supporting earlier researchers' claims that such understanding may not develop until 7 years of age. Here, the comparison between the two groups was not statistically significant.

How was the study positivist?

- It expressed a two-level model of the world. Szarkjowicz examined apparently random surface appearances in order to deduce an underlying order; and her results reinforced that two-level model of the world. Specifically, she examined randomly assembled young children's responses to questions about a story in order to deduce the existence (or not) of the cognitive ability to understand false belief. We can't see that underlying order (that cognitive ability)—we only deduce its existence from surface appearances. Consequently, Szarkjowicz didn't just ask children, 'Do you have the cognitive ability to understand false belief?', but instead sought to deduce the answer from the children's responses to other questions about 'Magic Carpet'.

- It used scientific research methods. Szarkjowicz sought to measure something that she had elicited in carefully controlled conditions and she expressed the result mathematically. That statement may evoke a scientific experiment in a laboratory, because it describes the methods of the scientist, as follows: 'Szarkjowicz sought to measure something.' The 'something' was whether context influenced young children's ability to hold a false belief 'that she had elicited'. She elicited it by asking questions about false beliefs 'in carefully controlled conditions'. She randomly assigned each child to one of two groups, each of which experienced the story—in video or book form— in similar conditions, that is, firstly uninterrupted, secondly interrupted at salient points, 'and she expressed the results mathematically'. Szarkjowicz deduced the existence of an underlying law from the statistical significance of her results: '$t(45) = 3.71$, $p<.05$'.

INTERPRETIVISM

Interpretivism seeks to explain how people make sense of their circumstances, that is, of the social world.

Interpretivist knowledge

For interpretivists the social world is not just 'out there' waiting to be interpreted, but 'in here' or 'in us'—it *is* our interpretations. Interpretivists argue that rather than simply *perceiving* our particular social and material circumstances, each person continually makes sense of them within a cultural framework of socially constructed and shared meanings, and that our interpretations of the world influence our behaviour in it. Interpretivists believe that we continually create and re-create our social world as a dynamic meaning system, that is, a system that changes over time. As we continually make sense of our circumstances, we continually negotiate with others the meanings of our own actions and circumstances, of their actions and circumstances and of social and cultural institutions and products. In short, interpretivists believe that our social world is not just waiting for us to interpret—it is always already interpreted. (Positivists, in contrast, regard the social world as an extension of the 'natural' world—'out there' awaiting interpretation by a scientist using methods and theories invented for the task.)

Interpretivist methodology

The interpretivist researcher's task is to understand socially constructed, negotiated and shared meanings and re-present them as theories of human behaviour. This requires more than just asking people, 'What do you think you're doing?' It requires the researcher to actively make sense of people's behaviour—including their own. One way to make sense of behaviour is to regard it as rule-bound. To interpret a specific individual's behaviour, we ask how closely it conforms to some social rule. An action makes sense to others to the extent that it follows a social rule; and we explain what a word or an action means by describing the rule-bound (or rule-breaking) way that we use it (Winch, 1958, pp. 121–33). Another way to interpret behaviour is to argue that we *interpret* our circumstances using some form of language, rather than simply perceive them. In this approach, language is much more than just a window on a world that exists independently of it. Instead, language *creates* our social world.

Interpretivist validity

For interpretivists, knowledge is valid if it is authentic, that is, it is the true voice of the participants in their research. A common way of demonstrating the authenticity of people's responses is to triangulate them, or to elicit them using more than one research method and checking whether the responses are consistent. Interpretivists don't use triangulation to produce knowledge that is valid whenever, wherever and by whomever it is produced, as positivists do. Interpretivist knowledge is always 'local' and specific to a particular research project conducted in particular circumstances with particular participants. Thus, interpretivist knowledge is valid only within tight limits . . . but interpretivist researchers must still be able to demonstrate the validity of their knowledge, even within those limits.

The following example of interpretivist research on children and the media can serve as a case study of interpretivism in practice. I will summarise the study, then explain what makes it interpretivist.

CASE STUDY

Interpretivism in research on children and media

Hengst, H. 1997, 'Reconquering Urban Spots and Spaces? Children's public(ness) and the scripts of media industries,' *Childhood*, vol. 4, no. 4, pp. 425–44.

Background

Heinz Hengst's complex German study derived from his argument that contemporary German childhood features an interrelationship between two phenomena:

- 'Sportification'—the increasing tendency in Germany for young sports fans to seek in their everyday lives the action, adventure and enjoyment they find in sports;
- 'Mediatization'—the influence of media 'scripts' (including, for example, stories, scenarios or characters) on children's 'thoughts, imagination, daydreams, entertainments and games' (p. 425). (NB: 'media' includes publishing, broadcasting, cinema, sportswear and other leisure corporations.)

These two phenomena come together in games through which children seek to claim territories in public spaces:

> The fashion, media and leisure industries process subcultural scripts about sport into 'style packages' for a global public of children for whom sport becomes something you do to be watched by others in your peer groups. In the process of negotiating those sports/media scripts, children struggle to take over and retain urban spaces (p. 434).

Hengst was especially interested in how children make sense of media 'scripts' in their 'sportified' play. He called that sense-making process 'negotiation', highlighting the possibility that a child (or group of children) may interpret a script in a way unintended by its 'author'—the media corporation that produced it. This reflects the interpretivist view that we continually and actively make sense of our circumstances, asserting their meaning or equivocating over it and continually (re-)creating our social world:

> Media analysis, as a form of cultural analysis, focuses on . . . how publics assign meaning . . . According to this understanding of culture, individuals and social groups (in this case children) are thought of within significant networks of meanings . . . These networks of meanings are the world from which people draw or create their orientations, but they also

contain the assumptions from which people distance them-selves (p. 426).

Aims

- General: to show that people make sense of media products with-in social networks, rather than media products having innate or implicit meanings.
- Specific: to show how children negotiate media scripts in the process of defining themselves as a 'public' with its own urban spaces.

Methods

Hengst spent 15 years observing 8–13-year-old children's play and asking them about it. He was especially interested in how chil-dren negotiated media scripts in the games through which they sought to claim territories in public spaces. As an interpretivist, he sought to discover what children's play meant to them. Thus, while he observed children's play, he asked these interrelated questions:

- how and with what do children play?
- how does their play create and maintain their social networks?
- how do children 'negotiate' media 'scripts' in their play?
- how do they claim 'territories' in and through their play?

Results

Hengst produced a range of results, illustrated in two vignettes, each centred on a film. The first vignette centred on the enormous popularity of BMX bikes, which Hengst found was an age-specific response to the film *ET*. One point in the film was crucial to the subsequent media script. In it, a group of adults in lum-bering, awkward armoured cars unsuccessfully pursue a group of children on their agile, manoeuvrable BMX bikes. The children escape, 'flying' over a road-block via the 'magic' of ET. Hengst found that the children negotiated this script in two ways. First, they sportified BMX bikes, calling their bikes 'machines' to differ-entiate them from toys by making them items of sporting equip-ment in a fast-moving sport. Second, they saw in the *ET* scene a metaphor for child–adult relationships, especially adults' tendency to constrain children's ambitions and activities—and their public spaces. The second vignette centred on the equally popular skate-board as an age-specific response to the film *Back to the Future*. The children negotiated this script in much the same ways as the *ET* script. They redefined the skateboard as an item of sports equipment, rather than a toy or plaything; and they saw in *Back to the Future* a metaphor for their continuing battles with adults to win new public spaces . . . in which to skateboard. As Hengst put it, "It is beyond question that children (and youths) view media and consumption industries as allies (for example, against the dictates of the educational project)' (p. 442).

Finally, Hengst regarded these specific children's negotiations with these two specific media scripts as an instance or illustration of the room for individuality within an increasingly global entertainment industry:

> Scripts devised by the media and consumption industries exert a decisive influence on when, where and how children's publicness is shaped in the urban setting (agenda setting). Children derive individual scope through the fact that the scripts are produced for a global market but must be put into practice at a local level (p. 442).

How was the study interprevitist?
- It rested on the belief that we continually create and re-create our social world as a dynamic meaning system (one that changes over time). Hengst's study rested on his belief that children actively make sense of their circumstances and that they do so by continually (re-)creating social networks of meaning through their play. He sought the *children's* explanations of how and why they (re-)created those social networks, rather than explaining their significance himself, because he sought to understand how *they* (re-)created their social world.
- It examined how people make sense of their circumstances, paying particular attention to the possible influence of media scripts on that sense-making process. Hengst regarded children's negotiations of media scripts as part of the broader process through which they made sense of their circumstances. Consequently, while he paid particular attention to those scripts, he sought to understand their significance for the children, rather than explaining their significance himself.

STRUCTURALISM

Structuralists regard the world as a collection of systems of law-governed relationships.

Structuralist knowledge

Structuralists explain the meaning and significance of something not in terms of its inherent qualities or characteristics but in terms of its relationships with other elements of a system. For a structuralist, meaning doesn't lie *within* something, waiting to be discovered through careful observation or experimentation. Instead, meaning lies in the non-observable system of relationships *between* that 'something' and something else. For example, an image, a word or a gesture doesn't mean anything in itself and by itself. Instead, its meaning is the result of its relationships with other images, other words or other gestures. Different writers have expressed this idea differently. For example:

> [A] structure is *not* a reality that is *directly* visible, and so directly observable, but a *level of reality* that exists beyond the visible relations between men, and the functioning of which constitutes the underlying logic of the system, the subjacent order by which the apparent order is to be explained (Godelier, 1974, p. xix; original emphases).

> Structuralism probes like an X-ray beyond apparently independently existing concrete objects, beyond an *item*-centred world, into a *relational* one (Sarup, 1984, p. 50; emphases added).

> Structuralism shares . . . attention to relations and systems as the framework for explanation. Instead of treating the world as an aggregate of things with their own intrinsic properties, structuralism and physics respectively seek to account for the social and physical world as a system of relations in which the properties of a 'thing' (be it an atom, a sign or an individual) derive from its internal and external relations (O'Sullivan et al., 1983, p. 227).

A structuralist would argue that nothing inherent in a child explains who or what s/he is; nor is there anything inherent in a child's video game that explains what it is. Instead, a structuralist would explain the meaning and significance of a child watching a video in terms of a complex system of law-governed relationships, including those between:

- the visual and audio signals that make up the video
- the sounds and images on the video and the narrative (story) they present
- the video and other media such as television, books and computer games
- the child, the video and those other media.

The term 'structuralism' refers not to a single, coherent paradigm but to a diverse collection of works in a diversity of disciplines including linguistics, anthropology and sociology. Structuralists within these different disciplines argue that we can best understand the world not by interpreting individuals' experiences, but by elucidating the impersonal systems of relationships that bind the world together. Indeed, a structuralist would go further and argue that the world *is* those systems of relationships—they *constitute* the world and, therefore, constitute each individual as part of the world. In other words, the individual doesn't explain the system of relationships—the system 'explains' the individual.

Structuralist methodology

Structuralism's different strands are bound together by the assumption that the truth is out there, waiting to be discovered by the assiduous structuralist researcher. As Harland (1987) put it:

> The Structuralists, in general, are concerned to *know* the (human) world—to uncover it through detailed observational analysis and to map it out under extended explicatory strands. Their stance is still the traditional scientific stance of Objectivity, their goal the traditional scientific goal of Truth (p. 2; original emphasis).

Linguistics—especially the work of linguist Ferdinand de Saussure (1959)—has influenced much structuralist research. Saussure regarded each language as a system, consisting of elements defined by their relationships with each other, that is, by their similarities to and differences from each other:

> [L]anguage has neither ideas nor sounds that existed before the linguistic system, but only conceptual and phonic differences that have issued from the system. The idea or phonic substance that a sign contains is of less importance than the other signs that surround it (p. 120).

Thus, many structuralists argue that an idea, an act, an event or an institution is an element of a language (system); that it does not and cannot exist 'outside' of a language; and that each element's meaning and significance arises from its relationships with other elements of that language. For example:

- The meaning of a word or phrase derives from its relationship to other elements of a particular language (for example, English, Thai);
- The meaning of a sound derives from its relationship to other elements of a sonic 'language', such as a particular type of music; and
- The meaning of a visual image derives from a visual 'language', such as a particular style of painting.

Thus, when we communicate by talking or singing or painting, for example, we express only what a particular language allows us to express. In this way, what we can communicate depends not on our wishes or intentions, but on the language we use. Further, structuralists argue that each of us does not ('subjectively' and 'intentionally') create a language when we use it. Instead, the various systems of relationships (languages) that make up our society and culture create us as individuals. Consequently, who we think we are depends on the language(s) we use to describe ourselves. Thus, a structuralist would explain our understandings and feeling about urban life and rural life, for example, by examining the systematic, mutually defining relationships between the two ways of life. They wouldn't examine people's experiences, views and sensibilities about urban life and rural life, because they regard each as defining the other: each means something because of its contrast with the other, neither means anything in the absence of the other. Some people criticise what they see as urban life's complications and stress by contrasting it with rural life's (alleged) simplicity and healthiness; other people criticise what they see as rural life's repetition and routine by contrasting it with urban life's (alleged) excitement and differences. This urban–rural relationship underpins innumerable film and television storylines.

Structuralist validity

A structuralist approach to validity resembles a positivist approach, in that both regard knowledge as 'out there' waiting to be discovered. However, while a positivist regards meaning as inherent or innate in something, a structuralist regards it as relational—a phenomenon derives its meaning or significance from its status as an element of a system of relationships. Consequently, to prove the validity of our knowledge of something, a structuralist demonstrates the nature of its relationship with other elements of a system, and shows how each element's meaning or significance derives from its relationships with other elements.

The following example of structuralist research on children and the media can serve as a case study of structuralism in practice. I will summarise the study, then explain what makes it structuralist.

CASE STUDY

Structuralism in research on children and media

Buckingham, D., Davies, H., Jones, K. and Kelley, P. 1999, 'Public Service Goes to Market: British children's television in transition'. *Media International Australia incorporating Culture and Policy*, No. 93, pp. 65–76.

Background

In Britain, much of the discussion about children's television has been couched in structuralist terms. Specifically, it has been based on 'relational meanings', that is, meanings derived from systematic relationships *between* two (or more) phenomena, rather than from any features or qualities *within* each phenomenon. The meaning of each derives from its relationship with (its similarity to, and difference from) the other. Those (invisible) systematic relationships exist beyond the visible relations between people and between objects. Therefore, Buckingham et al. didn't try to 'find' them by, for example, conducting experiments on viewers. Instead, they demonstrated the existence of those relationships by showing how they had 'structured' visible relationships between people who discussed children's television.

Aim

To show how systematic relationships between opposites have structured discussions in Britain about children's television, creating alliances between critics that the critics would not consciously/voluntarily create.

Methods

Buckingham et al. examined various texts about children and television that had been produced in Britain, seeking relational meanings expressing (invisible) systematic relationships that structured (visible) relationships between people. They found a series of relational meanings (see Results) and showed how these had structured discussions about children's television around a contradictory model of child audiences, and had created alliances between groups of critics who saw themselves as occupying quite different positions to each other.

Results

Buckingham et al. found three instances of relational meaning. They showed that three mutually defining oppositions have underpinned discussions about children's television in Britain:

- British children's television versus American children's television (nationalism);
- 'Culture' versus commerce (commercialism);
- Children as discerning consumers versus children as vulnerable to commercial pressures (consumerism).

Those three oppositions had had three effects on the discussions. First, they had structured the discussions as debates between advocates of opposing value-judgements. How? In each opposition, the first element is 'good', the second 'bad':

- Proposition: 'British children's television is (or should be!) a form of "Culture" to be appreciated by discerning consumers' (Good).
- Opposition: 'American children's television is a form of commerce thrust upon vulnerable consumers' (Bad).

Secondly, those oppositions (especially commercialism and consumerism) had supported a model of child audiences that contradicted itself:

> On the one hand, children have always been seen as a 'special' audience . . . whose particular characteristics and needs require specific codes of practice and regulation . . . Yet, on the other hand, [in] the 'discovery'—or at least the increasingly intensive targeting—of children as a consumer market . . . children . . . have become sovereign consumers, competent to make their own choices and to express their own wants and needs . . . [T]here is a fundamental contradiction here. On the one hand, children appear to have become a valuable, sought-after audience; on the other, the assumption that they can be bought cheaply still remains (pp. 66, 69).

Third, those three oppositions conflate nationalism and class: British 'Culture'—associated with the ruling class—is defined through its opposition to American popular (commercial) culture, which is associated with the working class. For instance:

> [T]he British tradition is aligned with quality live-action drama and educational programming, while the American invasion is of trashy animation and mindless entertainment . . . [I]t is hard not to perceive such arguments as the defensive response of a coalition of cultural elites—as yet another patrician condemnation of the limitations of popular taste (p. 68).
>
> . . . [W]e do not wish to fall back into a simplistic dichotomy between 'culture' and 'commerce' which often characterises debates in this field (Buckingham, 1995). Attacks on commercialism in children's culture often reflect a patrician distaste for 'trade' and a puritanical notion of what is 'good' for children (Seiter, 1993, p. 74).

This conflation created unlikely alliances between advocates of greater protection for children from commercial pressures and cultural elitists who dismiss popular ('American') tastes by invoking a so-called golden age (1950s) of British children's television. These alliances were created behind the backs of the people involved, as it were. They were the visible relationships between people, but they expressed invisible systematic relationships between nationalism, commercialism and consumerism—the language within which children's television was discussed.

How was the study structuralist?
* It expressed and reinforced a relational, systematic model of

the world. Buckingham et al. used the idea of relational meaning to explain both the form (adversarial) and the content (oppositions concerning nationalism, culture and commerce) of the continuing discussion in Britain about children's television.

- It presented people's views and behaviour as structured by their language. The study showed that people were both adversaries in debates and unlikely allies because their relationships with each other were not under their conscious control. Instead, those visible relationships were expressions of the invisible relationships that made up the language they used—a language that created them, rather than vice versa.

POSTSTRUCTURALISM

Poststructuralism is even more diffuse and complex than structuralism and its adherents can adopt such different perspectives on the world that it can be hard to see just what unites them. A further complication is that 'poststructuralism' is sometimes used interchangeably with **postmodernism**—an equally diffuse and complex term!

Poststructuralist knowledge

For the sake of simplicity, but at the risk of over-simplifying, I suggest that both poststructuralists and postmodernists regard the world as fundamentally incoherent and discontinuous; but where poststructuralists focus on individuals, postmodernists focus on society as a whole:

- Poststructuralists regard the individual as fundamentally incoherent and discontinuous. Consequently, they reject the view (shared by structuralists and positivists and, to an extent, by interpretivists) that individuals can develop coherent and continuous meanings of the world. For poststructuralists, everything and everyone can—and does—shift and change all the time and the task of the researcher is to explain this constant instability without attempting to 'capture' or stabilise it.
- Postmodernists regard human societies as fundamentally incoherent and discontinuous. They reject the (modernist) view that each society is at a particular stage of a journey by humanity towards some ill-defined goal or endpoint (**telos**). They also reject the (positivist) idea that science assists us on our journey by revealing more and more about the world, enabling us increasingly to control it. Instead, postmodernists argue that we can only understand the world at a local level, because as we try to generalise our understandings, we rely on 'big pictures' or **grand narratives** about humanity's progress on its journey.

45

I have separated poststructuralism and postmodernism to distinguish between them, but the poststructuralist idea of the incoherent and discontinuous individual makes no sense apart from the post-modern argument that societies are incoherent entities following no particular journey of progress or development. Therefore, when I refer to poststructuralism I am referring to a close association between poststructuralism and postmodernism.

Those complexities mean that my characterisation of poststruc-turalism as a paradigm consists of three cautious generalisations about poststructuralism, each differentiating it from other paradigms.

First, poststructuralism's research focus. Poststructuralists seek to understand the dynamics of relationships between knowledge/meaning, power and identity. (Contrast this with a positivist, who would seek to capture those knowledge–power relationships in a fixed and compre-hensive formula.) Kenway and Willis (1997) put it thus:

> For post-structuralists, meaning, power and identity are always in flux. They shift as different linguistic, institutional, cultural and social factors move and stabilise together. The emphasis in post-structuralism is on the discourses which make up social institutions and cultural products . . . [I]t is through discourse that meanings and people are made and through which power relations are maintained and changed. A discursive field is a set of discourses which are sys-tematically related (pp. xix–xx).

The second cautious generalisation concerns languages (in the broad sense of 'a system defined by and governed by a set of rules'). Poststructuralists believe that individuals are social products of lan-guages, rather than having an essence ('the real me') separate from their social existence. They regard the individual as *un*stable, referring to her/him as a 'subject', 'subject position' or 'subjectivity'. The subject's instability derives from their status as both a product and a producer of languages—unstable systems in which something's meaning can never be finally fixed because it may have several, different, mutually defining others. Thus, the subject is continually (re-)constructed by her/himself and others, adopting one or more 'subjectivities' that may be mutually contradictory; and s/he understands the world in ways that may be inconsistent or incoherent.

Davies (1989) argued that individuals are not unitary, coherent and stable, but complex, contradictory and dynamic:

> The individual is not . . . some relatively fixed end product, but one who is constituted and reconstituted through a variety of discursive practices . . . Individuals, through learning the discursive practices of a society, are able to position themselves within those practices in mul-tiple ways and to develop subjectivities both in concert with and in opposition to the ways in which others choose to position them (p. xi).

Clearly, poststructuralists reject the structuralist argument that languages are stable systems of fixed meanings, in which something's meaning derives from its relationships (similarity and difference) with other elements of the system; and that languages' stability, consistency and coherence enable them to create stable, consistent and coherent individuals.

My third cautious generalisation concerns relationships between meaning and circumstances. Poststructuralists believe that a subject's understandings of the world are associated with their particular experiences of the world—themselves associated with their social and material circumstances, such as their class, gender and race. For example, a poststructuralist might seek to show that a child's understanding/s of a film are associated with their experiences as a member of a specific class, gender and race. This explanation is oriented more to the viewer than to the film. It seeks to show how factors external to the film—such as class, gender and race—are associated with how a subject understands it. In contrast, a structuralist might seek to show how a film's genre (action–adventure, romance) predisposes viewers to interpret it in certain ways. This explanation is oriented more to the film than to the viewer. It seeks to show how factors internal to the film—such as genre (a system)—influence how an individual understands it.

Poststructuralist methodology

In summary, poststructuralists study relationships between knowledge/meaning, power and identity, and they regard those relationships as dynamic, unstable results of interaction between:

- an unstable and dynamic 'subject' whose identity is never fixed;
- unstable and dynamic 'languages', in which meaning is never fixed; and
- a world whose meanings are never fixed but are instead associated with the subject's social and material circumstances.

Poststructuralism's fundamental uncertainty about the world contrasts sharply with positivism and structuralism, each of which is certain that the truth is out there, waiting to be discovered; and with interpretivism, which is equally certain that the truth is in here—always already-interpreted by people.

Further, poststructuralist researchers don't just feel uncertain about the world—after all, any researcher seeks to reduce uncertainty. Instead, poststructuralist researchers reject the idea that we can *ever* be certain about the world because its complexity and dynamism defy encapsulation, categorisation and closure. Seeking certainty about the world is as futile as trying to hold a river in your hand—its dynamism precludes its capture and whatever you capture is no longer dynamic. Thus, our understandings of the world can only ever be provisional—

it is unattainable because it is ephemeral. Poststructuralists regard phenomena such as social institutions, relationships and individuals as products of the discourse(s) within which we think about them; but each discourse exists only in its difference from others. Consequently, poststructuralist researchers seek to demonstrate how discourses produce phenomena and how a phenomenon's meaning and significance is associated with the particular discourse(s) within which people encounter it.

Poststructuralist validity

Like interpretivists, poststructuralists judge the validity of knowledge according to the authenticity of the research participants' voices. However, poststructuralists' emphasis on the local nature of knowledge means that the limits they place on the validity of knowledge are even stricter than interpretivists'. For example, where a structuralist would judge the validity of knowledge by situating it with a grand narrative of progress or development, a poststructuralist would regard something as valid to the extent that it expressed the discourse(s) that produced it.

The following example of poststructuralist research on children and the media can serve as a case study of poststructuralism in practice. I will summarise the study, then explain what makes it poststructuralist.

CASE STUDY

Poststructuralism/postmodernism in research on children and media

Zanker, R. 1999, 'Kumara Kai or The Big Mac Pack? Television for six to twelve year olds in New Zealand,' *Media International Australia incorporating Culture and Policy*, no. 93, pp. 91–102.

Background
Zanker argued that the instability and incoherence brought about by the crisis in children's television in New Zealand invited critical examination of some founding assumptions of local children's programming. She showed that recent discussions in New Zealand about children's television have expressed poststructuralist/postmodern perspectives.

Aim
To critically re-appraise some founding assumptions of local

children's programming—'the child', 'the nation' and 'the national culture'.

Methods

Zanker examined closely the history of recent discussions in New Zealand about children's television. She showed that the radical deregulation of New Zealand television in the mid-1980s increased the proportion of (relatively cheap) imported programming at the expense of local production, creating, 'a monoculture where short bursts of local material wrap around global cartoons' (p. 99).

Zanker also examined the content of those discussions, which had rested on the argument that the founding assumptions of children's television in New Zealand—'the child', 'the nation' and 'the national culture'—are likely to disappear, or at least to change beyond recognition in the absence of locally funded and locally produced programmes. She regarded this argument as the foundation of 'modernist white middle-class content, genre and even formatting' (p. 94) and suggested that two developments in New Zealand society challenged it.

The first was postcolonial cultural fragmentation. Zanker questioned the value—even the validity—of terms such as 'the nation' and 'the national identity' at a time when New Zealand's population is becoming increasingly diverse: 'Identity in post-colonial New Zealand is becoming increasingly diverse, whether reflecting the resurgence of traditional tribalisms of Maori, voices from immigrant Anglo/Celtic/Pacific diasporas, or as expressed within the postmodern tribalisms of gender, ethnicity and consumerist lifestyles' (pp. 94–5).

Secondly, the argument was challenged by market-driven popular culture. Some imported programmes for children, for example, Nickelodeon's *Rugrats* and the BBC's *Teletubbies* consistently out-rated local programmes. These imports were widely regarded as 'quality' programmes and critics of publicly funded broadcasting used their popularity to question the need to fund local ('quality') programmes for children from the licence fee.

Results

After examining the history and content of the arguments about children's television in New Zealand, Zanker characterised them as instances of the broader, continuing arguments between supporters of commercial and public service approaches to broadcasting, and the difference between what we would call modern and postmodern paradigms.

Zanker suggested that advocates of increased, publicly funded local programming for children invoked a lost golden age based on a consensus about the child, the nation and the national culture and, therefore, about the aims and content of children's television. That golden age consensus rests on the modernist view that the child, the nation and the national culture are unitary, coherent and consistent entities, defined in opposition to a global popular culture that threatens to obliterate it. In contrast, Zanker argued that children can actively transform the products of global popular culture in the light of local circumstances if there are local spaces in which to do so:

> There may be more effective means of ensuring media rights for a new 'media-centric' generation of children than nostalgically jumping back into national quotas or public-service channels . . . Popular culture *is* global and children demonstrate by their choices that it is important for them to play out in the 'forever new' breaking news of global popular culture. But it is equally important for them to have access to local spaces in which to explore, play with and transform global culture . . . These will constitute the new public spaces for children (p. 101).

To support her argument, Zanker cited Massey's view that commodified cultures built around brand names (such as Nike, Barbie, Nintendo) can offer children new identities by offering them new spaces and ways in which to be children:

> Could it be also that many children are finding their own public spaces away from parental surveillance and the constraints of a modernist childhood within the brand tribes of commodified culture? Once children had secret passwords to peer group secrets; now children's—like youth—culture is increasingly defined by postmodernism and unstable 'constellations of temporary coherence' of global fashions and local peer-group response' (p. 101 [citing Massey, 1998]).

How was the study poststructuralist?

- It examined the dynamics of relationships between knowledge/meaning, power and identity. Zanker examined how 'golden agers' in New Zealand sought to accrue power by presenting themselves as guardians of a national identity (based on particular modernist meanings of child, nation and national culture) allegedly threatened by a global popular culture.
- It presented the individual as a fundamentally incoherent and discontinuous social product of languages, continually (re-)constructed by her/himself and others as one or more 'subjectivities'. Those subjectivities may be mutually contradictory and may understand the world inconsistently or incoherently, but

their understandings of the world are associated with their social and material circumstances. Zanker presented children as unstable 'subjects' continually (re-)constructing themselves. She argued that children can use television programmes and other popular cultural products (local and imported) to explore different ways of being; that when they do, they transform global cultural products into local ones; and that they need new public spaces in which to do so.

- It sought to explain the subject's constant instability without attempting to 'capture' or stabilise it. Zanker did not pose a definitive alternative to the stable, coherent model of the child implied in the modernist golden age. Instead she posed the child as a subjectivity in a constant process of re-construction, evading any definitive explanation. Rather than seeking a new (antimodernist) consensus that *This* (not that) is who the child *is*', Zanker said, 'This is how the child *can be*' . . . and left the possibilities open.

LINKS BETWEEN PARADIGM, METHODS AND RESULTS

When we choose a particular paradigm, we also (implicitly) choose particular methods of investigation. Let us look at this in each of the four paradigms we have considered, again using children's relationships with the media as the research topic.

- A positivist will investigate children's relationships with the media by, for example, surveying random samples of target populations of children, collating the data and tracking any patterns or regularities within that data. Their data will concern broad trends in their target populations, rather than the particular attitudes and actions of specific individuals within them; but their data should be broadly applicable to anyone within their target populations.
- An interpretist will investigate children's relationships with the media by trying to understand how specific young children make sense of specific media products. Thus, they will probably observe and interview children, their friends, carers and families. Their data will concern the particularities of specific children's relationships with specific media products, rather than broad trends in the population; other people should be very cautious about using that data to explain how any other children relate to other media products.
- A structuralist will investigate children's relationships with the media by tracing the systematic relationships between different programmes, advertisements, promotions and so forth, and

between them and other cultural products such as computer games, shopping malls, clothes and sports equipment. Their data will show how each item's meanings and significance derives from its (systematic) relationships with the others; and their data should be broadly applicable to any child who encounters one or more of those products.

- A poststructuralist would investigate children's relationships with the media by examining associations between specific media products, the influences of a particular viewer's class, gender and race on their encounters with those products; and the unstable, dynamic 'language/s' within which the child understands those experiences and expresses them. Their data will concern the diverse ways in which specific children draw on their specific experiences and 'languages' to make sense/s of specific media products; and the consequences of their sense-making activity for these products' social meaning/s and significance/s. Consequently, their data should be broadly applicable to anyone who shares those experiences and languages. However, the links between experiences and the languages within which they are understood and expressed can be very complex, so the applicability of the data to other people in similar circumstances would have to be demonstrated in each case, rather than assumed.

QUANTITATIVE OR QUALITATIVE RESEARCH?

Researchers often use the terms 'quantitative' and 'qualitative' to describe different methods of research, whereas in fact the terms describe different *approaches* to research, each characterised by the specific type of knowledge it produces. In general terms, quantitative research aims to produce facts and figures—some form of numerical, possibly statistical data—about something. A very simple example of a quantitative approach to research would be counting how many people behave in certain ways. A researcher could ask a group of parents if they put their children to bed in the afternoons and then count how many say 'yes', how many say 'no' and how many give another response. The resulting knowledge would be quantitative—the numbers (the quantity) of people who responded in particular ways to the question. This very simple exercise is the basis of all quantitative surveys, each of which counts how many people respond in particular ways to particular questions.

As its name implies, quantitative research is concerned with quantities—how to measure phenomena and how to express those measurements. A researcher who takes a quantitative approach to investigating a topic—such as children's relationships with the media—

aims to learn more about it. Their research is guided by the belief that our knowledge of something increases over time, step by step, piece by piece. We could say that they regard knowledge like gold dust—as you collect more and more, you get richer and richer. Taking a quantitative approach to research implies asking questions about phenomena that have answers that can be counted. For example: How frequently does a particular event occur in a society? How many people in an occupational group behave in a particular way? How much influence does an institution exert? Consequently, researchers who take a quantitative approach often work within positivism, as this paradigm frames the world as a collection of apparently independent phenomena to be counted, measured and otherwise catalogued as the prelude to deducing the rules or laws underlying them and giving them coherence.

In contrast, a researcher who takes a qualitative approach to investigating a topic aims to understand it differently. Qualitative researchers generally aim to show something's meaning or significance to particular people or groups of people. A very simple example of a qualitative approach to research would be asking people to explain their attitude to a particular issue. A researcher could ask a group of parents if they regularly encourage their children to sleep in the afternoon and then ask those who said 'yes' to explain their reasons. The resulting knowledge would be qualitative—detailed descriptions of how and why individual parents responded to their child's sleeping pattern. This very simple exercise is the basis of much qualitative research, which seeks to explain events and actions through the eyes and in the words of the people involved.

As its name implies, qualitative research is concerned with the quality of the data it produces, rather than just its quantity. A researcher who takes a qualitative approach to investigating a topic—such as children's relationships with the media—aims to learn about it in terms of the people involved. In a sense, a qualitative researcher doesn't seek to learn more about the topic itself, but about how people understand and make sense of the topic. Consequently, researchers who take a qualitative approach often work within interpretivism or poststructuralism, as each of these paradigms frames the world—in its own way—as the outcome of people's continuing negotiations.

Cutting across the distinction between quantitative and qualitative approaches is the distinction between deductive and inductive methodologies. Deductive research is a 'top down' approach: you start with a hypothesis (an idea about an issue) and collect data to prove or disprove it: 'What can I deduce about my hypothesis from my data?' Inductive research is 'bottom up': you collect data about an issue or an idea with no clear, preconceived view about the significance of that data for your issue or idea. Then you see whether your data will enable you to form an hypothesis about the issue or idea.

In summary:

- quantitative research produces 'facts and figures'
- qualitative research produces 'meanings and understandings'
- deductive research proves or disproves a hypothesis
- inductive research may suggest a hypothesis.

SUMMARY

This chapter has suggested that a researcher's choice of paradigm influences their research methods and the sort of knowledge s/he produces.

- Positivists explain their surroundings by observing and recording apparently random events and appearances and then deducing the law or laws that caused them.
- Interpretivists explain their surroundings by observing and recording how each person continually negotiates the meaning of their behaviour with others; how their interpretations influence their behaviour; and then showing how negotiations and interpretations continually re-create the world as a dynamic system of meanings.
- Structuralists explain their surroundings by re-presenting them as systems of law-governed relationships, in which something's meaning and significance isn't inherent but derives from its non-observable relationships with one or more other elements of the same system.
- Poststructuralists explain their surroundings by examining the dynamic, unstable relationships between knowledge/meaning, power and identity, and deriving those relationships from the interaction between a dynamic 'subject', dynamic 'languages' and a world where meanings are associated with the subject's social and material circumstances.

QUESTIONS FOR REFLECTION

Choose an issue that you have encountered as a student and/or staff member in early childhood services. The issue might concern, for example, your relationships with colleagues, how others see your work, or how your college, university or workplace is run.

- Using this chapter's definitions, explanations and case studies concerning positivism, interpretivism, structuralism and poststructuralism, briefly outline how a researcher within each of the four paradigms might investigate the issue.
- Using this chapter's material on the links between paradigm, methods and results, suggest the sort of knowledge about the issue that each paradigm would produce.

- Ask yourself which approach would be most likely to reso[l]
  issue to your satisfaction.

FURTHER READING

May, T. 1998, *Social Research: Issues, Methods and Process* (2nd edn)
Allen & Unwin, Sydney. An overview of some of the major paradigms used by social researchers and the links between theory, data
and values. Part Two relates those theoretical issues with research
practices, including surveys, interviews and observation.

Guba, E. G. (ed.) 1990, *The Paradigm Dialog*, Sage, Newbury Park,
CA. A collection of multi-disciplinary articles about the role of
paradigms in research.

4

Doing research for the first time

Sharon Ryan and Sheralyn Campbell

In this chapter we explore some of the challenges involved in learning to do research for the first time by sharing our own stories (Ryan, 1998; Campbell, forthcoming) as beginning researchers who have recently completed **poststructuralist** doctoral studies in early childhood. We highlight the key issues we faced through a conversation that interweaves our research stories. For more detailed discussions of poststructuralism in research, see Chapters 3, 14, 16 and 17.

FINDING A RESEARCH FOCUS, FINDING POST-STRUCTURAL THEORY

Sheralyn: My project grew out of my interest in social justice and equity, and my desire to ensure fairness was part of children's lives in early childhood settings. I wanted to investigate whether a 'pro-diversity disposition' (Derman-Sparks, 1993–94; Carr, 1997) was a useful way of thinking about how to help each child develop and internalise characteristics enabling her to choose to be fair in her relationships, and pro-active in her encounters with bias. However, two sets of literature suggested my concept of an equity disposition needed rethinking.

The first set included the work of researchers using feminist post-structuralism to analyse how gendered relations of power operated within (and through) what was understood, said and done in early childhood services (for example Davies, 1993; Mac Naughton, 1995). In these accounts, what each child understood to be possible, desirable, powerful and pleasurable in her play and relationships was constituted by the discursive politics of being a boy or girl. From this perspective, a child's disposition to be fair was constituted by the complex relations of power–knowledge that potentiated and constrained what each person was able to think, feel, say and do in the classroom. The second group of readings raised questions about significant silences around gender, race, class, ability and sexuality within traditional early childhood theory and developmental practices (for example, Lubeck, 1994; Silin, 1995). Thus, a dispositional view of the child in which pro-active fairness was a characteristic of the individual became problematic because it did not foreground issues of context and culture. These debates, about how fairness operated, suggested that finding ways to create change might best be explored in what happened in the daily life of a children's setting using the lens of feminist poststructuralism.

Sharon: Like you, Sheralyn, reading the early childhood reconceptualist literature (for example, Kessler and Swadener, 1992; Silin, 1995; Tobin, 1997) got me thinking about critiques of the developmental knowledge base and the potential of alternative knowledges for rethinking our practices. When I read this literature I became concerned that much of the criticism was theoretical and not grounded by empirical data, thus I chose my topic to redress this imbalance in the literature. Specifically, I became interested in the notion that a child-centred education based on developmental principles did not necessarily ensure an equitable education for all children because the developmental discourse is based on eurocentric, middle-class and masculine values (New and Mallory, 1994).

As I wanted to explore the politics of child-centred education, I chose poststructuralism, particularly the work of Michel Foucault because he theorises about power relations within social life. I then narrowed my focus on child-centred education to student choice in the curriculum, looking at the power relations exercised, negotiated and contested by a group of children and their teacher during choice or activity time, small groups and circle time.

Conducting a poststructural study was not foremost in our minds when we both began focusing our interests on a problem that could be investigated empirically. Rather, we came to poststructuralist theories through an intensive process of reading, trying to name and frame the problems we wished to study. Reading critiques of the developmental knowledge base in early childhood education led both of us to frame problems and to ask research questions concerned with equity, identity and the politics of classroom life. Coupled with the fact that we were teachers interested in integrating theory with practice, we needed to determine how to bring new theoretical frames into our research. This meant changing from modernist developmental frames of the child to those built from postmodernism.

CREATING DIFFERENT DESIGNS AND METHODS

For many in the field of early childhood, research is usually seen as a knowledge-generating endeavour, a process in which researchers, most often from a university, look in on classrooms trying to explain educational phenomena (Hatch, 1995; Graue and Walsh, 1998). In general, two pathways to producing knowledge in early childhood exist: positivist, quantitative studies aimed at measuring outcomes and determining relationships between different variables, and interpretivist, qualitative studies that seek to describe and explain educational phenomena in depth, and often from the perspectives of research participants. (See Chapters 7 and 8 for more in-depth discussion of these differences.)

In contrast to these research approaches, poststructuralists assume that the research process itself enacts relations of power that privilege the researcher (Cannella, 1997). Poststructuralists therefore not only employ procedures that enable them to gain insight into educational questions but employ methods to interrogate the research project itself, especially the lenses and the actions of the researcher (Lather, 1991). However, relatively little has been written about the methodologies that might contribute to this kind of a self-reflexive research design and few poststructural studies of education exist that might act as a guide for new researchers (Marshall, 1990). Complicating matters further for novice researchers is the dominant discourse of research circulating in early childhood texts and practices that gives more credibility to experimental or correlational studies than to interpretive ones. Qualitative inquiries are often seen as having little utility or functionality. As one reviewer of a conference proposal that Sheralyn submitted put it, 'I am not sure that data from a single inner urban Australian children's centre has a great deal of generalisability or relevance for the conference audience'. Consequently, as beginning researchers we were faced with a dual set of challenges. First, we had to develop poststructural research studies that would be seen as valid and relevant by those working in the academy, as well as the early childhood field. Second, these research designs had to provide spaces for our work as researchers to be criticised, although there was little guidance about how we might do this.

These challenges were met somewhat by participating in research classes that taught us as much about what we didn't want to do as they did about creating a poststructural research design. For Sharon, the task was somewhat easier because her supervisor, Celia Genishi, was an experienced qualitative researcher who also taught a class on qualitative inquiry. Not only did this class give Sharon access to a range of designs and methods but also introduced her to the work of scholars developing new forms of postmodern inquiry. Sheralyn's research training involved learning about quantitative design and methods which were in opposition to a study aimed at examining values and politics in the early childhood curriculum. However, under the supervision of Glenda Mac Naughton who had conducted her own action research studies (see Chapter 14), Sheralyn was introduced to what is called **fourth generation action research** (for example, McTaggart and Garbutcheon-Singh, 1988) and to a six-week research methodology class dedicated to this form of inquiry. These experiences led us to create quite different designs using poststructuralism to study issues of equity in early childhood practice.

Sheralyn: As a feminist, I was committed to making involvement in my research project by the early childhood staff and children emancipatory. I spent over twelve months in the children's room observing, talking with children, and videotaping and audiotaping their play. The action research team met at least once a week to revisit what had happened in the classroom. We talked about our understandings of how equity was practised in the interactions between children and adults, and the other possibilities revealed through a critical feminist lens. The emerging contradictions enabled us to map new courses of action in which we attempted to disrupt how unfairness appeared to operate in the classroom. We learned from our successes and failures that children were active participants in this process, able to co-opt or subvert our attempts to work for equity. We looked for ways to include their voices as we revisited life in the classroom and created change. My action research design allowed me to foreground the voices and actions of my collaborators in cycles of critical reflection on what was happening in the classroom, followed by planning, implementing, and evaluating changes to our equity and anti-bias **praxis**. In this way it worked in the interests of, and was owned and validated by, those who were researched.

Sharon: In response to the criticism that most researchers fail to address the effects of the research process on those who are being researched, I created opportunities for multiple readings of the research texts by the teacher and a group of her students. I still used qualitative methods of field notes, audiotaped and videotaped observations to collect data on classroom social relations. But in order to prevent my poststructural orientation and subjective biases from being the sole lenses through which data were gathered, examined and presented, I created opportunities for the teacher and students to provide their own readings of classroom events.

The first set of multiple readings was gathered through interviews structured around videotaped episodes of free play in which I asked the children and teacher to talk about what they saw. A second set of multiple readings was gained by asking the teacher to act as a critic of research texts, both of my talk and actions in the classroom and the written products I created. Alison provided feedback about the effects of my methodology on classroom life such as the timing and pullout of students for interviews. As I drafted the report, Alison provided further analyses of classroom events, often contradictory to those of my own. Both sets of readings were included in the final report to create a multi-vocal text in which the voices of the children, the teacher and the researcher are heard.

Despite being able to overcome the problem of creating a design and method that was in keeping with the poststructural orientation we were drawing on, as beginning researchers we quite often felt incompetent. In opening up our practices to question and criticism, and by inviting those we were researching to participate in data collection and analysis, there were times that we felt we were not taking on the appropriate identity of 'the researcher'. This tension was particularly pervasive when it came to collecting data in our chosen early childhood settings.

DEVELOPING COLLABORATIVE RELATIONSHIPS IN CLASSROOM-BASED RESEARCH

Often when one reads research texts and participates in methods classes, being a participant observer seems unproblematic. Supposedly, the 'good researcher' maintains the position of the quiet and interested observer, documenting classroom life by becoming a member of the culture but not to the point where one might begin to alter teaching and learning-as-usual. As we sought to enact collaborative research designs where the distance between researcher and researched is lessened, this image of the 'good researcher' became difficult to maintain.

Sheralyn: In retrospect I laugh at the simplistic vision I had of myself as a participant observer, who would objectively record what was happening, stepping untouched from the classroom into the meeting room where I could focus our later discussions on equity and anti-bias issues. Understanding myself as a feminist, novice researcher, critical friend and early childhood educator constituted competing and contradictory possibilities for each moment that I was in the classroom. Was it ethical for me to intervene on behalf of the girls who were defending their 'shop' from the attacks of the Lego 'drill'-wielding boys, while their teacher was caught up in comforting a child distressed by the departure of his parent? There was no simple 'yes' or 'no' answer.

As we reviewed and discussed the videotapes of children's play

many differences emerged between our readings. Because our relationships were built on the basic action research premise of equal invest-
ment and participation in the research, these contradictions became
essential to our conversations—opening dimensions that were more
complex, critical and trusting. These levels of engaged dialogue were
essential to creating new possibilities for understanding our praxis (and
ourselves) and creating change. None of this was described in any text
that I had read. Thank goodness for the experiences of my supervisor
and her perceptive guidance, which helped me to negotiate the pitfalls
that come as professional and personal boundaries blur. Glenda helped
me to maintain a balance between staying on track with what I had
to do (a PhD) and ensuring that what I was doing continued in the
interests of those who were central to it.

Sharon: I also went into the classroom assuming that I could easily
take on the role of a participant observer but, like you Sheralyn,
I found that my position changed from day to day and sometimes from
moment to moment. Quite often I was an assistant to children's efforts,
performing minor tasks like tying shoelaces while I took notes. At other
times I found myself in the position of teacher, directing individual
children, reading stories to the group or intervening in a conflict of
some kind. This is where I found the theory I was using invaluable
because it gave me a framework for understanding that my researcher
identity could shift and change. Poststructuralism was not always
helpful however, when it came to my collaboration with Alison.

I thought giving Alison numerous opportunities to read and criticise the report, and recording our differences in the text, would demonstrate to her how seriously I respected and valued her insights. Yet in
many ways she still felt I was using language and theory that she would
not use to describe her own practice. In other words, Alison positioned
me as a typical researcher who looked in and made assertions over
which she had no control. I am still wondering about what I could have
done differently so that Foucault's vision of research in local sites
having the potential to create change might have been realised.

It is rather paradoxical that as beginning researchers we had
chosen to challenge doing research-as-usual and yet so often we struggled with what it meant to be a 'legitimate researcher'. In trying to be
collaborative, we broke away from the notion that the researcher has
sole authority over the knowledge produced in a study and yet, at the
same time, our collaborations were not necessarily equal. These studies
were our doctoral projects. We were asking these individuals to engage
with issues that we were interested in, to collaborate on studies that we
designed and that would eventually lead to our being awarded the
status that goes along with being named 'doctor.' Although there have
been papers and presentations where Sheralyn's collaborators have had
equal status as co-authors, as researchers we probably gained the most.

Therefore, despite our dialogic and self-reflexive designs, as beginning researchers we have also learned that research can have unintended effects.

SUMMARY

Our stories illustrate that research is a complicated, messy and ever-changing political process. Research, regardless of its theoretical orientation, is a social activity and when people come together in class-rooms and educational settings, challenges and tensions are inevitable. Navigating the contradictions and pitfalls of this journey have led us to make some suggestions for those about to embark on research for the first time. From our experiences, learning how to do research involves four basic elements:

- The support and wisdom of a supervisor or mentor. This person can both direct you to a range of theoretical and practical ways of investigating your problem as well as assist you to deal with the complex relationships that emerge during the research process.
- Being organised. A simple suggestion but an essential one. Always have a pen and paper handy. Ideas come at the oddest times and places, and every thought may offer an important contribution to the process. Set yourself up with bookshelves, filing cabinets, computer facilities, Internet access and your own workspace where you can leave work in progress. Try to provide yourself with consistent blocks of time to think and work uninterrupted and develop a big chart with deadlines and processes that must be followed. Invest in technology (qualitative analysis packages, transcription machines) that enable thinking time to be spent reflecting on, rather than managing, data.
- Being self-reflexive. To design and enact a study that will be seen as valid and relevant you need to constantly re-examine and criticise your understandings and actions. From day one, keep a personal research journal of your impressions, questions, problems and ideas. *How* things are written in this journal doesn't matter as much as that they *are* written. It is hard to remember all the nuances of what happened and early impressions can have important ramifications for later analyses.
- Being collaborative. Despite some of the tensions inherent in seeking the criticism of others, there is much to be gained from involving research participants in the study. Your findings will have more significance for others if you talk about, write about, test and problematise your ideas with those involved and with others in wider forums like conferences. Seeking input from others is not just about getting feedback, it also involves thinking about the

benefits of your research for your collaborators and what they stand to gain and lose from participating in the study.

QUESTIONS FOR REFLECTION

Choosing a supervisor

- What do you and others know about the scope of expertise of your supervisor, her interests and her politics?
- Do you feel able to trust, question, dialogue and critically engage with your supervisor?

Researching
Have you:

- Started a journal?
- Got a list of questions in place that will encourage you to critically reflect on what you are doing and how you are doing it at each step?
- Prepared and organised yourself conceptually and ethically for what might happen in the process of researching?
- Got effective management systems in place for dealing with data and information?
- Set out a time line for your study that allocates time for data collection, data analysis and the writing of the report?

FURTHER READING

Graue, M. E. and Walsh, D. J. (eds) 1998, *Studying Children in Context: Theories, Methods and Ethics*, Thousand Oaks, London.
Hatch, A. (ed.) 1995, *Qualitative Research in Early Childhood Settings*, Praeger, Westport, CT.

These books provide a general introduction to methodology from a critical and qualitative perspective and offer specific examples of studies that new researchers might find informative as they design their research projects.

5

Ethics in early childhood research

Margaret M. Coady

'. . . the only safe way to avoid violating principles of professional ethics is to refrain from doing social research altogether' (Bronfenbrenner, 1952, p. 453).

This statement about ethics by one of the leading theorists of child development is challenging. Though research is essential if our understanding of human development is to be advanced, the history of research is littered with examples of harm caused by researchers to their subjects. Bronfenbrenner's comment was made soon after the Nuremberg War Trials had revealed the horrors of research in the Nazi concentration camps. As a result of these revelations the Nuremberg Code (Appendix B, Grodin and Glantz, 1994) was promulgated and has been incorporated into many codes governing research. The first statement in this code is that in research 'the voluntary consent of the human subject is absolutely essential'.

Children are heavily represented among victims of research, as are other socially powerless groups, such as prisoners, the mentally disabled and those living in poverty. The likelihood of being a research victim increases if one experiences more than one of these vulnerabilities. While most of the horror stories of research come from the medical field, unethical research in the social sciences can also result in extreme harm, even though in many cases researchers are genuinely trying to establish important data. One example is of a 13-year-old girl, found in Los Angeles in the 1970s, who had been severely deprived of social contact. For researchers, 'Genie', as they named her, presented an ideal opportunity to test the hypothesis that there is a sensitive period for language learning. Genie was finally returned to very unsatisfactory care conditions when the research grant ran out (Rymer, 1994).

In this case the focus shifted from benefit to the child to benefit to research. In David Elkind's words (quoted Rymer, 1994, p. 206) 'the child was the centre of people's careers and grant-getting'. This is just one case that demonstrates the difficulties of combining the role of researcher with that of carer, teacher, doctor or therapist. Researchers may well be interested in benefitting the subject and finding important data for social good, but inevitably part of their motivation includes furthering their career and status. Research institutions also have an interest in grants and status as well as in producing socially valuable data (McNeill, 1993), and the good of the research subject can be forgotten.

INFORMED CONSENT

Informed consent of the subject, as the Nuremberg Code stressed, is the key to ethical research. The idea of informed consent is based on the ethical view that all humans have the right to autonomy, that is, the right to determine what is in their own best interests.

Requirements for informed consent

The subject must be told, in words they can understand:

- the nature of the research
- exactly what will be expected of them
- any possible risks of the research
- that they can withdraw from the research at any stage and withdraw any unprocessed data.

In addition, the subject:

- must not be pressured by financial or other inducements to take part in the research.

Most research institutions require that the method of gaining informed consent be in writing and approved by the institutional ethics committee in advance.

CHILDREN AND CONSENT

If we were to take the Nuremberg Code literally, no research using children as subjects would be admissible. Not all early childhood research involves children as subjects—early childhood staff, parents or some other adults are the subjects in many studies. Much important research does involve children as subjects, however. According to legal definitions children cannot give consent, but the child's legal guardian can give consent on behalf of the child. It is good practice, however, and in keeping with the United Nations Convention on the Rights of the Child, to ask the child also to give consent, or 'assent' as it is known in these circumstances.

While in almost all cases it is imperative to gain the consent of the child's parents, there can be problems with parental consent. There have been cases where parents have agreed to children being subjects of research that has had poor outcomes for the children (Lederer and Grodin, 1994). In addition the parents may not be present for all of the research and so not fully aware of what goes on and not be able to exercise their right to withdraw the child. This is particularly true where the research is conducted in an institution. It is desirable that the child's state be monitored during the course of the research, ideally by somebody outside the research team—a parent, a teacher or a carer—in order to ensure that the child's best interests are paramount.

People who are experienced in working with children may need to be involved in the gaining of assent. Pictures and diagrams are sometimes used by researchers to convey the nature of the research, and by the child subjects to indicate feelings about involvement.

DECEPTION IN RESEARCH

If subjects are deceived as part of a research project, they cannot give proper consent, since they have not been fully informed. While most codes of research ethics see deception of the subject as an ethical problem, some important research could not be carried out without some form of deception. In fact, the process of approving pharmaceutical drugs demands so-called 'double blind' experiments which constitute a form of deceit of the subject. The subjects are randomly assigned either to the treatment group or the placebo group. While these kinds of studies are more common in medicine, they frequently occur in education or psychosocial research, and there is a 'scientific' justification for them. The experiments may be ethically acceptable if potential subjects are told about the treatments and the placebos. The subject can then agree to be deceived, or at least to not be fully informed, to this extent.

Other types of research involve more serious deception, which may be justified by the importance of the findings. One example involved covert video-recording of parents interacting with their children in hospital (Southall et al., 1995). The children had been admitted for what is termed ALTE (apparent life-threatening events). The video evidence showed that in 33 of the 39 cases, parents abused their children in hospital to the extent of attempted suffocation or poisoning or breaking of limbs. Since a majority of the parents were later diagnosed with mental illness, and since the admitted children had siblings who would also presumably have been helped, if not saved, by this knowledge, it was argued that the great benefit obtained through this experiment outweighed the deception. However, it was a very controversial piece of research.

What of research where children are deceived? One such case (Hoagwood, Jensen and Fisher, 1996) had as its aim the examination of children's eyewitness memory. Four-year-olds were videotaped playing individually with a research assistant posing as a baby-sitter. A week later half the children met individually with a research assistant posing as a police officer who suggested to them that the baby-sitter the previous week may have done some 'bad things', and asked for their account of what had happened. Later all the children were questioned by members of the research team. One of the hypotheses in the research was that those who had met with the authority figure would be more likely to say the baby-sitter had acted badly.

Some of the questions that need to be asked about research involving subject deception are:

- Is the research important?
- Can information be gained in any other way that does not involve deception?
- How would the children be affected by being deceived?
- Should the children be 'dehoaxed' after the research?
- Should the parents be informed in advance of the deceptive nature of the research, thus possibly contaminating the research by suggesting the truth to the child subjects?

CONFIDENTIALITY AND PRIVACY

Most professionals working in the early childhood area are aware of the need to maintain confidentiality about children and their families. Out of respect for the privacy of the subjects, confidentiality is also promised in most consent forms for research.

In research, procedures are needed to keep data confidential. These procedures include:

- Coding of data and keeping the key to the code separate from the data.
- Keeping data in secure, locked storage.
- Ensuring that only those researchers authorised by the appropriate ethics committee have access to the data.
- Ensuring that reports, articles and conference papers do not contain identifying material.

What is often forgotten is that subjects can be identified through photos, videotapes and audiotapes. If such materials are to be used in publications or conference presentations, consent to this needs to be given by both parents and children. Even then it can be tricky, since charming children agreeing at age three to be shown on videotape may object strongly to the same video at age eight when they believe that they look foolish!

Confidentiality and child abuse

For researchers there is a strong presumption in favour of confidentiality. However there are also reasons in some cases for overriding this presumption and breaching confidentiality. It is quite possible, for example, that the researcher will come across evidence which suggests a child is being abused. In such a case the researcher needs to consider the following questions:

- Am I **mandated** to report suspected child abuse?
- If I am, have I made this clear when getting informed consent from the subjects? The researcher should point out to subjects, in advance of their giving consent, where there are legal limits to keeping matters confidential.
- If I am not mandated to report child abuse, should I nevertheless report?
- How serious is the promise of confidentiality made to the subjects? Does the potential damage to the child, and the possibility that reporting the suspected abuse can prevent it continuing, outweigh the promise of confidentiality?

In research connected with child abuse it is important to ensure that the research does nothing to make a bad situation worse.

The risk/benefit equation

In approving a research project, an important factor is the risk/benefit equation. The idea here is that the greater the benefit to be gained from a piece of research, the more the risks are acceptable. If a piece of research was almost certainly going to lead to a cure for childhood leukemia, the risk of a small amount of pain to child subjects who gave blood for the research would be allowable. If the value of the research will not be high, then any risk, even a slight one, would be questioned.

Risks of research on children can include psychological risks, ranging from a feeling of temporary worry to longer lasting emotional disturbance, and the upsetting of relationships within a family. In research on attachment the temporary upset shown by a baby separated from its mother would probably be acceptable, but only if the research was seen as providing new and significant data. Researchers cannot go around tormenting babies just to demonstrate their research skills! Risks in research on families can include legal risks, breakdown of relationships and even physical risks where there are violent members in the family. Risks in research on professionals include damage to workplace relations, loss of jobs, loss of reputation and legal risks following from these.

CULTURAL ISSUES IN ETHICAL RESEARCH

Some researchers treat minority groups as curiosities rather than as people, or as *objects* to be researched rather than *subjects* with all that entails about subjectivities. This kind of attitude was prominent in much nineteenth-century research into indigenous peoples—but it is a phenomenon which still exists.

Cultural differences may lead to misunderstanding by the researcher as well as by the subject. The subject may misunderstand because of language difficulties (in many cases having a translator is absolutely essential) or because of cultural understandings. The subject may believe that access to educational and other important benefits may depend on agreeing to participate. Researchers may misunderstand the different cultural understandings of family and family responsibilities, of relationships and of appropriate behaviour in different situations and may, as a result, unintentionally insult, offend or terrify the subject.

Some argue that informed consent procedures should vary from one cultural group to another. In one sense this is obviously true. Subjects must be informed about the research in a language that they understand. But some writers further suggest that some cultural groups do not value informed consent or that the leader of the family or of the tribe should give the informed consent. It is argued that the idea of autonomy or the right of the individual subject to consent is a western middle-class notion.

An important study in this regard was conducted in the Gambia (Leach et al., 1999). The subjects were mothers who were asked to consent to their children being given the *Haemophilus influenzae* type B (Hib) vaccination. Interviews were conducted with the 137 mothers who had agreed to the vaccination and the 52 who had refused. In spite of being from a 'developing' country, having very little education and living in rural areas, these women showed a good understanding of the consent procedure and its rationale. They valued autonomy and wanted to be free to give informed consent or refusal to their children having Hib vaccines. The researchers conclude that this community affirmed the principles of informed consent. It is easy and dangerous to underestimate or prejudge the abilities and concerns of the subjects in a situation that is very different from that experienced by the researcher.

RESEARCH INVOLVING INDIGENOUS GROUPS

Because of histories of lack of understanding and lack of respect of researchers for indigenous peoples, research on such groups is now very sensitive. In Canada, the Social Sciences and Humanities Research Council Code of Ethical Conduct for Research Involving Humans makes special provision for consulting what it terms 'vulnerable collectivities' which includes indigenous peoples. This policy is available at the website: http://www.nserc.ca/programs/ethics/english/policy.htm

In Australia, the National Health and Medical Research Council has set up formal guidelines on ethical matters in Aboriginal and Torres Strait Islander health research. These guidelines are available on the web site: http://www.health.gov.au/nhmrc/ethics/asti.pdf

These guidelines cover full consultation with the community, gaining consent both from individual subjects and the community, ensuring that Aboriginal women are present during all work dealing with children, and the use of any pictures strictly in accordance with the community wishes.

PUTTING IN ETHICS APPLICATIONS TO ETHICS COMMITTEES

Research undertaken within an institution will probably need to be approved by the institution's ethics committee. If more than one institution is involved in the research, there may be applications to both hospital and university, for example, or to school and university. Though the requirements of the institutions may be slightly different, they should be compatible and will cover areas such as the vulnerability of subjects, informed consent, risk assessment and confidentiality.

Ethics committee application reminders

- Try not to regard your ethics application as just another legalistic hurdle to be crossed. Ideally, ethics committees should be encouraging ethical research rather than acting as obstructive police. Such committees are certainly important in providing another perspective to researchers whose main concern is successful completion of the research.
- Give a thorough but concise description of what you plan to do, avoiding jargon and technical detail, particularly in the

plain language description of the project. Include exactly what will be expected of the subjects and how much of the subjects' time it will take. It is important to include how much of children's time it will take. The fact that children are 'captive' in institutions does not mean their time can be used at the whim of others.

- Do not forget that videotapes and audiotapes are identifying material. Show how you intend to maintain confidentiality if you are using such tapes.
- The form will ask you whether you are in a **dependent relationship** with any of the subjects. It often happens in early childhood research that the researcher wants to use as subjects the children and/or families in the centres in which they work, or the colleagues with whom they work. In these cases you need to *show*, not just assert, that the subjects will not feel any pressure to participate and, in the case of colleagues, that their working conditions can be in no way adversely affected by their agreeing to be subjects.
- Remember that the subjects, whether they are school children, children in child-care, or adults, are doing the researcher a favour by agreeing to take part in the research.

RESEARCH METHODOLOGIES

The application forms for most institutional ethics committees are better geared to quantitative research, often of a medical nature. However, ethics committees are now more sensitive to a range of different research paradigms. If the research involves open-ended in-depth interviews, most ethics committees would be satisfied with a description of why this is necessary and an account of the kind and scope of questions to be asked.

While feminist thinkers, in particular, have been sensitive to the inequalities of power between researcher and subject, the attempt to remedy these inequalities through collaborative research and building reciprocity into the research design (see Chapter 17) needs to be carefully managed. For example, a researcher may want all those employed in a child-care centre to share ownership of research being conducted by the researcher in their centre. In such a case the researcher needs to be realistic about the inequalities of power involved in a particular employment situation that may prevent some staff from refusing involvement. All staff should be fully informed in advance of the details of the research and the expectations of the different roles. Special care needs to be taken in acknowledging in any publications or presentations the contributions of each member of the research team.

SUMMARY

Attention to the ethical aspects of research can in some instances impede research. There are even certain pieces of research which are 'forbidden' in the sense that, while possibly yielding valuable data, they are so harmful to the subjects that they should not be performed. In other cases research has to be limited out of respect for the subjects, for example when accepting a subject's right to withdraw. In general, however, concern for ethics in both the planning and the execution stage of research can add to the quality of the research. While at the time it seems an added burden, even the submission of an ethics application means that the researcher must think through the whole process of the research and its implications before commencing. The result is better-thought-out research and greater protection of the rights of the subjects and of all those affected by the research.

QUESTIONS FOR REFLECTION

- Have you ever been invited to be a subject of research? Did you consent to taking part? If so, what were your reasons for taking part? If not, why not?
- What kind of benefits could ethically justify subjecting a child to some risk?
- On what occasions can you envisage having to breach confidentiality in a research study?
- If you already have in mind a possible research topic or question, what sorts of issues of an ethical nature do you think it raises?

FURTHER READING

Beauchamp, T. L., Faden, R., Wallance, R. and Walters, L. (eds) 1984, *Ethical Issues in Social Science Research*, Johns Hopkins Press, Baltimore. Although not recent, this book provides detailed cover of most ethical issues in research in the social sciences.

Grodin, M. A. and Glantz, L (eds) 1994, *Children as Research Subjects*, Oxford University Press, New York. This book, entirely devoted to the topic of children as subjects, is particularly useful on issues of risk to children in research. Its appendices include several of the most influential codes that cover research.

The research departments of most research institutions can provide lists of principles to be followed in research and particular requirements for making submissions to the relevant institutional ethics committee.

Part II

Analysis and design

6

Design issues

Alan Hayes

PLAN YOUR WORK AND WORK TO YOUR PLAN

Research design is a matter of planning. It is all very well to have a good idea for research, and to develop a set of incisive research questions, but these may not necessarily translate into a feasible study. The design process considers the many options and alternatives for planning the study, with a view to developing the most appropriate blueprint for the project—the investigator must consider, among other things, what is to be researched and how, when and where the research is to take place, who will participate, what data will be collected and how these will be analysed.

This chapter provides a foundation understanding of design. It seeks first to define the concept of research design and to explore the link between research questions and decisions about design. Some of the major options available (experimental, quasi-experimental and non-experimental) are discussed, focusing on the concept of causation. The discussion also addresses the dimension of time, considers retrospective and prospective approaches and compares and contrasts cross-sectional and longitudinal designs. A discussion of who is to participate in the research focuses on sampling issues (random sampling, stratification and two-stage random sampling, along with non-random techniques such as systematic, purposive and convenience sampling). Specific methods of data collection are not discussed, as these are covered in later chapters. The final section briefly addresses some further practical considerations in the design process. Throughout the chapter studies undertaken by the author and his research students, involving research on participants from infancy to adolescence and set within family and community contexts, are used as brief illustrations of the design issues discussed. The chapter aims to demystify design and make it accessible to students who have a minimal background in research.

Setting the discussion in context

At the outset, it is important to acknowledge the research tradition that underpins this chapter. The discussion is framed within the positivist paradigm of research, reflecting the background and experience of the author. Nonetheless, many of the issues raised, and how they might be approached from a design perspective, are relevant for those working within different paradigms. Useful insights into design issues for research framed by non-positivist paradigms are also provided elsewhere in this book (see Chapter 8) and in other publications (Goodwin and Goodwin, 1996; Bogdan and Biklen, 1998). Early childhood research can be informed by and combine elements of these various approaches. All frameworks, and the methods each one favours, provide valuable insights into the important questions that early childhood researchers address. Chapters 7 and 8, which follow, outline quantitative and qualitative designs and analyses, respectively.

DESIGN DEFINED

Research, like other aspects of life, is a matter of options and choices. Research design is the creative process of translating a research idea into a set of decisions about how the research will proceed in practice. The design process seeks to achieve a balance among several factors. These include the focus of the study, the original idea and its translation into a question or a series of questions that can feasibly be researched, the work that has been undertaken previously on the topic, the methods that seem most appropriate to the project and the means of interpreting and communicating the findings.

In the social sciences, and in fields such as early childhood, there is rarely a single correct way of conducting any research project, although some projects will clearly be better designed than others. Unlike the 'definitive experiment' in the physical sciences, research in the social sciences confronts considerable lack of capacity to control the phenomena of interest—people and their behaviour. This lack of precise control means that there is always some degree of uncertainty surrounding the inferences and conclusions that are drawn from even the most carefully designed study. Of course, the physical sciences also confront issues of uncertainty and lack of control, although these may too often be conveniently overlooked.

In texts on research methods, design is often presented in a way that seems complex and unduly surrounded by scientific and statistical mystique. In fact, research design is a straightforward, practical process of logically considering the relative merits of a range of approaches to the problem to be researched. It is the process by which the topic is turned into a researchable project. Following consideration of key issues such as whether the topic is within the researcher's competence, the design process involves identifying the possible alternative ways in which the project might be undertaken and evaluating their relative merits (see, for example, Bell, 1993; Patterson et al., 1993; Tuckman, 1994; Booth, Williams and Williams, 1995; Hubbard and Power, 1995; Gall and Borg, 1996; Gay, 1996; Kumar, 1996; Mauch and Birch, 1998).

THE 'WHAT' AND 'HOW' OF RESEARCH

How research is to be designed and undertaken depends on the specific focus of the investigation. The first step in design is clarifying the topic and identifying the specific focus of the research (Kumar, 1996). Just as an architect cannot design a house until the clients are clear about their requirements, research cannot be well designed unless what is to be researched is clear. Many projects may involve stages that successively build upon one another but, at the very least, the initial stage of the project must be clarified to ensure that it is researchable and feasible.

Refining the topic

Having decided on a general area to research, the design process begins with refinement of the general topic. Typically, the initial formulation of the area of interest is too broad to be researchable within the resources and time available to the researcher. It may also involve too many facets to be addressed within a single study.

The researcher needs to break the general topic into a number of subtopics and consider the logical order in which these might be addressed. This process is illustrated in the following discussion of the development of knowledge about the links among young children's social experiences in early life, their brain development and their social behaviours.

77

CASE STUDY

The development of knowledge: Some old foundations of the new brain research

The broad topic

To what extent is brain development in early childhood influenced by social experience and the quality of early nurturing?

The significance of the topic

In its broadest sense, this topic casts light on the relationship between heredity and environment. If brain development can be shown to be influenced by experience, this would provide important evidence of how inherited characteristics are modified in interaction with the environment and the particular experiences it provides. More specifically, it would demonstrate the importance of early childhood as a time in which changes occur that influence later development in fundamentally important ways.

The old foundations

Until recently, it was not possible to examine brain structure and functioning directly. The recent explosion of interest in brain development in the early years of life has been stimulated by rapid advances in imaging technology. These advances have enabled direct observation of brain functioning and the production of high resolution images of the brain.

The recent research is built on some older research that provided the important first step in addressing the larger question posed above: To what extent is brain development in early childhood influenced by social experience and the quality of early nurturing?

To establish that infants can be influenced by social experience required research into their competencies, particularly their sensory and perceptual capabilities. The early research was based on clinical observation and the development of infant tests by Gesell (1952) and others (Cattell, 1934).

In the 1960s and 1970s there was a renewal of interest in infant development (White, 1971) and a series of ingenious experiments laid the foundations of knowledge of infant visual acuity and perceptual development, demonstrating their capacity to identify familiar and novel faces from the first weeks of life. Much of this work had built on equally groundbreaking research by Hubel and Weisel (1962) into the role of experience in shaping the visual system of cats. Again, a well-designed experiment enabled these researchers to show that the early experiences of kittens directly affected their visual development. These studies also showed that some of the earlier clinical observations had, in fact, underestimated the pace of development and the degree of competence that infants demonstrate at birth and in the first year of life.

In parallel, researchers examined infants who had been deprived of social contact in early life and compared and contrasted their development with children growing up in families where social contact was appropriate.

Some possible directions for further research

What design options are there for further research building on the accumulated knowledge of brain development in early life? At the outset, it might be necessary to develop a valid and reliable scale to measure social experience, given the possible shortcomings of the existing scales. The first study might involve the assessment of the newly developed scale against previous scales and of its capacity to identify reliably differences in the quality of children's social experience, as well as the relationship of scores on the scale to other measures, such as observational data on the characteristics of their home environments.

In addition, it might be important to evaluate a range of methods for accurately capturing social behaviours of the children. The range of possibilities might include parent or early childhood staff reports of their direct observation of the child's experiences within the home or early childhood services. These aspects of the project would need to be completed before the main study could be undertaken.

The above discussions highlight how a process of investigation can involve stages of development of the topic, parallel strands and a range of design options to address the questions at each stage and within each strand.

For a recent review of the brain research literature and the historical development of knowledge in this area see Cynader and Frost (1999).

Two broad types of research

In general terms, research can be classified as either non-experimental (sometimes termed 'observational') or experimental (Tilley, 1996). The difference between the two, broadly speaking, comes down to the extent to which the researcher actively controls the situation. A continuum exists from unobtrusive observation in naturalistic settings, where the researcher remains as aloof as possible from the action, to experimental methods, where the researcher directly controls the situation. Between these extremes are approaches that differ in the extent of involvement and control exercised by the researcher.

In the popular imagination, research is synonymous with experiments controlled by the stereotyped 'mad scientist'. This conception of science ignores the fact that scientific knowledge is predominantly built on foundations of observation. In the social sciences this is typically of the behaviour of children and/or adults, including observation, recording and analysis of their verbal behaviour (the cornerstone of much qualitative research). The choice of whether to base the research on experiment or not comes down to whether the study is focused on explaining the causes of events and as such addresses causal hypotheses, or not.

Hypotheses or not?

The extent to which the topic can be framed as a set of hypotheses needs to be the first consideration (Mauch and Birch, 1998). Not all research projects involve the testing of hypotheses. Much valuable research involves observing or documenting things that occur in everyday life.

Hypotheses are predictive statements containing a possible explanation of some phenomenon. They are typically, though not exclusively, couched in terms of cause and effect and presented as a statement such as: 'That parental neglect negatively influences brain development'. In this instance the cause, neglect, is presumed to have an effect, in this case on brain development in infancy.

The original hypothesis might derive from clinical observations of young children who have experienced severe neglect and/or abuse (see, for example, the research by Weatherburn and Lind, 1997). But how does the presumed effect of neglect impede brain development in infants? Is it a product of their nutrition, their mothers' nutrition during pregnancy, or both? Is it a product of impaired attachment relationships that typify neglectful families? Or is it an interaction between nutritional and social factors? What is the relationship between neglect and abuse? Does neglect increase the probability of abuse? Given that it is estimated that 190 million children, or 40%per cent of the world's population of children under 5 years, are currently living in circumstances that provide inadequate nutrition, this is a most important research topic.

How might one address such a topic? There are several possibilities, but some of these are ethically constrained. For example, it would be highly unethical and, moreover, illegal to neglect children for the purpose of research.

80

Experimental designs

One possible design for such a study might involve an **experiment** using non-human subjects. For example, animals such as rats could be reared under systematically different conditions and their brain development evaluated after a standard time, controlling for as many relevant factors as possible (including the strain of rats, their genetic character- istics, nutrition during pregnancy and the rearing conditions since birth). The rats would be randomly assigned to the different conditions (or treatments) in the experiment. Random assignment means that each subject has an equal chance of being assigned to a particular treatment group. By controlling as many of these relevant factors, and randomly assigning the animals to treatments, the researcher seeks to increase the chance that the effect that is measured can only be attributed to the hypothesised cause, or combination of causal factors.

In the simplest form of experimental design there will be two groups (Pedhazur and Schmelkin, 1991; Tilley, 1996). In the example above, the rats assigned to the **treatment group** (in this experiment it might be a low level of nutrition, as one indicator of neglect) will be compared and contrasted with a **control group** that receives a level of nutrition within the range normally needed by rats of this age and body weight. Nutrition would be regarded as the **independent variable**.

Rearing conditions (such as cage type, lighting, temperature, noise levels, food type and presentation, and any other relevant variables) would be controlled to be, as far as possible, identical for each group, as previous research might have shown them to influence the behaviour of this strain of rats. These factors are called **relevant variables.**

The effect of nutrition on brain development would be the focus of this particular small group study. Brain development would be hy- pothesised to vary depending on the level of nutrition, the variable that is free to be controlled by the experimenter. The outcome, in this case brain development, would be regarded as the **dependent variable** as it 'depends' on nutrition.

If the effect can be demonstrated, under very similar circumstances, by other researchers, one can be confident of the causal role of early experience on early brain development. The process of repeating the experiment, ideally with different researchers conducting the experi- ment in different laboratories, is called replication (Pedhazur and Schmelkin, 1991). In science, and especially in the social sciences, replication is necessary to ensure that the results were not a product of chance factors or because of some causal factors, unrelated to the hypothesis, that occurred in conducting the experiment on the first occasion. If the results from different researchers in different locations are similar, one may have greater confidence in the initial hypothesis.

The animal experiment might be regarded as valid in its design and in the way that it was conducted, but still might be of limited value in understanding human infants and the effect of early experience on their brain development. Of course, important ethical constraints also apply to the experimental use of animals.

Quasi-experimental designs

Most readers of this book will be more interested in studying children than rats! Given the ethical and legal constraints that apply to experimental manipulations of children's nutrition and social experience, however, how might one study this topic in early childhood? One way might be to conduct a quasi-experiment (Cook and Campbell, 1979). The defining feature of such a design is that random assignment to treatments is not possible, although in real life groups can be identified that naturally vary in their levels on the variables of interest.

With reference to the present example, it might be possible to describe precisely differences in nutritional levels and social experience in various groups of young children and measure each child's brain development, using the new imaging techniques. From this the researcher might be able to infer that any differences that are detected in brain development across the groups are caused by the pre-existing differences in nutrition and social experience.

While providing a less powerful demonstration of the cause and effect relationship, in many areas of the social sciences, education and early childhood, the most that can be aspired to is quasi-experimentation. The problem with not being able to assign participants to treatment groups randomly is that many other factors may be systematically related to the groups. A group that is malnourished for example, may have associated medical problems or be at higher risk of other problems such as abuse (Weatherburn and Lind, 1997).

Non-experimental designs

Often it might not be possible to conduct even a quasi-experiment. It might be feasible, however, to measure the variations that occur within a group of children and explore the relationships of these variations to the measures of their brain development. One such non-experimental design, that analyses the relationship but does not conduct an experiment to determine that one variable (or set of variables) causes the other, is called a correlational study.

Unlike a controlled experiment, a correlational study is not capable of concluding that one factor is the cause of the other. The hypothesis might be: 'That early experience of neglect is related to brain growth'. The difference in these two ways of stating the hypothesis may seem subtle, but it is fundamentally important. It is a major temptation to interpret correlation as causation (Pedhazur and Schmelkin 1991; Tilley, 1996). To say two things are related or associated does not provide evidence that one causes the other. They may be related via a third variable. Neglect and brain growth, for the present example, might be related to the third variable of social experience. Correlational approaches seek to ascertain the extent of relationship of variables within a group.

Qualitative studies

As argued above, in the social sciences there may be far more uncertainty and lack of control than in the physical sciences. For example, the key variable may actually be the interpretation of experience, more than the experience *per se* (Bogdan and Biklen, 1998). Rather than conducting an experiment or undertaking a correlational study, the researcher might wish to conduct a qualitative study to provide information about the perceptions or beliefs of mothers who differ in the quality of their care for their infants (from identified neglect to high quality care). The survey might probe the mothers' knowledge and ideas about child development, attachment, play, nutrition, behaviour management and other potentially relevant dimensions of parenting. Alternatively, it might seek to explore the beliefs without imposing any frame on the data collection, by using an interviewing technique without previously determined categories (Strauss and Corbin, 1990). Such a study is less likely to be framed in terms of hypotheses about cause and effect.

An example of the integration of research types in a doctoral project

The topic
Is motor development in young children showing clumsiness or intellectual disability delayed or different, when compared to the development of children not showing any motor problems? If delayed, then while the rate of development may be slower, the manner of development should be similar to that of typically developing children. Difference implies that some or all of the characteristics of development deviate from the typical pattern.

The design
Comparison across groups of children (4–7 years and 8–11 years) varying in their motor development were studied using a variety of approaches:

- Qualitative description of movement patterns, as reflected in walking, running, jumping, catching and throwing, involving filming of children and comparison of patterns across groups.
- Quantitative analysis of motor performance on a norm-referenced test of motor development.

- Experimental study of motor control processes using a laboratory task (launching rockets to strike targets at different distances, using different hands, in response to a signal). This experiment was designed to measure reaction and response times as well as accuracy of movement.

The project found that different patterns of motor development were evident depending on the aspect studied and how it was measured. Development was *both* delayed and different—a finding that has considerable implications for the design of early childhood movement programmes for young children with motor problems.

(Further information concerning this study can be found in O'Brien and Hayes, 1995).

THE 'WHEN', 'WHERE' AND 'WHO' OF RESEARCH

Time, place and persons are other key aspects of research design. With regard to time, studies can focus on the past, the present or the future, depending on the nature of the research questions being addressed and the purpose of the project. Place is important, particularly in studies of young children, as settings and contexts may exert considerable influence over children's behaviour, especially when children are not familiar with them. Who participates is also a key dimension and, again, relates to the focus of the study as well as the extent to which the conclusions of the research are representative of the wider population and whether the findings can be generalised to groups other than those who participated in the research.

Time's arrow: present, past and future orientations

Much research is focused in the present, as time and its passage tend not to be key dimensions of many studies. The research might explore current behaviour, attitudes, beliefs or values. The exception is research that focuses on developmental phenomena, which are inherently bound to time. Developmental research can be regarded as a 'time science'.

Of course, researchers face the same realities of limited time that confront most of us and this in part explains the appeal of designs that can be completed in a short time-frame. In order to truncate the time required to undertake studies of development, **cross-sectional designs** are often the option of choice. These typically involve selecting groups of participants at different ages and interpreting differences in performance across the age groups as evidence of developmental

84

change. The simplest of these designs might involve comparison of two groups (say younger and older infants or children). More complex designs might involve multiple age groups.

The difficulty with such designs is that differences across the groups might not be solely the result of developmental changes related to age (Miller, 1987). Other variables, such as life circumstances or experiences, might also differ for different age groups. Changes in obstetric practices or approaches to infant care might result in systematic differences in infants that might be confounded with 'true' developmental changes (changes due solely to age). If the age groups span years, as has often been the case in projects studying trends in intellectual development or cognitive processes such as memory, the effects may be even more marked. A group of 6-year-olds may have a fundamentally different set of early life circumstances and developmental experiences to a group of 90-year-olds who have lived through the Great Depression, two world wars and a radically different set of early childhood and later educational experiences. To make matters even more complex, the 90-year-olds represent the sample of those from their birth cohort who have survived to that age and may be a small proportion of those who were alive when they were six years old. Differences across age groups are referred to as cohort effects (Baltes and Schaie, 1974; 1976; Miller, 1987). While these differences may be real, the conclusion that they illustrate the process of development may not be valid.

Another strategy to study developmental effects involves exploring the past experiences of groups and reconstructing their developmental pathways. Research that focuses on the past collects information retrospectively (retrospective studies). Historical information is commonly collected and is an example of retrospective data. Using the example related to brain development, the study might take children who are showing signs of impaired brain development and focus on their previous history of care and nutrition. While it is tempting to see such **retrospective research** as providing evidence of causation, this risks reaching inappropriate conclusions. Hypothetically, it might be the case that many children who suffer early deficits of nutrition and/or care do not go on to show lasting impairment of brain development. Again, as Sameroff and Chandler (1975) argued some time ago, retrospective data may not provide valid evidence of developmental causation.

Studies designed to follow the participants through time can provide compelling evidence of causation (Miller, 1987; Pickles and Rutter, 1991). Prospective studies are a powerful way to establish the causal pathways for outcomes in children's development. Such studies can involve experimental designs with measurement before some intervention (pre-testing) and of outcomes following the intervention (post-testing). With regard to the brain development example, a pre-test/post-test design might involve initial measurement of at-risk children's brain development prior to their involvement in a social stimulation intervention project along with nutritional supplementation and follow-up assessments, after involvement in the intervention for a period of say a year. Comparison of measurements at the same times for matched comparison groups receiving either nutritional supplementation or social stimulation (but not both) would provide a test of the relative contributions of each factor separately.

Another type of prospective design involves longitudinal research. A longitudinal study, as compared to an experimental follow-up study, typically involves investigation of naturally occurring changes on repeated occasions over a substantial period of time (Miller, 1987). What constitutes a substantial period of time depends in part on the period of development under study. In early infancy, for example, the rate of change may be so rapid that a longitudinal study can be undertaken over a period of months or weeks, depending on the focus of the study. The key advantage of prospective, longitudinal designs is that they enable the behaviour and capabilities of individuals to be tracked as they develop. They also provide an elegant way of addressing questions related to stability and change in development both for individuals and for groups (Olweus and Alsaker, 1991; Pickles and Rutter, 1991). Of course, if only a single cohort is involved, the results are specific to that group.

An ingenious way of enhancing the power of a longitudinal study is to recruit multiple cohorts (say those born in 1994, 1996 and 1998, or 6-, 4- and 2-year-olds) at the commencement of the study in 2000 and assess their development at regular intervals, say every three months, until they enter school (Bergman, Eklund and Magnusson, 1991). In this way, any similarities and differences in development among the cohorts can be explicitly measured as well as the stability and change within each cohort as time passes. Like all matters of design, the manner in which time is handled depends on the topic and the resources available for the study.

An example of a project using both cross-sectional and longitudinal designs

The topic
Facial gaze in mother-infant social interaction.

The approach
A structured observational study in a Community Health Clinic.

The cross-sectional design
Two studies examined the gaze behaviours of mothers with infants aged 4–15 weeks and 16–30 weeks (Study 1) and 20–33 weeks and 34–54 weeks (Study 2), respectively.

The results
While the percentage of time mothers spent in facial gaze remained similar, irrespective of infant age, infant facial gaze decreased from the youngest to the oldest age groups.

The longitudinal design
A third study recruited groups of mothers and their infants aged 8, 10, 12 and 14 weeks and followed each group at fortnightly intervals (10, 12, 14 and 16 weeks and 12, 14, 16 and 18 weeks). The design enabled comparison of the facial gaze of each group, across ages (for example, for the youngest group at 8 then 10 and 12 weeks) and between ages at any single time of observation (for example, of the groups aged 8, 10, 12 and 14 weeks on the first occasion they were observed, as well as the second and third times).

The results
The design showed that the behaviours of mothers and infants were different on the first occasion each group was observed, most probably as a result of lack of familiarity with the setting. For each group, however, the trend to stable percentages of facial gaze for the mothers and diminishing levels for the infants, that had been observed in the cross-sectional studies, was confirmed.

(For further information please see Hayes, 1980.)

An example of a retrospective design

The topic
The developmental and educational history of a boy with late diagnosed Asperger's syndrome, a disorder showing social skill deficits, language and communication difficulties, clumsiness, obsessive preference for routine and a preoccupation with idiosyncratic interests.

The approach
A case study of a boy aged 17 years at the time of the research using a combination of current standardised psychological tests and interview data along with retrospective data based on existing records and interviews with the boy and his parents.

The results
The study provided greater insight into the possible developmental pathway for persons with Asperger's syndrome and explored some of the reasons why it had been late diagnosed in this particular boy. It could not, however, provide evidence of the precise cause(s) of the condition.

(For further information please see Gilmore & Hayes, 1996.)

THE IMPORTANCE OF PLACE

In the lay imagination, research often conjures images of experiments conducted in musty laboratory settings, cluttered with strange apparatus. In practice, however, research takes place in as many settings as one can imagine. In early childhood, research is more likely to occur in settings other than laboratories, such as children's homes, early childhood services or schools.

The advantage of laboratory settings is that they allow greater standardisation and control of the conditions for the experiment. In turn, standardisation and control mean that the experiment ought to be able to be replicated across laboratories, provided the same physical and procedural conditions are established for the research. The disadvantage is that the conditions in the laboratory may not match those likely to apply in the world beyond.

In research with young children (and people generally), their behaviour may be altered by the laboratory environment and they may act in ways that they normally would not in their own surroundings. Typically, early childhood researchers will seek to study behaviour in naturalistic settings, and as unobtrusively as possible, as everyday settings can suffer similar problems to those of laboratory settings if children are required to perform activities and tasks that are out of the ordinary (Hayes, 1980). The issue of place is complex and depends on the purpose of the research and the extent to which issues of generalisability of the findings to everyday settings are focal.

An example of the importance of place

The topic
The teaching behaviours of younger and older children with Down syndrome and their siblings when observed in play at home and in a laboratory setting.

The approach
This study observed the same children under two conditions:

- Playing spontaneously at home.
- In an observational setting in a university while taking part in spontaneous play and structured tasks designed to elicit teaching behaviour.

The results
The rates of teaching behaviour observed were much lower for all children in the home as opposed to the laboratory setting although, at home, the younger brothers and sisters of children with Down syndrome were observed to teach their older siblings to a greater extent than observed in any other group.

In the laboratory setting the older children (irrespective of whether they had Down syndrome or not) taught significantly more than when in spontaneous play, at home.
(For further information see Senapati, 1989.)

SELECTING PERSONS TO PARTICIPATE

Addressing the what, how, when, and where questions takes place with reference to a further question: 'Who will participate?' In early childhood research the possibilities for participants are extensive. Infants or young children might be the focus although, depending on the purpose of the study, the participants could also be members of their family, peer group or people from their neighbourhood, early childhood staff, students training to work with young children or members of the wider community, among others. It is not uncommon for more than one of these groups to be involved. This is particularly the case if interactive phenomena such as communication, including teaching or learning interactions, are the focus of the study. The participants in this instance might be a mother or father and their young child, or a toddler and her carer, or a preschool student and his teacher.

In considering the participants, variables such as age, gender, family structure (two-parent versus single-parent families, families with only one child or couples without children), social status (as indicated by educational background, occupation and/or income level), ethnicity, home language and any special characteristics (such as giftedness or disability or specific medical conditions) may need to be taken into account, among others. The participants might also be defined by where they are rather than who they are and the key characteristic might be for example, whether children are currently attending early childhood services or not. In short, a wide range of characteristics of the participants may need to be considered in designing the project.

The number of participants is another aspect that must be decided. The options here span from a single individual (Hersen and Barlow, 1976; Tawney and Gast, 1984), if the study is to be a case study of one person, through to a large-scale study of an entire population. It is rarely possible, however, to study all of the members of a population, such as the world's 3-year-olds. It would require time, money and personnel beyond the realms of possibility. A population is all of the members of some group (Fraenkel and Wallen, 1996). Of course, populations vary greatly in size and some, such as children with a rare medical condition, are by definition small.

When study of a population is not feasible, researchers resort to sampling from the population. Earlier in the chapter the concept of the **random sample** was introduced in discussing experimental designs. The defining feature of such a sample was that each member of the population has an equal chance of being selected to participate in the study. While it is beyond the scope of this chapter to provide a detailed discussion of sampling, the major types of sampling will be described briefly.

It is not always possible to sample individuals randomly. For some purposes, one wants to ensure that the sample is representative, in terms of the proportions of the sample from each subgroup within a given population (Fraenkel and Wallen, 1996). For purposes of illustration, 30 per cent of a given population might be from homes where a language other than English is spoken. The sampling strategy would ensure that these subgroups, or strata, are proportionally represented in the sample (70 per cent from an English-speaking home background and 30 per cent from non-English-speaking homes). Within these two strata, the sampling would still be random. This approach is described as **stratified random sampling**.

Again, when random sampling of individuals is not possible, it might be necessary to sample some whole group, or cluster of individuals, randomly. The group might be from some particular early childhood service. This technique is referred to as **cluster random sampling** (Fraenkel and Wallen, 1996). Another variant combines cluster and individual random sampling in a two stage process. For purposes of illustration, the researcher might randomly select twenty child-care centres and within each randomly select five children to give a sample of 100 children in total.

At times, however, random sampling will not be possible for a range of reasons, some related to practical limitations, others related to the purpose of the study. The options for non-random sampling include systematic sampling, say of every fifth child on a class list; convenience sampling, say of two child-care centres that are accessible to the researcher; or purposive sampling, where the sample is based on prior knowledge of the group, say of children who demonstrate particularly creative play and are selected for a study comparing them to a sample of those who are regarded as closer to the average (Fraenkel and Wallen, 1996). Unlike random sampling, however, each of these techniques is more likely to have the risk of bias in the sample (Hopkins, Stanley and Hopkins, 1990).

Again, the issues of who will participate in a particular study involve many decisions that relate to other aspects of the project such as purpose, approach, time and place.

Sampling methods illustrated in the studies cited above

- Purposive sampling: O'Brien and Hayes (1995); Senapati (1989)
- Convenience sampling: Hayes (1980); Gilmore and Hayes (1996)

GETTING REAL: FROM THE ABSTRACT TO THE CONCRETE

The process of designing a research project is one of turning abstract ideas for research into a set of feasible, practical research procedures. It involves a set of decisions that take the researcher from imagining an ideal study to addressing the complexities of real research, with real people, in real settings and with real limits on resources.

Design is a process of choice among many possibilities. It requires logical consideration (and elimination) of alternatives. The order of these decisions is not necessarily as presented in this discussion. As has been illustrated, the decisions are interdependent and there is great scope for flexibility. Design is the 'thought work' prior to deciding on an approach, methods and procedures for a research project. From personal experience, conducting a small-scale trial, or pilot, of the chosen approach, methods and procedures is a vital step in reassuring oneself that the choices and decision are the most appropriate and practically feasible ways to address the research questions for the project. Ultimately, however, issues of feasibility, practicality and ethics are the key determinants of whether a particular design can be implemented or not.

SUMMARY

Design involves the processes of:

- Refining the topic and framing researchable questions ('what' will be researched).
- Deciding among alternative approaches to the research ('how' the research will be undertaken).
- Considering issues related to time, place and persons ('when', 'where' and 'who').
- Choosing methods of data collection and analysis.
- Evaluating the feasibility and practical constraints on the design.
- Modifying the design in the light of pilot testing.

QUESTIONS FOR REFLECTION

- Discuss the process of research design and compile a list of the factors that might need to be considered in designing a research project.
- Consider the topic: 'The effect of social play on children's development in early childhood'.

Complete the following tasks:
1. Develop a set of three researchable questions.
2. For each question choose two alternative approaches to research it.
3. For the project as a whole, consider the following:
   (a) the dimension of time and how this will be handled;
   (b) the place, or places, where the research might take place in order to address the research questions you have framed;
   (c) the likely participants, their characteristic and a sampling strategy to guide their recruitment;
   (d) with reference to the other relevant chapters of this book, the data collection methods and techniques that might be used in your project; and
   (e) the practical limitations that need to be considered in implementing your research design.

FURTHER READING

Fraenkel, J. R. and Wallen, N. E. 1996, *How to Design and Evaluate Research in Education*, McGraw-Hill, New York. This volume provides a very clear discussion of issues related to sampling and design options for educational research.

Miller, S. A. 1987, *Developmental Research Methods*, Prentice-Hall, Englewood Cliffs, NJ. The specific focus on developmental design and research issues has considerable relevance to early childhood.

7

Quantitative designs and statistical analysis

Linda Harrison

This chapter summarises the main features of quantitative research and associated methods of statistical analysis. Underlying assumptions of quantitative research, types of measurement and statistical procedures are illustrated by drawing on examples from the author's longitudinal investigation of child-care. It is anticipated that the reader will come to appreciate the purpose and benefits of quantitative research designs, understanding not only the reasons this approach is the preferred choice for some sorts of research questions but also its usefulness in addressing a range of issues.

Example: Child-care research

The research examples that will be drawn on throughout this chapter are from a longitudinal study of non-parental child-care and its effects on children's development (Harrison, 1999; Harrison and Ungerer, 1997, 1999, 2000). The impetus for the study was twofold. First, we sought to address the challenge put forward by Belsky (1988), based primarily on US data, that early and extensive experience of child-care had negative outcomes for children, in particular, a greater likelihood for insecure infant–mother attachment relationships and more aggressive, non-compliant behaviour at preschool. Second, we wanted to test the expectation that Australia's system of formal, government-regulated and federally-subsidised child-care, which has been favourably compared to child-care in the United States (Wangman, 1995), would not be detrimental to children's socioemotional and cognitive development. In keeping with international research on this topic, a non-experimental quantitative design was used.

CHARACTERISTICS OF QUANTITATIVE RESEARCH

Readers will have already gained some insights into the features of quantitative research from previous chapters; specifically, its location within a positivistic paradigm, its connection with experimental designs and the importance of researcher-imposed controls. Quantitative research proceeds systematically through a series of stages—defining the question and the variables, selecting the sample and appropriate assessment measures, applying the assessment measures and analysing the data. Throughout this process, there is a reliance on data that are numerical in form. Measurement and statistical analysis are essential to quantitative designs. In most studies, data are summarised and analysed using computer software packages such as SPSS (Statistical Package for the Social Sciences) or EXCEL. Readers wishing to use such software might turn to Burns (2000), Cramer (1998), Foster (1998) or other recent statistics texts for details of these procedures.

ASSUMPTIONS OF QUANTITATIVE DESIGNS

Quantitative research draws on the assumptions of the traditional scientific approach, that is, 'objectivity, reliability, generality and reductionism' (Burns, 2000, p. 4). Questions of interest are invest-igated objectively, giving·due attention to alternative explanations of observed events. Phenomena are defined, or reduced, to a set of spec-ific, measurable components or variables. The methods used to assess these variables are scrutinised as to the reliability of the information they provide, and the results are examined as to their relevance, or generalisability, to the population as a whole. Quantitative studies must attend to these four key assumptions.

Objectivity

By being objective, the researcher aims 'to discern *what actually is the case*,' such that even if a hypothesis seems to have support, alternate hypotheses will also be tested (Burns, 2000, pp. 4–5). The researcher must give due attention to alternative explanations by attending to a range of possible influences on the phenomenon being studied. This is a major challenge for the researcher. The solution is to introduce 'controls' into the research design, which may be done in any of the three following ways.

Controlled conditions

The researcher can control or manipulate the conditions of the investigation and randomise the assignment of subjects to different conditions in order to eliminate or limit other possible influences on the outcome. This is the approach taken in true experimental research.

Control variables

When random assignment is not possible, as in quasi-experimental or non-experimental studies, the researcher can control or neutralise the influence of pre-existing differences in subjects by limiting the scope of the study to a specified group. Control variables hold constant the effect of particular independent variables.

Statistical controls

The researcher may take account of pre-existing differences in the sample population by including a range of relevant variables in the research design, in addition to the variables of primary interest. Preliminary stages of data analysis are used to assess the relationships between these relevant variables and the independent and dependent variables. In the final analyses, statistical procedures are used to systematically control for the effects of relevant variables while testing the effect of the independent variables on the outcome, the dependent variable.

Example: Child-care research

The effects of child-care were examined in combination with other important factors, such as maternal, family and child characteristics, which were included in the design and controlled for statistically. We restricted the sample to firstborn children to control for the child's position in the family.

Reductionism

In quantitative research, phenomena of interest are reduced to a set of specific, observable components or variables that can be tested: that is, the researcher 'operationalises' the research question by reducing constructs to their measurable components. An operational definition 'assigns meaning to a construct or a variable by specifying the activities or "operations" necessary to measure it' (Kerlinger, 1986, p. 28).

Example: Child-care research

Child-care was 'reduced' to three aspects: type, amount and stability. Type was defined as formal government-regulated child-care services, such as child-care centres and family day-care, and informal arrangements, such as baby-sitters, relatives and nannies, which are not regulated. Amount of care was defined in terms of number of hours per week. Stability of care was based on the number of changes to care arrangements. Child outcomes were defined as key developmental tasks: quality of the infant's attachment relationship with the mother at age 1 year; social competence with peers and non-parental carers at age 2.5 years; children's academic and behavioural adjustment to the first year of school at age 6 years.

Reliability

Reliability relates not so much to the research question itself, but to the means used to test it and whether these methods meet criteria for scientific rigour. The information provided by the assessment instruments must be accurate, consistent and predictable. These instruments must also have **internal validity**; that is, the assessment items should describe the construct that the measure purports to assess. The requirements for establishing reliability and validity in assessment are complex and cannot be fully covered within the scope of this chapter, but the basic premise is that instrument reliability is a description of the amount of measurement error. Clearly, the researcher must aim for a low level of error. One of the best ways for the researcher to ensure this is to use published methods that have met criteria for reliability and validity.

Example: Child-care research

Recognised measures were used to assess developmental outcomes. At age 1, we used the Strange Situation technique to code infant–mother attachment (Ainsworth et al., 1978). At age 2.5 years, we observed children's social interaction with peers using procedures outlined by Howes (1980), Wright (1983), and White and Watt (1973). At age 6, we included standardised tests, such as the Peabody Picture Vocabulary Test, and questionnaire measures to rate children's behaviour and abilities. Trialling these measures and establishing reliability were essential steps in the initial stages of the research.

Generality

Generality refers to the assumption that the research [...] ity, that is, the findings should have relevance or '[...] other settings, populations, and conditions' (Goodv [...] 1996, p. 53). To meet the requirements for ext[...] researcher must select a sample that is representative of the wider population to which the findings will be generalised. Consideration must also be given to any bias in the results that may arise from the sample, the procedures or the administration of the procedures.

Example: Child-care research

The following three criteria ensured that the study sample would be representative of the wider population of women likely to use child-care for their infants, but manageable within the confines of resources and funding realities.

Sample size
A large sample, 150 women and their partners, was selected in order to offset sample attrition and to ensure sufficient numbers of children in each of the four infant–mother attachment groups.

Sample variability
Variability was reduced by selecting only English-speaking mothers expecting their first child, and by retaining only those children whose delivery was full-term and who showed no abnormalities at birth.

Representativeness
Maternal psychological well-being, which had been identified as a significant determinant of children's socioemotional and cognitive development (Belsky and Isabella, 1988; Belsky, Rosenberger and Crnic, 1995), was seen as a critical factor in the selection of the sample. A two-stage procedure was used to ensure that the sample was representative of a wide range of personality functioning. Initially, 453 mothers were screened on a measure of maternal psychological functioning. Using the full range of scores on this measure, a stratified sample of 157 women was selected, retaining subjects who scored in the lower, intermediate and upper thirds of the range of scores (see Ungerer et al., 1997).

DEDUCTION AND INFERENCE

The approach taken in quantitative investigations follows the processes of deductive reasoning. The researcher identifies a set of specific ations, expectations, or hypotheses, along with specific methods by which these will be measured. Resulting data are analysed in relation to the research question to prove or disprove the researcher's hypotheses. Explanation, interpretation and significance of the findings for the wider population are deduced through this process of analysis. When the assumptions of quantitative research are wholly adhered to, the researcher is able to infer cause and effect relationships. **Causation** is not an essential component in quantitative research (many studies describe relationships without testing causal effects) but quantitative designs are required when the researcher seeks to establish causation. Cook and Campbell (1979) identify three criteria as necessary for inferring cause:

- A significant relationship between the presumed cause and the effect, that is, between the independent variable(s) and the outcome, the dependent variable(s).
- Evidence that the cause precedes the effect.
- The need to control alternative causes or rule out alternative interpretations.

They emphasise that the researcher should examine probable causal connections; it is not possible or even desirable to explain all causal forces.

Example: Child-care research

Our aim was to examine possible causal relationships between child-care and children's development. The impact of early child-care was conceptualised as having separate but overlapping effects on mother and baby. For the infant, child-care was seen as an extension of the parental system to include other adults and other settings, requiring the infant to adapt to the caregiving style of persons other than the parents. The impact of this experience on children's developing attachment relationship with mothers was seen as directly related to the quality of the care setting (for example, Howes, Phillips and Whitebook, 1992). For the mother, child-care was seen as a separation from the baby and, as such, an emotionally charged experience. Quality of care was expected to have an indirect effect on mother–child interaction and the infant–mother attachment relationship, through the child's level of adjustment to care and the mother's confidence with the care arrangement.

We hypothesised that child-care that supports and reassures the mother in her maternal role, and that meets the infant's emotional needs, would be more likely to foster a mutually responsive relationship and a secure attachment between mother and child.

Conversely, child-care that is unsatisfactory for the mother, and which does not provide the infant with adequate emotional support, was expected to cause anxiety for the mother–child dyad and reduce opportunities for responsive interaction between the two.

In order to test this hypothesis, we constructed a detailed record of each child's experience of care and assessed each mother's perceptions of care. We asked mothers when they started using child-care, what type and amount of child-care they used, why they made these choices and how satisfied they felt about their care arrangements. We also recorded the number of care arrangements used each week and the number of changes to these arrangements.

NUMBERS, MEASUREMENT AND NUMERICAL RELATIONSHIPS

In quantitative research, dependent, independent and relevant variables are described in numerical form. Some variables may be easily defined or measured; others are more abstract and difficult to define. Whatever the construct, quantitative research requires it to be transformed into numbers. In social research, four main types of measurement are used. The simplest are nominal and ordinal measures, which use non-metric categories to describe variables. Interval and ratio measures are higher level measures which use metric scales to quantify variables.

Nominal

Nominal measures code, or assign, labels to variables based on a common or shared quality. Numbers are assigned to distinguish different categories; they do not represent a unit of measurement, hence the term 'non-metric'. Codes may also be used to denote the presence (1) or absence (0) of a characteristic.

Example: Child-care research

Sex-of-child was coded girls = 1, boys = 0. Type of child-care was coded father = 1; informal care with relatives or non-relatives = 2; family day-care = 3; child-care centre = 4; mixed formal and informal = 5. Nominal codes were also assigned to mothers' reasons for choosing a type of care. Responses were coded as 1 (giving) or 0 (not giving) any of four independent reasons.

Ordinal

Ordinal measures assign rank to the nominated categories in either ascending or descending order. This type of measure describes the level of a characteristic in terms of more or less, but does not quantify it. Ordered ratings are used in self-report or observer-rated questionnaire measures; for example, rating scales such as the 5-point 'strongly agree' to 'strongly disagree' Likert scale and the 100-point Thurstone scale. These scales assume an equal difference between one ranking and the next and can be treated like interval measures (Tuckman, 1999).

Example: Child-care research

Mother's level of emotional satisfaction with child-care was coded negative, dissatisfied = 1; accepting, reassured = 2; positive, happy = 3. Occupational status was ranked from 1 to 7 in accordance with Daniel's (1983) system for Australian workers. Maternal self-report questionnaires, based on Likert scales, were used to collect information about maternal well-being and infant temperament.

Interval

Interval measures quantify variables in terms of units of measurement. The scale assumes equal distance between intervals and a defined arbitrary starting point, zero. These higher level measures can be combined to form ordinal or nominal measures.

Example: Child-care research

Interval measures included years of post-secondary education, number of hours of child-care per week, number of carers per week, number of changes to care. Interval data for hours of care was collapsed to form ordinal categories: none = 0; minimal, up to 10 hours per week = 1; part-time, 11–30 hours per week = 2; full-time, over 30 hours per week = 3.

Ratio

Ratio measures are similar to interval measures but have an absolute zero point. Apart from naturally occurring ratio scales, such as age and time, this type of measurement is rarely used in educational research (Tuckman, 1999).

ASSESSMENT AND ANALYSIS

The type of assessment measures determines both the extent to which the data can be compared and the type of statistical analyses that can be applied to these comparisons (Hair, et al., 1998). Metric measures allow the full range of mathematical procedures to be applied, whereas non-metric measures are restricted in their use. Methods of statistical analysis are classified as **parametric**, for metric data, and **non-parametric**, for non-metric measures. The following section will introduce and illustrate some of these techniques. For a more detailed explanation, readers should turn to Huck, Cormier and Bounds (1974), Cohen and Manion (1985), Hair et al. (1998), Tuckman (1999) or Burns (2000).

Types of measurement and associated statistical analysis techniques

Metric, continuous measures	Parametric statistics
ordinal scales (e.g. Likert) interval scales ratio scales	mean, standard deviation t-test, analysis of variance correlation, multiple correlation multiple regression
Non-metric, categorical measures	**Non-parametric statistics**
nominal codes ordinal codes	chi-square distribution rank order correlation logistic regression

---

Know your data

This is the challenge for the researcher at the analysis stage of quantitative research. The more complex the data set, the more rigorously this maxim must be adhered to. Data analysis is a systematic process. The researcher starts with descriptive methods, which summarise the distribution of each variable and identify relationships among the set of variables, and then progresses to inferential techniques, which assess the significance and applicability of the results.

Descriptive analyses for the set of independent and relevant variables

Metric measures: Parametric statistics

Distributions for continuous data are presented as frequency counts for each interval point of the measure, represented graphically as a histogram. Data are summarised in terms of the range of scores (lowest to highest), the mean score (M), and the variability of the scores or standard deviation (SD). Relationships between measures can be correlated, and illustrated as a scattergram (see Kumar, 1996, and Hair et al., 1998, for examples of histograms and scattergrams).

Example: Child-care research

Initial analyses examined key characteristics of the sample. Table 7.1 presents the distribution, expressed as means (M) and standard deviations (SD) for each variable, and the relationships between the variables, expressed as bivariate correlations (Pearson's r).

The mean (M) is the average score for all subjects; for example, mothers' average age was 29 years. The standard deviation (SD) is a measure of the variability of the sample scores, calculated as the average amount of difference between individual scores and the mean score. For example, the standard deviation for mothers' ages was 4.1, meaning that on average mothers' ages varied around the mean of 29 by about 4 years. When numerical data is presented in its raw state, means and standard deviations are expressed in real terms; for example, the data in Table 7.1 refer to mothers' years of education, ratings of marital relationship, number of close relationships, etc. Raw data can also be transformed, using mathematical computations, into new measurement variables. For example, maternal depression and child temperament, which were assessed using a number of measures, have been computed as standardised scores (z score). The sample mean for these measures is zero, and individual scores are expressed as the number of standard deviations away from the mean; SDs are either positive, above the mean, or negative, less than the mean.

Table 7.1 also summarises the relationships between the set of independent variables. The strength and significance of each relationship was tested using Pearson's product–moment correlation.

Correlation analysis compares subjects' scores on one measure with scores for another measure. The strength and direction of each relationship is expressed as a correlation coefficient (r). Pairs of variables which have a positive correlation are directly related; that is, as the scores on one variable increase so do the scores for the other. Variables which are negatively correlated have an inverse relationship, that is, as the scores on one variable increase the scores on the other decrease. When there is no relationship between variables, this is described as a zero correlation.

Table 7.1 Means, standard deviations and bivariate-correlations between relevant maternal, child and family variables

	1	2	3	4	5	6	7	8
Demographic:								
1. Maternal age								
2. Maternal education	.46**							
3. Family socioeconomic status[a]	.46**	.85**						
Maternal personality:								
4. Depression (z score)	-.11	-.16	-.18					
Child characteristics:								
5. Temperament (z score)	.03	.05	-.03	.26**				
Social support:								
6. Positive marital relationship	-.14	-.11	-.04	-.43**	-.24*			
7. Negative marital relationship	.09	.12	.09	.40**	.28**	-.82***		
8. Availability of close relationships	-.09	-.16	-.18	-.30**	.26**	.46**	.46**	
Mean	29.08	5.42	9.59	0.00	0.00	6.15	2.56	7.21
Standard deviation (SD)	4.10	1.86	2.37	0.67	0.85	0.81	0.85	0.94

Notes: [a] the measure of socioeconomic status was formed by computing a composite from mothers' and fathers' years of education and occupational status (Hollingshead, 1975).

* $p < .05$
** $p < .01$
*** $p < .001$

The significance of the relationship between variables is expressed as the degree of probability (*p*) that the observed relationship has not occurred by chance. A *p* value less than .05 means that the odds of the relationship happening by chance is less than 5 in 100, or 5 per cent; a *p* value less than .01 is less than a 1 per cent chance, a *p* value less than .001 is less than a 1 in 1000 chance. Significance is conventionally set at $p < .05$.

The correlation matrix for the set of independent variables (Table 7.1) showed that within the demographic and social support domains, variables tended to be significantly correlated with each other. For example, mother's age was positively correlated with years of education ($r = .46$, $p < .01$), and positive and negative marital relationship measures were inversely correlated ($r = -.82$, $p < .001$). We also noted significant correlations across domains. Mothers who reported more depressive symptoms perceived their infants as being temperamentally more difficult ($r = .26$, $p < .05$), felt their marital relationship was less positive ($r = -.43$, $p < .01$) and more negative ($r = .40$, $p < .01$), and reported fewer close relationships ($r = -.30$, $p < .01$).

Non-metric measures: Non-parametric statistics

Distributions for non-metric data are presented as frequency counts for each category, either as whole numbers or a percentage of the total number of subjects. Relationships between categorical variables are examined by comparing percentage distributions.

Example: Child-care research

Non-metric measures were used to code type of child-care and mothers' reasons for choosing care. Table 7.2 presents the proportion of mothers who nominated each reason for each of the five child-care groups.

Inspection of the distributions in Table 7.2 suggested that there was a relationship between type of care and mothers' reasons for choosing care. A higher proportion of mothers using father or informal child-care gave characteristics of the caregiver as a reason for choosing that type of care compared to mothers using formal and mixed care (.50 and .65 versus .29, .11 and .14). In contrast, more mothers using formal settings identified aspects of the environment as a reason compared to mothers using father and informal care (.50 and .58 versus 0 and .19). The strength of these differences was examined using chi-square analysis.

Table 7.2   Proportion of mothers nominating reasons for choice of care by child-care type

| | Reasons for choice of care | | | |
	Carer qualities	Environment qualities	Benefits for the child	Practical needs
Father (n = 12)	.50	.00	.00	.17
Informal (n = 52)	.65	.19	.21	.21
Family day-care (n = 14)	.29	.50	.29	.21
Centre care (n = 19)	.11	.58	.37	.26
Mixed care (n = 7)	.14	.57	.29	.43

Chi-square analysis provides a test of significance for the number of responses, or subjects that fall into two or more categories. The test compares the 'expected' distribution, that is, the number that would be expected to occur by chance, with the 'observed' or actual distribution. The chi-square (χ^2) statistic is a measure of the probability that the observed distribution differs from the expected distribution by more than chance. The significance of χ^2 is dependent on the **degrees of freedom** *(df)*, which is calculated as the number of categories minus 1.

Four separate chi-square tests were conducted, one for each category of reasons, to compare the proportion of mothers giving each reason across the five child-care groups. Degrees of freedom for each test were calculated as 5–1, *df* = 4. The chi-square tests achieved significance for two types of reasons, qualities of the caregiver, $\chi^2(4)$ = 22.15, p < .001, and qualities of the environment, $\chi^2(4)$ = 19.86, p < .001.

Descriptive analyses for the dependent variable

Example: Child-care research

This stage of the analysis examined the relationships between the dependent variable, infant–mother attachment security, and the set of independent and relevant variables. Note that the dependent variable was nonmetric; we used nominal codes to categorise children into one of four attachment groups: insecure–avoidant (A), secure (B), insecure–ambivalent (C) or disorganised (D).

Table 7.3 Descriptive statistics for independent and relevant variables by infant–mother attachment (A, B, C, D) classification

Section 1	Avoidant (n = 9) A		Attachment classification Secure (n = 65) B		Ambivalent (n = 22) C		Disorganised (n = 8) D	
	M	SD	M	SD	M	SD	M	SD
Demographic:								
Maternal age	28.22	4.66	29.62	4.11	28.36	3.67	27.63	4.57
Maternal education	5.11	2.37	5.71	1.77	4.68	2.01	5.50	1.20
Family socioeconomic status	9.61	2.77	9.85	2.20	8.91	2.85	9.31	1.77
Maternal personality:								
Depression (z score)	−.01	.69	.00	.58	.24	.60	.37	1.27
Child characteristics:								
Temperament (z score)	−.28	1.14	.00	.75	.00	.92	.28	1.06
Social support:								
Positive marital relationship	6.32	.58	6.10	.84	6.20	.80	6.21	.80
Negative marital relationship	2.12	.82	2.62	.86	2.56	.75	2.59	1.04
Availability of close relationships	7.11	.93	7.37	.72	6.77	1.31	7.25	1.17
Child-care variables:								
Age of entry to care	5.2	3.7	5.7	3.4	6.3	3.7	5.6	2.7
Number of changes to care	1.3	0.5	1.6	0.8	1.5	0.8	2.1	1.0
Number of carers/week	2.1	0.3	2.3	0.5	2.2	0.4	2.8	0.9
Mother's satisfaction with care	2.9	0.4	2.2	0.7	2.3	0.6	2.0	0.9

Table 7.3 *continued*

Section 2

| | Attachment classification | | | |
	Avoidant (n = 9) A	Secure (n = 65) B	Ambivalent (n = 22) C	Disorganised (n = 8) D
	%	%	%	%
Sex of child:				
Boys	7.0	64.9	22.8	5.3
Girls	10.6	59.6	19.1	10.6
Child-care variables:				
Mother's reason for choice				
Carer qualities	67.0	48.0	32.0	38.0
Environment quality	11.0	34.0	36.0	13.0
Benefits for child	00.0	28.0	27.0	00.0
Practical needs	11.0	26.0	23.0	13.0
Type of child-care:				
Father	16.7	50.0	25.0	8.3
Informal	11.5	55.8	21.2	11.5
Family day-care	0.0	100.0	0.0	0.0
Child-care centre	5.3	63.2	31.6	0.0
Mixed informal/formal	0.0	57.1	28.6	14.3
Amount of child-care:				
Minimum, 1–10 hours/week	19.2	34.6	30.8	15.4
Part-time, 11–30 hours/week	0.0	73.9	19.6	6.5
Full-time, > 30 hours/week	12.5	68.8	15.6	3.1

Table 7.3 presents results for the four attachment groups. The first section of Table 3 shows the means (*M)* and standard deviation (*SD*) for continuous variables: demographic, maternal personality, child temperament, social support and some aspects of child-care. The second section gives percentage distributions for categorical variables: sex of child, child-care type, amount of care and reasons for choice. Because of the small numbers of subjects (less than 10) in the insecure–avoidant (A) and insecure–disorganised (D) categories, statistical analysis to test these relationships were limited to comparisons of secure (B) versus insecure (A, C, D) groups. However, these tests could only be conducted when the pattern of results was sufficiently consistent across A, C and D subgroups to justify combining them into a single insecure group.

Metric measures: parametric statistics
Examination of the means for each of the four attachment groups (Table 7.3, section 1) showed a consistent pattern for mothers of secure (B) infants to be older, more educated, to have a higher family socioeconomic status and to report a greater availability of close relationships compared to mothers of insecure (A, C, D) infants. These differences between secure versus insecure groups were tested using analysis of variance. Results were significant for two variables: mother's level of education, $F(1,102) = 3.04$, $p < .05$, and availability of close relationships, $F(1,102) = 5.05$, $p < .05$.

Analysis of variance (ANOVA) is used to test the significance of the difference between mean scores for two or more groups. Results of ANOVA tests are expressed as *F*, which is a measure of the variability of the means for each subgroup (between groups) compared to the variability of the overall sample mean (within groups). The significance of the *F* value or *F* ratio is determined by the degrees of freedom, which is determined by the number of subgroups and the size of the sample, and must be included when reporting *F* values. Degrees of freedom (*df*) are expressed as two numbers; the first is the number of subgroups minus 1; the second is the number of subjects in the sample minus the number of subgroups.

Non-metric measures: non-parametric analysis
Table 7.3, section 2, presents percentage distributions of secure (B) and insecure (A, C, D) infants across the categories of sex of child, mother's reasons for choice of care, type of child-care and amount of care. The figures suggested that secure (B) attachments were more likely when children had attended family day-care (100% secure) or child-care

centres (63.2% secure) compared to informal settings (55.8% secure). Security was also associated with part-time (73.9% secure) or full-time (68.8% secure) hours of care, compared to minimal hours (34.6% secure). To test the significance of these differences, family day-care and child-care centres were combined to form a formal care group, which was compared with the informal care group. Chi-square analysis comparing the numbers of secure (B) and insecure (A, C, D) children in these two groups was significant, $\chi^2(1) = 4.68, p < .05$. Chi-square comparison of the distributions of secure and insecure children in minimal versus part-time versus full-time hours of care was also significant, $\chi^2(2) = 11.72, p < .01$.

Inferential analyses

Inferential analyses are required when the researcher seeks to test hypotheses, establish causation or make generalised statements about the significance of the results for the wider population. Inferential analyses draw on multivariate methods of analysis to simultaneously assess the contribution, and significance, of a number of independent and relevant variables to the dependent variable. Pathways of influence, that is, whether a variable has a direct or an indirect effect on the dependent variable, can also be tested. Multivariate methods of statistical analysis are highly complex and readers are advised to look at other texts, such as Cook and Campbell (1979), Hair et al. (1998), or Huck et al. (1974), and to Baron and Kenny (1986) for an explanation of moderator and mediator effects in causal pathways.

Example: Child-care research

Inferential analysis was used to test the effects of child-care on infant–mother attachment in combination with other relevant maternal, child and family variables. The technique chosen for this test was multiple regression, specifically logistic regression.

Multiple regression is a statistical technique that can be used to assess the combined effects of a number of independent variables, or predictors, on an outcome. The contribution of each independent variable to the dependent variable is specified in the final statistics. This method allows the researcher to statistically control for the effects of a number of alternate predictors while assessing the unique contribution of key variables. Multiple regression is suitable for outcomes that are continuous measures (see Edwards, 1976; Hair et al., 1998).

109

Logistic regression is the preferred method for multiple regression when the outcome measure is non-metric, specifically when a binary or 2-category measure is used. Logistic regression assesses the likelihood of obtaining the observed outcome distribution in relation to the predicted or expected distribution. The overall statistic tests the 'goodness of fit' or the effect of all variables included in the model; this is expressed as the model chi-square (Hosmer and Lemeshow, 1989).

Because the dependent variable, infant–mother attachment, was a binary measure, logistic regression analysis was used, coding secure = 1 and insecure = 0. Initial analyses tested the effect of the set of relevant maternal, child and family variables on the outcome measure. Maternal education and availability of close relationships were the only significant predictors of attachment security, at $p < .05$; therefore, these two variables were retained in all further analyses. Second-stage analyses tested the additional effects of child-care on attachment security in a series of three logistic regression tests, or models. Model 1 tested the contribution of amount of care; Model 2 tested the effect of formal versus informal care; and Model 3 tested the combined effects of amount and type of care variables. Results of these analyses are presented in Table 7.4.

For each of the three tests, the chi-square for the overall model (model χ^2) achieved a high level of significance, $p < .001$ or $p < .01$. The Wald statistic indicates the effect for each variable after controlling for all the other variables in the model. The odds ratio is the ratio of odds that an outcome will be secure to the odds that it will be insecure. Odds ratios less than 1.00 indicate reduced odds for secure attachment and greater than 1.00 indicate increased odds for secure attachment. The closer the odds ratio is to zero, the smaller the effect.

Models 1 and 2 confirmed that amount of child-care and type of care were significant predictors of secure versus insecure attachment, and that these made a contribution to the outcome over and above the effects of maternal education and mother's level of social support. Children who were in part-time or full-time child-care had increased odds for secure attachment compared to children in minimal hours of care (odds ratios = 9.04 and 4.82 respectively). Children attending formal child-care had increased odds for secure attachment compared to children in informal child-care (odds ratio = 3.84).

Model 3 showed that when both amount and type of child-care were included in the model, these variables made independent contributions to attachment security. Children attending formal care had increased odds for security (odds ratio = 3.78), regardless of the hours attended. Children attending part-time care had increased odds for secure attachment compared to children in minimal hours of care

Table 7.4 Logistic regression analysis for predictors of secure versus insecure attachment classification

	Wald	p	Odds ratio
Model 1 (n = 104). Model $\chi^2(4) = 25.13, p < .001$			
Maternal education	4.94	.026	1.33
Availability of close relationships	8.85	.003	2.33
Hours of child-care	13.36	.001	
Part-time vs. minimum	12.87	.000	9.04
Full-time vs. minimum	6.86	.009	4.82
Model 2 (n = 85). Model $\chi^2(3) = 13.12, p = .004$			
Maternal education	4.04	.045	1.32
Availability of close relationships	4.11	.043	1.73
Type of child-care			
Formal vs. informal care	5.78	.016	3.84
Model 3 (n = 85). Model $\chi^2(5) = 20.99, p = .001$			
Maternal education	3.91	.048	1.34
Availability of close relationships	5.58	.018	2.08
Type of child-care			
Formal vs. informal care	4.58	.032	3.78
Hours of child-care	7.09	.029	
Part-time vs. minimum	7.05	.008	6.54
Full-time vs. minimum	1.97	.160	2.66

(odds ratio = 6.54), regardless of whether they were attending formal or informal care. However, the effect of attending full-time care compared to minimal hours of care was no longer significant after accounting for the effect of child-care type.

CONCLUSIONS, CAUTIONS AND QUALIFICATIONS

The conclusions and recommendations that the researcher is able to draw from inferential analyses depend not only on the results of statistical techniques, but on research design features such as hypotheses, sampling and assessment measures. As Goodwin and Goodwin (1996, p. 103) point out, 'statistical significance is not the same as practical significance'. At the final stage of a quantitative study the researcher must make objective comments about the value and applicability of the findings.

Example: Child-care research

The results achieved a high level of significance, $p < .01$ in the final analyses, and confirmed some of the proposed hypotheses and causal connections. Recall that we had hypothesised that child-care that supports the mother and meets the infant's emotional needs would be more likely to foster secure attachments between mother and child. As expected, secure attachments were significantly higher in the group of children who had received care in formal settings, which are governed by standards for quality and rely on qualified early childhood staff, compared to those receiving informal care. Furthermore, secure attachments were more likely when care was more than ten hours per week. This outcome pointed to the benefits for the infant of having sufficient time in care to feel emotionally reassured and better able to manage the experience of separation from the mother. Our results met the criteria for cause-effect relationships. There was a significant relationship between the cause (child-care) and the effect (security of infant–mother attachment); the cause (child-care in the first 12 months) preceded the effect (attachment at age 12 months); and the relationship between child-care and attachment held up after taking account of alternate explanations (maternal education and personal support).

We had also hypothesised that mothers' sense of reassurance with infants' child-care arrangements would be part of the causal process. Our data did not support this expectation. Mothers' satisfaction and reasons for choosing care were not related to attachment security. Our rejection of this hypothesis must be qualified, however, by the limitations of the measures. It may be that more specific questions relating to child-care and the mother's sense of feeling supported in her relationship with the child might have tapped this dimension of maternal reassurance more accurately. Also, interviews with carers might have provided a fuller sense of the interconnections between mothers' experiences of care and the quality of the infant–mother attachment relationship.

This study has provided important findings for child-care policy-makers and practitioners alike. While formal care was found to have benefits for children's development, we noted that a large proportion of mothers preferred to use informal care for their babies. We would not want our research to be used to denigrate this choice. Rather, we would argue that informal care is an important section of Australia's child-care system and, as such, deserves the level of government recognition and support that the formal sector has been given. Similarly, we need to qualify the finding that part-time and full-time hours of care were more supportive of secure attachments than minimal hours of care. Although we stand by our argument that regular, predictable care is beneficial for children, there may be other explanations for the poorer outcomes for minimal hours of care. Our results suggest other interpretations that might be explored in future studies. For example, could it be the case that mothers who keep their child-care hours to a minimum feel more conflict and greater anxiety about leaving their babies, and might this be a marker for a more problematic mother–child relationship?

STRENGTHS AND LIMITATIONS OF QUANTITATIVE RESEARCH

The major strength of quantitative research designs is the potential for generalising the findings from the sample population to the larger population it represents. The assumptions of objectivity and generality, when met, enable the researcher to consider wider applications of the research findings. The potential for describing cause and effect relationships also has implications for practice. In sum, well-designed quantitative research studies have the power to influence decisions across a wide range of areas in early childhood education.

When undertaking and reporting quantitative studies, however, the researcher must be aware of the limitations of this type of design. The assumptions of reductionism and reliability imply certain limitations. Quantitative designs reduce, or operationalise, complex constructs to a set of measurable activities or events. The results of the research must therefore be seen within the limited frame of these operational definitions. Likewise, the reliability of the measures determines the strength and applicability of the findings. The quantitative researcher cannot generalise beyond what has been measured and how well it has been measured.

The significance and generalisability of quantitative research rely on statistical analyses. This can be seen as both a strength and a limitation. Results that are based on a reasonable sample size and an acceptable level of probability are accepted as 'real'; they are unlikely to have occurred by chance and therefore, the hypothesis is 'proven'. However, the conclusion is based on the sample, not on the wider population, and errors are possible. In some cases, a hypothesis is accepted as proven when it should be rejected (Type I Error) and, in others, a hypothesis is rejected when it should be accepted (Type II Error). Quantitative researchers must familiarise themselves with these types of errors and other statistical constraints (see Huck et al., 1986; Burns, 2000).

Example: Child-care research

The multivariate nature of the research design and the significance of the results allowed generalisations to be made for child-care policy. One of the rewards of this research has been the response that the study has attracted from the early childhood community, State government legislators and the media. Nevertheless, there were limitations that also need to be acknowledged. Our design provided a broad overview of the use and outcomes of child-care, but wasn't able to probe mothers' individual experiences of child-care or give a deep insight into the processes of the care experience. We might have achieved this by including qualitative methods, such as an extended interview with the mothers or observation of infants in their child-care settings. Our operational definitions also point to some of the limitations of the study. Quality of care was defined by formal versus informal types of care. A more specific definition would be one based on observable events and interactions. A further concern was that assessment of infant development was based on one measure, the Strange Situation procedure. While this is a robust measure, and one that is recognised internationally (NICHD, 1997), reliance on one outcome has its limitations. The longitudinal nature of the study, however, which has enabled the use of multiple assessment methods at different stages of children's development, is a major strength of the research.

SUMMARY

Quantitative research is based on the following assumptions:

- Objectivity, which introduces controls into the research design.
- Reductionism, which operationalises the research question to a set of measurable variables.
- Reliability, which determines the accuracy of these measures.
- Generality, which sets criteria for sample selection.

Measurement is a key feature of quantitative designs:

- Independent, dependent, and relevant variables are defined in measurable terms.
- The nature of the measures determines the types of statistical analyses that can be applied to the data.
- Non-metric measures, that is, nominal and ordinal codes, name but do not quantify variables and are analysed using non-parametric statistics.

- Metric measures, that is ordinal, interval, and ratio scales, quantify variables and are analysed using parametric statistics.

Analysis of data proceeds systematically:

- Descriptive analyses summarise the distributions for each variable and identify relationships among the set of variables.
- Inferential statistics test the extent to which the results can be generalised to the wider population.

At the final stage of a quantitative study, the researcher interprets the value, applicability, and limitations of the findings.

QUESTIONS FOR REFLECTION

- Using Table 7.1, find the correlation coefficient that describes the relationship between mother's education and mother's ratings of child temperament. Is it a direct, inverse or zero correlation? Consider why this might be so?
- Using Table 7.2, find the proportion of mothers using mixed formal and informal care who gave 'practical needs' as a reason for their choice of care. Is this figure higher, lower or the same as those mothers using other forms of care? Consider why this might be so.
- Using Table 7.3, find the percentages of children classified as avoidant, ambivalent and disorganised who received minimal hours of child-care per week. Calculate the total percentage of children in this group who were insecure $(A + C + D)$. Do the same for children receiving part-time and full-time hours of care. Draw up a 3×2 table summarising amount of care by percentages of secure and insecure attachments. Now look at the results for the chi-square test that compared these outcomes $(\chi^2(2) = 11.72, p < .01)$. This test compares the expected distribution of secure to insecure children with the observed distributions of secure to insecure children, across the three care groups. Consider why the chi-square test was significant.

FURTHER READING

McMillan, J. H. and Wergin, J. F. 1998, *Understanding and Evaluating Educational Research*, Prentice-Hall, Englewood Cliffs, NJ. This introductory text categorises quantitative research as experimental and non-experimental, and presents a useful summary of the key principles of each. Three research articles drawn from educational research are included in each section to illustrate different methodologies and statistical techniques. Readers are led through a series of questions to analyse and criticise these studies.

Goodwin, W. L. and Goodwin, L. D. 1996, *Understanding Quantitative and Qualitative Research in Early Childhood Education,* Teachers College Press, New York. This very accessible text includes two chapters on quantitative research design and methodology, drawing on a range of examples from early childhood research. The final chapter makes a compelling argument for combining quantitative and qualitative components into research design.

8

Qualitative designs and analysis

Anne Edwards

SOFT RESEARCH FOR SOFT TOPICS?

This chapter starts with a health warning. Qualitative research is not the easy option. Whatever version of qualitative design and analysis we select, we will find ourselves getting to grips with the complexities of the social world of early childhood. This is as true of an exploration of the pedagogy of early childhood staff as it is of a focus on children's experiences. Qualitative research is therefore demanding, but thoroughly worthwhile. It gives us access to the web of interactions between, for example, child, family, early childhood services and the community, and between these and the intellectual and material resources available to each. In short, it allows us to build up a picture of the actions and interpretations of children and adults and locates them in the shifting networks of complex interactions that make up the contexts providing the constraints and possibilities for action and interpretation.

Of course single-handed researchers cannot look at everything in the web at once. As individual researchers we have to select what we want to foreground and what we will treat more lightly. While this selection is a subjective one, it is not as subjective as the selection made by the experimental researcher in the laboratory, because one virtue of all qualitative research is that the process demands that the researcher is continuously open to fresh interpretations of familiar events. In summary, qualitative research tries to be responsive to what the evidence tells the researcher. Responsiveness can be seen in both design and analysis. For example, we might decide to look at the language use of a group of 3-year-olds at home and in preschool and subsequently discover differences in their parents' beliefs about child-rearing that brings our attention to how parents use the resources available in their homes. The analysis of the evidence will explain how the design developed to include a particular focus on parents and the language opportunities they provide. Qualitative research has to start somewhere, however. The starting point of a qualitative study largely determines how the study is designed, the methods of data collection and their analysis and what the researcher is likely to be alert to as the study proceeds.

FROM QUESTION TO DESIGN

Let us begin with an apparently straightforward practitioner concern: 'the children in this preschool rarely settle down with books'. How might we deal with this issue as qualitative researchers? A feminist researcher using a qualitative research approach might frame the research question so that the focus is placed on the different experiences of boys and girls with books in the preschool. A developmentalist would want to explore the children's previous experiences of books. Someone interested in sociocultural approaches to learning would be wondering what the children do with books. A linguist might ask, 'Where else are the children getting experience of text?' These are all very different questions, demanding different research designs and levels of detail in the analysis of the evidence gathered. Each question is also, to some extent, driven by a different theoretical framing of the situation.

We can look at how we might tackle some of these questions to give some foretaste of the range of design options that we loosely call qualitative. The developmentalist might frame her study as a cross-sectional study of 2 to 5-year-olds (see Chapter 6) and select a small sample of children in each year for fine-grained observations at home and in child-care services. The socioculturalist would focus on a small group of children as a case study and undertake detailed observation while the children interact with or relax without books in the preschool and at home. She would also interview parents and staff and build a picture of the relationship between the children's experiences of books at home, in school and in the community. The feminist and the linguist might also opt for a case study approach, but their focus in observations and interviews would reflect the theories that inform their specialist perspectives. For instance, the feminist would focus on gender and the linguist on language structures.

118

QUALITATIVE RESEARCH: ALL KINDS OF EVERYTHING?

Qualitative research has a very respectable history, but definitions of it have changed over time and so have the debates around its purposes and usefulness. In an overview of twentieth-century versions of qualitative research, Denzin and Lincoln identify five overlapping phases or 'moments' in its development over the last one hundred years (Denzin and Lincoln, 1994). They describe the first four decades as the 'traditional period' during which anthropologists used ethnographic techniques (see Chapter 13) to create objective accounts of the lives of 'others'. The others were usually alien and strange and ethnographers had considerable power over how these others were revealed, as a result of their claims to objectivity and the analytic frames through which they developed and wrote their accounts. Critics of this early phase argued that these accounts were based on positivist views of social science (see Chapter 3) and seemed to colonise the experiences of the cultures being studied by reducing the diversity of the fields of study so that they would fit the researchers' frames of eference.

The second phase, lasting from the 1940s until the 1970s and which Denzin and Lincoln label 'modernist', saw the emergence of what has become a continuing tension in qualitative research. Some of the work in this period built on the first phase by more overtly seeking to meet positivist research goals such as trying to tease out causal relationships in their data (see Yin, 1998, for an example of this). At the same time the period saw the development of the social sciences in universities, while qualitative researchers began to work with more interpretative theories of, for example, symbolic interactionism, feminism and phenomenology. There was a growing concern with the 'voices' of those being studied and a desire for a liberationary social science. Yet these aims were frequently subsumed within a concern to ensure that qualitative field work was as rigorous as that produced by experimental studies. It is in this period that the distinction between qualitative and quantitative research is so clearly shown to be a false one, as great efforts were made by some researchers to use qualitative evidence from their studies in quantitative ways through, for example, fine-grained **content analysis**.

A number of researchers, including the author of this chapter, continue to work with frameworks that originated in this modernist phase, which marked the emergence of new priorities that have continued to be of relevance. A number of very influential early childhood studies (for example, Tizard and Hughes, 1984; Wells, 1986; Dunn, 1988) were undertaken during this phase and usefully combined both qualitative and quantitative analyses to produce detailed and distinctly challenging accounts of the experiences of young children at home and in preschool settings.

The tensions of the modernist period, between the rigour of quantitative analysis on the one hand and the excitement of a liberationary social science and proliferating theoretical developments on the other, led eventually to the third phase, termed 'blurred genres' by Denzin and Lincoln, which was pre-eminent in the 1980s. Here we find the theoretical and methodological diversity that makes qualitative research so difficult to label. Research methods using a qualitative approach now included biography, case study and action research informed by theories that included **feminism, structuralism** and interactionism. This pluralism encouraged boundary crossing, so that insights from the theories and methods found in the arts and humanities permeated the work of qualitative researchers in the social sciences. It is at this point that an interest in, for example, the work of Bakhtin was seen in the analysis of textual data (Wertsch, 1991). Parallels between the representational power of researchers and of authors of fiction led some researchers to question their right to interpret the stories told by the field. Instead, they argued, attention should be paid to gathering thick descriptions of the field and social science should limit itself to producing what Geertz (1983) suggests is 'local knowledge'. That is, rich information about locally embedded ways of understanding and acting in the world.

The fourth phase Denzin and Lincoln label 'a crisis of representation', a crisis which arguably is still with us. This phase in qualitative research approaches is marked by the encouragement of a more reflexive form of writing that makes the researcher's voice more evident and weakens any claim to the objective interpretation of the lives of others. One outcome of this development is that there may be no attempt to separate the researcher from the field of inquiry, from the analysis and how it is written for public discussion. Instead the writing process becomes part of a reflective research process. (Ryan and Campbell discuss this further in Chapter 4.) This integration of the identity of the researcher with the production of research texts has raised questions about the reliability of the text (that is, the extent to which another researcher would produce a similar representation of the field) and its more general usefulness. Mac Naughton in Chapter 14 discusses an approach to this in poststructuralist research. Denzin and Lincoln's fifth and final phase is forward-looking and points to emergent features of qualitative research approaches. These include jointly constructed hypertext, multi-disciplinary approaches, lack of certainty and increased reflexivity as qualitative researchers attempt to tell the stories of the field.

This overview of qualitative research in the social sciences in the twentieth century offers insights into some of the dynamics in qualitative research in the twenty-first century. It does not, however, fully tackle the purposes of qualitative research. This too is a contentious area, but nonetheless one that has to be considered when designing a qualitative study, as the purpose helps to shape the study. Let us look in turn at two rationales for qualitative research.

A focus on illumination

Here the emphasis is on research as a way of enlightening, for example, professional practice, by providing information which questions assumptions and offers fresh ways of interpreting familiar events. The information that research generates is thus seen as a tool to be used for clarifying our thinking about the world and how we act on it (Chaiklin, 1993; Hammersley, 1997; Edwards, in press). This constructivist intention can be met by qualitative research which ranges, for example, from a personal story about making applesauce in a Michigan classroom (Clark, 1990) to the quantified analyses of interactions between early childhood staff and children in Glasgow (Munn and Schaffer, 1993).

A focus on critical interpretation

This focus belongs to Denzin and Lincoln's fourth and fifth phases, just outlined. Whereas illuminatory research aims at informative and analytic descriptions of phenomena which attempt to map the territory, critical interpretative research places the subjectivity of the researcher as writer overtly at the center of the research process. There, researchers make immediate connections between phenomena in the field of study and their personal theorising of it. For example, a researcher's anger at the treatment of a child with disabilities in a child-care service would be legitimately written into the theorising account of the event. Lather argues that, rather than description, the concern is *inscription*, where researchers inscribe their accounts of the field of study with the meanings they bring to it (Lather, 1993). This approach to data interpretation is particularly prominent in research conducted from within a poststructuralist paradigm (see Chapters 14 and 17).

The range of purposes and priorities of qualitative research make a simple definition of the approach impossible. However, across this diverse field run a number of common themes. These include concerns about the power of the researcher in interpreting the field of study; an openness both to what the field is revealing and to other disciplines; and a self-critical awareness of the processes of research. In addition qualitative researchers usually need to attend to issues of feasibility, **reflexivity** and validity.

KEY ISSUES IN QUALITATIVE RESEARCH DESIGN

Feasibility

This is a priority for the single-handed researcher. Qualitative research can become so open-ended and engrossing that boundary setting becomes difficult and the researcher is seduced into gathering just that bit more information or looking closely at that relationship as well as at this one. If too many lines are followed the single-handed researcher will need a clone! If vast amounts of data are gathered, even if the focus is narrow, the analysis will become daunting. For instance, a one-hour interview may take an hour to arrange, need an hour for travel, 30 minutes for settling in and leaving, one hour for the interview, six hours to transcribe (or longer if the typist is not expert) and often several days to analyse. It is, therefore, helpful to draw a timeline for the duration of a project and use it to calculate the time available for each stage of the study, thus ensuring that enough time is allocated for analysis and writing.

Access to the sources of evidence is also a matter of feasibility. Ethical issues need to be considered (see Chapter 5). Sometimes parents' permission will be required if data on children are to be gathered. Promises of confidentiality may prove difficult to keep when writing up some studies, consequently the design may need to be adjusted to accommodate expectations of confidentiality. Some documentary sources, such as assessments made of children, may not be as readily available as might be believed. Some key informants (often the most senior ones) may decline the opportunity for a taped interview. It is therefore advisable to confirm access while designing the study and, where possible, to get written confirmation. Concern with feasibility can lead to a modification of grand designs but it usually ensures that the research is completed and written up.

Reflexivity

Reflexivity is common to most qualitative studies. The term carries a number of meanings, all of which are relevant to the design of a study and all of which enhance researchers' sensitivity to the field of study. Sometimes designs are left slightly open, allowing researchers to respond reflexively to unanticipated evidence by slightly reshaping the design of the study. For example, a research question might take the researcher initially to observations of how adults interact with children in early numeracy and literacy activities in several child-care services. The observations might pick up some distinct differences between the ways that the services organise their provision for the children, differences which may raise questions about, for example, staff supervision or key worker systems and lead to the collection of evidence on these topics.

Reflexivity can be built into the design from the outset. Case studies are frequently designed so that the analysis of evidence from one source informs how evidence is collected from another. Designs that combine large-scale surveys and case studies, often called mixed designs, sometimes ensure that surveys explore issues picked up by the more field-sensitive case studies and that case studies try to unravel some of the trends evident in the survey evidence. Reflexivity is clearly one of the major advantages of qualitative designs for examining the messy and constantly changing contexts of early childhood. However, it does require the researcher to see data analysis as a continuous activity and not something that can be left until after all the evidence has been collected.

A particularly demanding form of reflexivity is reflexivity in the analysis of the data. Here reflexivity can refer to the involvement of those who have been the focus of the study in checking and approving the researchers' interpretations of the evidence. This is extremely difficult to do, but is often considered an essential element of feminist and anti-racist research and research conducted from within a post-structuralist paradigm. Grieshaber (Chapter 9) discusses the importance of this for equity in research design.

Reflexivity can also refer to an understanding of the impact of the researcher on the study. The position of the researcher in the field of study has long been a concern in qualitative research, as the very presence of the researcher can distort the system being examined. Careful covert observation, where researchers became part of the field and hid their identities as researchers, was one early response. However, once the subjectivity of the researcher became overtly relevant, as it has done, for example, in feminist and anti-racist research, it was argued that the idea of the entirely neutral, disengaged human observer was a myth and therefore it was thought to be more honest to reveal one's starting points, both personal and theoretical. Having made that revelation, it is incumbent on the researcher to demonstrate that the best quality evidence the field could reveal has been gathered and subjected to rigorous analysis.

Self-aware, engaged and reflexive research has emerged in response to researchers' disquiet about the separation of professional researchers from the field of study and their unease about their ability to speak for those whose lives they have been studying. However, self-aware reflexivity has slightly different implications for those researchers who are practitioners in the field, for example as early childhood staff, and thus are already engaged with the field. For practitioner–researchers, reflexive self-awareness demands the capacity to separate oneself from the field of study and to gain the distance that allows a fresh examination of familiar events using the lenses offered by previous research studies and new theoretical perspectives. In addition, increasingly informed practitioners will change the dynamics of the field as they interpret it and respond in fresh ways. Quite clearly, all researchers working with qualitative designs need to be self-aware about the balance they want to achieve between engaged commitment to the field and the capacity to offer an informed and research-based interpretation of it.

Validity

Validity is often a vexed issue in qualitative research approaches. This is not because qualitative studies produce invalid findings. Indeed, qualitative researchers argue that the field-sensitive evidence gathered in qualitative investigations offers more valid representations of social worlds than that found in studies which reduce the lives of others to statistically significant generalisations. The problem lies in the competing ways validity is understood within different research paradigms. (Validity has specific meanings within each research paradigm, as discussed in Chapter 3). In more qualitative approaches to research, the meaning of validity is close to that commonly found in philosophy, that is, the truth-value in a statement. Validity in qualitative research is a matter of being able to offer as sound a representation of the field of study as the research methods allow. As we have seen, the development of qualitative research as a broadly distinct version of the research process has been based on attempts to offer valid interpretations of what a study of the field reveals.

In qualitative research the validity of the findings of a study does not, therefore, add to an argument for the probable generalisability of those findings to other settings. Instead, a statement about the validity of a study is a judgment about the extent to which it can be said that the research has captured important features of the field and has analysed them with integrity.

Capturing the features of social worlds often calls for a number of fixes on the shifts and variability of settings. The qualitative researchers' response, particularly from those who are happy with the 'modernist' label offered by Denzin and Lincoln (1994) is to attempt to build a robust picture of events through a process of triangulation. Triangulation, as the term implies, involves getting a purchase on the field of study by looking at it from a number of vantage points. Denzin's classic definition (Denzin, 1978) described four main types of triangulation.

- *Data triangulation*: the use of a variety of data sources in a study.
- *Methodological triangulation*: the use of multiple methods to study a single problem.
- *Investigator triangulation*: the use of several researchers.
- *Theory triangulation*: the use of multiple perspectives to interpret a single set of data.

Each version of triangulation is important, though not all studies will employ all of them and certainly the more reflexive and engaged accounts of the research process may dismiss them as all equally irrelevant. Patti Lather, for example, has produced five new forms of validity more in tune with a critically interpretative form of research, especially that from within a poststructuralist paradigm (Lather, 1993). Mac Naughton (Chapter 14) illustrates how she used Lather's work on validity in an action research study. But triangulation does help in the quest for rich data that attempts to reduce some aspects of bias. For example, in a study of work-based training, interviews with student child-care staff might give insights into how the students are benefiting from their work placements. On the other hand, interviews with other practitioners in the service and with the trainers can provide evidence that will inform interpretations of evidence from the students (data triangulation). Similarly, in a study of how children are supported as learners, observational data might point a researcher towards assumptions about how practitioners are approaching children as learners, but these assumptions need to be explored in interviews or by taping planning meetings to which the practitioners are contributing (methodological triangulation). Frequently, qualitative studies employ a combination of data and methodological triangulation. For example, in an exploration of how children interact with books, observations of children might be augmented by interviews with parents and the collection of planning and assessment documents produced by early childhood staff. With feasibility in mind, single-handed researchers need to decide what is to be foregrounded as the major source of evidence and what is to provide more background information. Despite the origins of the term, triangulation neither restricts nor requires the researcher to observe the phenomenon from three vantage points.

Investigator triangulation is another important feature of qualitative research. You can not always work with others when collecting evidence, but studies that claim to be robust within modernist parameters do need to demonstrate that the analysis of qualitative data has been reliable. Thus, for instance, as we shall see later in the chapter, it is important to show that a second researcher would have analysed the data from the field in a similar way when working with the analytic categories used in the study. (For discussion of reliability in postmodern/poststructuralist paradigms see Chapter 3.)

Theory triangulation is challenging and sometimes avoided even by the most established of researchers. In brief, it requires researchers to consider alternative interpretations of the data. It can usefully lead to caution in interpretation and so prevent over-claiming from the evidence. For example, a curriculum researcher might want to explain changes in children's behaviour in terms of the new curriculum she is evaluating. A developmentalist might explain the same changes as maturation. The alternative developmental explanation has to be acknowledged even if the design of the study had not allowed an exploration of the possibility. Indeed, the more openly reflexive and critically interpretative versions of qualitative research are often more likely to explore competing theoretical interpretations of evidence. Multiple readings of data are increasingly a hallmark of research conducted from within a poststructuralist paradigm (for example, Campbell, 1999).

Designing the study

Having considered the possibilities, tensions and constraints offered by qualitative research, it is time to design the study. Case study is the most broadly used form of qualitative research design. Here the term is to be used to include individual cases, illustrative and comparative cases and **lifestory**. They all attempt to answer the question 'What is going on here?' by focusing on the particularities of lives in context. The question does not rule out the capacity to reveal causal relationships, but the prime purpose of case study is to get below the surfaces offered by one method of data collection on one element of the field in order to achieve some purchase on the complexities of social worlds.

Types of case study

So what is a case? Cases are often referred to as units of analysis, the bounded systems which we explore in our study. A case can be, for example, an individual, a family, a work team, a resource, an institution or an intervention. Each case has within it a set of interrelationships that both bind it together and shape it, but also interact with the external world. Stake usefully describes a case as 'an integrated system' (Stake, 1994). Case studies can be longitudinal, but more often than not they provide a detailed snapshot of a system in action.

Case study is used for one of two broad purposes. Cases can be of *intrinsic* interest—for example, a study of the introduction of a new way of working in a child-care service. Or they can be selected as an *example* of phenomena occurring more widely, in the expectation that the fine-grained exploration that case study allows will assist our general understanding of the phenomena. An English example here would be a study of how 4-year-olds are coping with attendance at primary school.

Our expectations of each kind of case study are therefore different. In cases of intrinsic interest we would focus on one case and the interactions and meanings held by participants. We might choose to look at more than one case, but our focus is *inside* the case and comparison of the cases is not our main concern. We frequently find that an intrinsic case raises questions about wider issues, for example how policy is changed as it is integrated into practice, but we do not design intrinsic cases in order to generalise from them. An intrinsic case may be the starting point for further study. For example, experimental designs often start with case studies that allow the researchers to clarify their understanding of the area of study.

Cases that are selected as exemplary have the potential to tell us more about a wider population than might be gleaned in a survey. Exemplary cases can be selected to represent a particular category from a wider population. For example, a sample of cases in a study of the national implementation of an early childhood curriculum might include a private child-care service, a voluntary-run service and a State-run service. Here the function of the cases would be mainly illustrative, to show how each service made sense of the policy. This type of exemplary case is sometimes part of a mixed design, where cases are selected to clarify findings from a survey and perhaps to help shape the construction of a further survey instrument. In another project, exemplary cases all taken from a similar type of child-care service might be selected and the cases compared in order to build up an understanding of issues that are common to all the cases in that version of child-care. Here the function of cases would be comparative and their purpose the identification of common themes across the cases.

In both types of exemplary case study there may be a temptation to generalise from the cases to the wider population, that is, from the particular to the general. Most writers on case study urge considerable caution about generalisation, Stake (1995, p. 8) suggesting that the 'real business of case study is particularisation'. For most case study researchers the main benefit of case study is that the familiar is seen afresh as a result of rigorous examination. For others, for example Atkinson and Delamont (1985), the capacity that case study has for **theory building** through the comparative analysis of cases should not be forgotten, and indeed provides a major justification for the use of case study.

In brief, case study can be either a design in its own right or a feature in other research designs.

Case study research

- A research study can take an intrinsic case as its sole focus.
- Exemplary cases can be incorporated into mixed designs to provide illustrative evidence to inform understandings derived from surveys.
- Exemplary cases can be compared so that more general understandings of the field can be constructed from the ground up.

Identifying the boundary of a case can be difficult. This because once we see a case as a system it is, necessarily, connected into other social systems. Decisions on the foreground and background of the study are therefore essential. It is sometimes helpful to think of a case as a set of concentric circles in which the major focus is on the central circle with interest decreasing as one moves towards the outer ring. In an intrinsic case study of how adults and children in a child-care service interact after the introduction of a key worker system (that is, where each child has a designated member of staff as a key carer), the case would look something like this: At the centre of the case we would find the primary focus of study, children in interaction with their key workers. More than one pairing of adult and child at the centre would be needed as the case is the service rather than the child. The next circle would represent the early childhood staff's expectations and pedagogy in relation to the children and their practices. The next layer, still moving outwards from the centre, might be the early childhood curriculum, its implementation and management. The next layer might tackle parental perspectives and the outer circle might address issues relating to government policies on the early experiences of the under-4s and conditions of employment for early childhood staff.

The collection of evidence would centre on the interactions between the adults and the children. Consequently, high quality observational data would be essential here. Staff and parents would be interviewed and documentary sources would be gathered on policy, management and implementation. Exemplary cases look very similar to intrinsic cases, but feasibility is important when constructing several exemplary cases. If a number of cases are being explored it may be advisable to narrow the focus (for example to the two innermost circles in the example just given), to ensure that there is time to gather the good quality evidence required. There are few things more disheartening than to find that the evidence gathered from cases is too superficial to be informative.

The *timing of data collection* is crucial, as case studies are designed to allow exploration of interrelationships between elements of the study. Ideally, evidence from one source is analysed before themes from that source are pursued in other forms of data collection. This ideal is not always achieved, but at the very least case study researchers need to remain alert to emerging themes in their data and to write **analytic memos** as they gather and read through their evidence. **Research diaries** become a useful resource for qualitative researchers as a place to record their changing interpretations of the field of study over time. The diary can include insights from the field and from published studies.

GETTING THE BEST INFORMATION AVAILABLE

Case study calls for a balance between rigour and lightness of touch. Bromley (1986) summarises these demands when he suggests that case study requires the best information available. The words 'l 'available' are both important, as rich data are essential, bu the case study researcher has to take care to avoid overly distorting tne case by her presence. Qualitative researchers, therefore, do need to acknowledge that they will disrupt the case. Most ensure that participants in the case become used to their presence before starting to collect evidence. Sometimes the disruption can become part of the case. This can occur, for example, when the study is monitoring an intervention such as the introduction of a new set of practices. Observations of children and interviews with staff can assist the careful implementation of the new practices. Most case studies, however, are examining existing systems and researchers try to avoid too much disruption. Case study researchers therefore aim at low-intrusion data collection methods so that they can do justice to the story the case is telling.

Observations

The least obtrusive way of collecting evidence is observation (see Chapter 15 for more detail).

Broadly, observations can be:
- anecdotal (rich descriptions of a specific and informative event);
- event-sequenced (noting when a particular behaviour occurs); or
- time-sequenced (collecting information at regular intervals).

Anecdotal observations can be descriptive notes of an event that appears to offer some insight into the phenomenon being studied. For example, a quarrel in the book corner over whether or not it is girls' or boys' space, or a child's reluctance to leave her parent, can be written first in notes that capture the event, its context and its immediate antecedents. Subsequent behaviours are then written up more fully, perhaps as a vignette.

Event-sequenced observations can involve a simple count with an event counter or even a system of tally counting, for example, every time a child uses a particular resource. This is a fairly crude way of collecting evidence as it tells us nothing about the length of time or how the resource was used.

Time-sequenced observations that are useful for qualitative researchers in early childhood settings are photographs and Sylva's target-child method (Sylva, Roy and Painter, 1980). Both methods allow researchers to collect evidence from the field and analyse it inductively once it has been collected. Photographs can be used to collect time-sequenced data by taking a picture of the target child or adult at regular intervals, for example every 60 seconds. If a digital camera is used the pictures can be loaded on a computer for ease of analysis.

The target-child method, like photographs, involves selecting a target, which may be an adult or a child or even a small group (Edwards and Talbot, 1999). The researcher prepares an observation sheet after the style of the example below. The rows represent one minute of observation and five rows fit an A4 page.

The target observations method

Time	Observations	Analysis
10.00		
10.01		

In the first column the time is noted, in the second rectangle the researcher records everything the target does in one minute, the third rectangle in the third column is left blank for the analysis stage. At 10.01 the researcher moves to the second row and so on. This method is tiring, so a break after ten or fifteen minutes is recommended to enable the researcher to make sense of the scribbled notes and to record any background information on the settings that will assist later analysis. After a short break observation can resume. The number of observations will depend on how they are contributing to the design of the study. As a rule of thumb, more than one observation is made of a target, if observations are to be a major data source.

The target method can be used alongside tape recording, as the minute-by-minute breakdown allows the researcher to combine the real-time tape with the real-time observations. So why not use a video camera? The answer is that they tend to be disruptive if they are hand-held, and if they are fixed they see less than the more flexible human observer. The target method is not helpful if you need to know precisely how long a behaviour lasts, but it does allow you to capture broad sequences of behaviour and their contexts.

Interviews

Interviews (see Chapters 11 and 12) allow case study researchers to explore the meanings that lie behind observed behaviours or documentary evidence. In some cases the interviews will be the major data source and the observations will be prompts. In case study research it is commonplace to use observations as a starting point for interviews. Most interview schedules start quite broadly and then focus more narrowly on the issues that have arisen as the case has been explored. Case study researchers often use interviews to explore their interpretations of the data and the tentative links they have been making between elements of the case as part of a process of progressively increasing an understanding of the case. Of course here it is important to avoid leading questions. A simple tip is to ask 'What do you think about the key worker system?' rather than 'Do you think the system is working?' The researcher can focus the topic of the interview, but should avoid constraining the response.

Documentary sources

These are easily collected and can include material sent to users of the service, minutes of meetings, observations made of children by staff, curriculum policies and so on.

ANALYSING QUALITATIVE DATA

Being organised is an essential attribute for the qualitative researcher. To be drowning in data is not a pleasant experience. The physical sorting of data needs to start as soon as evidence starts to accumulate. An increasing number of qualitative researchers like to put as much data as possible onto computer databases and to manipulate them there. There are also growing numbers of computer programs aimed at assisting qualitative analysis. These should be treated cautiously, however, and only used if they give the help that is needed. Analysis should not be led by what the analysis program can do!

Qualitative analysis usually involves content analysis, that is, a process of combing the evidence. The comb can be quite fine, allowing detailed analysis of the transcribed interview text—for example, the type of language used to talk about children. Or it can be quite broad and pick up thematic responses—for example, beliefs about children as learners. Analysis can involve the entire text or simply segments of it. Much depends on the purpose of the study. Whatever method is used, the case study researcher needs to explain carefully how the analysis was carried out.

Sometimes the analysis is theory-led. In a study of mother–child interaction, for example, a researcher might record mothers' behaviours in the second column of the observation chart and use the third column to label the behaviours recorded, using the categories of mothering behaviour identified by Schaffer (1977). Schaffer's categories may not fit the data, perhaps because the mothers in the present study are from a different cultural background to those who generated the original categories. The researcher must then adapt some categories or create new ones in response to the data.

Sometimes the analysis is data-driven. Data-driven analysis is not easy to do well, as it involves constructing a category system from the evidence that has been collected. In fact, most data-driven analyses start with the researcher's beliefs about the focus of the study. For example, in a study of 3-year-olds and number activities, the starting point for analyses would be the researcher's own grasp of how young children learn to think and act with number in everyday settings. This understanding may have been informed, even implicitly, by earlier research, for example that of Saxe, Guberman and Gearhart (1987). Indeed, the study could not have been designed without some implicit theory of how children acquire numeracy.

Sometimes only analytic memos are required. The third column of the observation chart can simply be used for writing analytic memos which will alert the researcher to the topics to be followed up in later data collection when the mothers are interviewed. (If observations are photocopied they can be used for both categorisation and memos.) Similarly interview evidence can prompt analytic memos which help the researcher's developing interpretations of the case.

Developing a category system. This is where the modernist qualitative researcher's rigour is tested. A category system consists of the category labels assigned to observed behaviours or, in interviews or recorded conversations, to units of talk. Each category label needs to be supported by a description that distinguishes it from the other category labels. The descriptions need to be clear enough to enable another researcher to use them to categorise a sample of some of the data and achieve a high degree of match with the original categorisation. Above 85 per cent match on categorisation by two researchers on a 10 per cent sample of a data set is usually acceptable. If the second researcher finds the categories difficult to use they need to be refined and made clearer until they are usable. At the start of a project the category system is an evolving document as adjustments are made to descriptors in response to the data.

Applying the categories. The first task is to identify the unit of analysis to which the categories will be applied. One version of a unit of analysis is where the behaviour or utterance begins and ends. Identification is relatively easy in observational data where behaviour is labelled at the point when it starts. With interviews, units can be fine-grained 'meaning units' (Edwards, 1997), where a unit is defined as a string of words in which a meaning is carried. For example, 'she is often late/but she's keen when she gets here' contains two units. At the other end of the range of unit are large segments of text which represent a specific perspective on events in a more broadly thematic analysis. Again, much depends on how the data are to contribute to the story of the case.

However the evidence is analysed, the major virtue of qualitative studies is their capacity to tell a well-substantiated story. These stories are strengthened by using voices from the field, or detailed snapshots of the field, to bring to life the arguments being pursued in the research report. Organisation of qualitative evidence therefore has to allow the researcher to access easily the qualitative sources of the strong themes being discussed. For example, if a report identifies two perspectives on young children as learners in operation in one preschool, the researcher needs to be able to find examples of each interpretation to use them to illustrate briefly the argument being made. Systematic organisation of data cannot be overemphasised!

TELLING THE STORY

Qualitative data can be transformed into quantitative data through fine-grained content analysis, and findings can be statistically tested. But tables cannot represent the complexities and ambiguities of the field revealed in case study. One of the challenges of telling the tale elicited from the field is to provide an account of what is going on which is sufficiently coherent to retain a reader's interest but is also sensitive to the complexities and multiple perspectives revealed in the study.

The extent to which the story is a richly illustrated research report, or is a personal narrative, will largely depend on whether the researcher's aim is primarily to produce illuminating research or to offer a critical interpretation. Although these aims demand different modes of story-telling, the former often more like a traditional research report, the latter giving more opportunities for inventive representation, they will usually contain some common features.

> ## Common features in qualitative research
>
> - Openness about the researcher's theoretical and personal starting points;
> - An ethical concern for those whose experiences are being represented;
> - An attempt to reveal the richness of the field in the field's own terms;
> - A need for a careful system of data organisation to support the analysis; and
> - A critical awareness of what has been learnt during the research process.

QUESTIONS FOR REFLECTION

- Think of a practical issue that you would like to explore. Try to identify the questions that some of the following researchers might like to pursue when exploring the topic: a feminist; an anti-racist; a linguist; a developmentalist. Briefly outline the studies that two of them might undertake. How will their starting points affect how their study is designed?
- Where would you place yourself as a researcher in the 'moments' of qualitative research identified by Denzin and Lincoln (1994) and outlined in this chapter? How easy is it to categorise yourself? Can you think of a situation where, for example, you might be both a modernist and a critical interpreter? (The author of this chapter certainly can!)
- How would you explain to a civil servant who might offer you funds how your qualitative research will help the development of practice in early childhood services?
- What would be the ethical issues to be considered when designing a case study of how a preschool handles links with children's families? (See Chapter 5 and, for example, ethical guidelines available on the websites of national research associations and psychological societies.)
- Roughly how much time should you allocate on your timeline for data analysis, and to what extent can analysis be carried out before all the evidence is collected when planning a study which will involve the following: Six hours of interviews to be analysed to extract broad themes, three hours of written target-child observations (30 minutes on each of six children) which will be analysed in some detail, assessment data on the six children being observed and some background information on curriculum policies and planning.

FURTHER READING

Denzin, N. and Lincoln, Y. (eds) 1994, *Handbook of Qualitative Research*, Sage, London. This book is a classic. Hamilton's chapter, 'Traditions, preferences and postures in applied qualitative research', is a useful introduction to the labyrinth of debates around qualitative methods. Huberman and Miles' chapter, 'Data management and analysis methods', unravels the difficulties of organising qualitative data.

Dey, I. 1993, *Qualitative Data Analysis*, Routledge, London. This book is a very helpful guide on how to organise and analyse qualitative evidence.

9

Equity issues in research design

Susan Grieshaber

This chapter considers the idea of research as a cultural invention; discusses what equity, research and research design mean, and reviews several issues that need to be taken into account if the research process is to be guided by principles of equity.

RESEARCH AS A CULTURAL INVENTION

Research is a **cultural invention** of the white western (male) academic world and as such represents a privileged position. Along with this privileged position comes the dominant understanding about what research means in social science. This dominant understanding 'presupposes the possibility and desirability of an objective, neutral and a-political approach' (Schrijvers, 1991, p. 169). The approach taken in this chapter, however, is the obverse of the dominant position. I believe that research is subjective, never neutral and always political, hence the need for **equity** as a fundamental component of research design.

As well as research activity being a cultural invention itself, the focus of much research activity is other cultural inventions and social constructions. The concept of childhood is a pertinent example of a cultural invention. Kessen (1979) made this clear in the title of his publication, 'The American child and other cultural inventions'. A psychologist, Kessen wrote the article in order to challenge his students' assumptions concerning childhood and accepted ways of researching

young children. Hatch (1995) too, has argued that childhood is a cultural invention:

> There is no permanent and essential nature of childhood. The idea of childhood is defined differently in every culture, in every time period, in every political climate, in every economic era, in every social context. Our everyday assumption that the childhood we 'know' is and always has been *the* [emphasis in original] definition of childhood turns out to be false (p. 118).

Yet much time and money has been spent in researching aspects of childhood to establish parameters for what is considered the normal child. The influence of the normative view has been pervasive in some research from within developmental psychology. For instance, Weber (1984) has acknowledged that studies by researchers such as Gesell were instrumental in creating norms of physical, motor, social and mental growth. One of the difficulties associated with the normative view is that children of students and professors were used to establish the norms, which were then 'generalised to all children' (Weber, 1984, p. 60). Burman (1994) cautions against researching children using a culturally western, white and middle-class idealised model of the normal child to measure other children against. Her work calls attention to the inequities that can be produced if early childhood researchers treat developmental differences as developmental deficits.

In a similar vein to categorising difference as deficit, Mayall, Hood and Oliver (1999) have argued that the objects of social research are often members of 'socially, economically or politically disadvantaged groups and in need of help or redress' (p. 1). Such groups include children, the elderly, those with health problems and gay men. According to Mayall et al. (1999), these people are the object of research projects because they are constituted as economic problems and a remedy is needed to reduce the economic burden they present for government. Research activity, then, is a particular cultural invention of the western academic world that is aimed at investigating other social constructions and cultural inventions that are not necessarily located within the same culture, economic circumstances or historical period. Some of the difficulties encountered with this position include the imposition of western ways of researching on who and what is being studied.

The fact that a chapter about equity is being included in this book is an indication of how some in the academy have challenged traditional understandings of what research can be and how it can be undertaken. Inclusion of equity as an issue in research design is therefore a topic for both qualitative and quantitative researchers to consider, although it may be problematic if some of the differences between these two approaches are taken into account. For example, Oakley (1999), writing from a feminist perspective, has discussed the idea that the 'social sciences have themselves been gendered, and have thus spawned a gendered discourse about "qualitative" and "quantitative" methods' (p. 161).

The difference espoused by Oakley (1999) is that quantitative research approaches are aligned with masculine approaches while qualitative approaches are associated with feminine approaches. She points out other dualisms beside the association of qualitative research with feminine qualities and quantitative research with masculine qualities, contrasting understanding (feminine) and control (masculine), intuition and reason, soft and hard, subjective and objective and so on, and noting that dualistic thinking is a characteristic of western culture (p. 161). Despite pointing out these differences, Oakley believes the more important issues for all social research are **trustworthiness**, matching methods to research questions, and 'integrating a range of methods in carrying out socially useful inquiries' (p. 166). Whatever the approach adopted (qualitative or quantitative), equity ought to be considered from the beginning when the research is being conceptualised.

WHAT IS MEANT BY EQUITY, RESEARCH, AND RESEARCH DESIGN?

An understanding of equity involves notions of justice and fairness. It moves beyond equality, as equality signals understandings of parity, equivalence and making things equal, which do not necessarily equate with justice and fairness. In order to be just and fair, it is sometimes necessary to move beyond making things equal.

Both the nature of research and research design have been variously categorised. Although both terms conjure up many different understandings, research is conceptualised here as 'a systematic method of inquiry' (Drew and Hardman, 1985, p. 3) that is culturally specific. Research design means the plan for what is to be investigated. As Oakley (1999) said, it is important to match the research questions to the research methods that are chosen for the study. The research design is contingent on the research questions or the problem and is directly related to the data to be collected, and how this will be accomplished. This means considering who the participants will be, the selection process for participants and how the data will be collected (data gathering techniques). The research design also involves how the data are to be analysed, including measures of reliability, validity and generalisability, and how data are to be interpreted. Equity issues in research design therefore incorporate notions of fairness and justice in relation to the research investigation (the systematic method of inquiry) and how it is to be undertaken. Concerns probed here in relation to equity issues in research design include power relations, research based on a **deficit model**, the notion of **homogeneity**, and some ideas for the detection of **bias**. I begin with power relations.

ISSUES OF EQUITY IN RESEARCH

Power relations

Because researchers enact and participate in relationships of power, there can be no researcher neutrality. Undertaking any research activity alters the research site to an unknown degree. In more traditional approaches to research within a positivist paradigm, and in much quantitative research, the researcher is positioned more powerfully than those who are the objects of that research (Atweh and Burton, 1995). Approaches that attempt to relocate some of that power are more likely to be found within qualitative research, especially that informed by feminist and anti-racist theoretical perspectives. Lather (1991, p. 269) believes that 'we are both shaped by and shapers of our world' and that the choice of research paradigms reflects our beliefs about the world in which we live and the world in which we want to live.

Incorporation of the notion of equity into the relationships of power that are enacted between researchers and those who are researched means a redefinition of relationships involved in the research process. This can be difficult, as it involves 'the intersection of three sets of interests', including the researcher/s, the researched and 'those of socially dominant political structures, organisations, social groups and individuals' (Mayall et al., 1999, p. 1).

Although we need to move beyond simplistic notions of researchers being all-powerful, Williams and Stewart (1992), Atweh and Burton (1995), Smithmier (1996) and Mayall et al. (1999) maintain that the balance of power remains with the researcher. The traditional power associated with researchers can be redefined in several ways. These include sharing the power through collaborative approaches, such as fourth generation action research (see Chapter 14), where participants are able to negotiate issues including the research questions, research design, access, analysis and the recognition of rights. It also includes reflexivity, which is discussed in a later section of this chapter on detecting bias.

In relation to Australian Aboriginal educational research, Williams and Stewart (1992) present a compelling case for participatory action research involving community control, where disproportionate gains to individual researchers through 'one-way research' (p. 4) are reversed and Aboriginal communities benefit through research based on community control and self-determination (p. 1). This means negotiating issues of power and control from the inception of the project, and remains a challenge to all those committed to research that attempts to redefine relationships of power by locating power other than solely with researchers. The first stage of the process therefore involves gaining insight into the world view of potential research participants. Like Williams and Stewart (1992), Lather (1986) has argued that when designing the mode of inquiry it is essential that participants be 'actively engaged in the construction and validation of meaning' (p. 268). This form of participation also involves reflexivity, as accounts can be used for further analysis as well as enabling respondents to react to the perceptions of the researcher through provision of feedback to the researcher. Chapters 4 and 17 provide examples of this approach in action.

In their effort to redefine power relationships, Atweh and Burton (1995) described how they attempted collaboration among university researchers, teachers and school students in a project designed to facilitate equity and access to higher degree education. Despite the students being responsible for 'the choice of questions to research, the methods used, the analysis of their data, and the reporting of their findings' (p. 566), problems of the partiality of ownership were identified. These related to the fact that 'the original definition of the project was not theirs' (p. 574) and were complicated by time, trust and the location of the project at the school and not the university. Studies such as these are instructive as they highlight the complexities and intricacies involved in redefinition of issues of power and control and signal important aspects for other researchers to take into account.

In relation to those researched, Mayall (1999) argues that the analysis and presentation of data is an area where the researched have least power. Being reflexive can help researchers address these concerns in what is written and presented. The written aspects of any research project are inevitably a process of combining participants' experience and communication with that of the researcher and converting it into an academic text that adheres to the conventions and procedures of the genre of academic writing (Pels and Nencel, 1991). In other words, there should be an explicit recognition of the 'emphasis on writing as an enactment of the social relations that produce the research itself' (Lather, 1991, p. 112). This requires active and therefore written recognition of all aspects of the research process, including generation of the research problem, the researcher's participation in research sites and ongoing decisions about issues as they were negotiated throughout the project.

Researching using a deficit model

Research based on a deficit model involves the use of statements or norms developed with one group of participants and applied to another group. For example, Head Start programmes were initiated in the United States in the 1960s to provide compensatory early education experiences for children living in poverty. Cannella (1997) has argued that Head Start programmes were 'grounded in the assumption that particular groups of children are deficient, that parents are responsible for these deficiencies, and that outside intervention is necessary to overcome the problems' (p. 111). Since the 1960s these programmes have been the focus of continuous research, much of it aimed at showing how such programmes are beneficial. Although often demonstrating what have been called benefits, the research can make cultural, socioeconomic, racial, and ethnic differences appear as deficits. In Cannella's (1997) words, 'Head Start would provide an environment in which "disadvantaged" children would become like their middle-class peers, would be prepared cognitively for first grade' (p. 111). In a similar vein, Brennan's (1998) documentation of the origins of the Australian kindergarten movement evidenced a belief 'that the conditions of working class family life could be improved through voluntary, philanthropic activity' (p. 7).

Research based on assumptions of deficit or disadvantage often reflects 'Eurocentric normative and scientific principles' (Utley and Obiakor, 1995, p. 11). What Utley and Obiakor are referring to is the way in which 'the West has dominated the rest of the world both politically and scientifically' (Harris, 1991, p. 147). Utley and Obiakor (1995) make a strong case for investigating the underlying assumptions of quantitative research and methods, as they say that a cultural deficit model or blaming the victim model is used in most quantitative research conducted with racial and ethnic groups.

In their critique of **Eurocentric** approaches, Padilla and Lindholm (1995) have shown that the Eurocentric paradigm rests on three assumptions:

(a) the White middle class American (typically male) is the standard against which other groups should be compared; (b) the instruments used for assessing differences are universally applicable across groups, with perhaps only minimal adjustments for culturally diverse populations; and (c) although we need to recognize the sources of potential variance such as social class, educational attainment, gender, cultural orientation, and proficiency in English, these are nuisances that can later be discarded (p. 97).

Although Padilla and Lindholm are talking about quantitative educational research, their criticism is instructive for qualitative researchers as well, because it highlights the 'biases inherent in the paradigms themselves' (p. 97). Padilla and Lindholm are scathing in their analysis of how research with minority students is used, claiming that: 'when minority students are included in quantitative research, it is usually with the intent of documenting low achievement of Hispanic, African American, and, to a lesser extent, Native American students in comparisons to Anglo students' (p. 100).

The domination by the Eurocentric paradigm incorporates particular relations of power and knowledge that serve to locate as 'other' all those who do not have the particular 'Western middle-class political bias' (Huizer, 1991, p. 41) on which the research is based. This argument is similar to that made by Lubeck (1994) about developmentally appropriate practice (Bredekamp, 1987; Bredekamp and Copple, 1997), which is the dominant influence on early childhood education.

Lubeck (1994) has shown that through developmentally appropriate practice, much child development research has endorsed the belief that 'some cultural practices are preferable (and others, if not "deficient", certainly less desirable)'. Lubeck has also argued that the focus in developmentally appropriate practice on 'individuals (children and family members) [has been used] in an effort to rectify social ills' (p. 20). Focusing on the individual child or family locates the problem with the individual, rather than structural factors in society. The individual or family is then the target of programmes aimed at rectifying the social ills identified. This is an example of how the production of normative assumptions based on a distinct segment of the population (white middle-class children) has been used to promulgate norms that are then generalised to society as a whole. This can happen with both qualitative and quantitative research approaches, but is less likely with the former.

Constructing homogeneity

The notion of homogeneity can be likened to **essentialism** and is also linked to research based on deficit models. Homogeneity means using a major characteristic to group items or people. In relation to research activity, Alarcon, Erkut, Coll and Garcia (1994) talk about 'lumping together' information about Hispanic people, including 'white collar Cubans, Central American refugees, Mexican migrant workers and Puerto Ricans', simply because they are assumed to speak Spanish, and also point out that Puerto·Ricans have been treated as a homogenous group without taking into account factors such as differences in 'socioeconomic standards, acculturation, migration patterns and color' (p. 2). This would be a similar situation to including all Australian or British people who spoke English in the one group, combined with a lack of identification of any other factors such as ethnicity, class, gender, age, socioeconomic status and so on. Classing any group as homogeneous can therefore obstruct differences that are likely to be significant in research activity. This can impede the trustworthiness of the data, the data analysis and the validity of the research project as a whole.

Essentialism is understood as the possession of intrinsic or characteristic properties that constitute the true nature of something.

Essentialist understandings can be applied to a host of constructs including childhood, women, family, gender, man and Chinese people. However, as Hatch (1995) has argued, there is no permanent and essential nature of childhood. Likewise, there is no permanent and essential nature of woman, family, gender, man or Asian people. The humanist understanding of 'Man' for instance, is an essentialist notion because it 'occludes important differences between men and women and covertly supports male domination of women. Humanist discourse postulates a universal essence as constituent of human beings which operates to enthrone socially constructed male traits and activities (such as reason, production, or the will to power) as essentially human' (Best and Kellner, 1991, p. 206).

This essentialist understanding of 'Man' locates women as other and sets up a binary division between women and men. Earlier, I referred to Oakley's (1999) discussion of this binary division in relation to qualitative and quantitative research. There are many differences among women (race, class, sexuality, age, to mention a few) which cannot be reduced to an essential understanding of who and what all women are, particularly when those differences have been essentialised as binary oppositions to male characteristics. The postmodern project and its associated research paradigm has been valuable for those (including women and others from so-called minority groups) who have been marginalised by essentialist understandings of 'Man' that privilege truth, reason and objectivity. They have been able to draw on the 'postmodern emphasis on plurality, difference, otherness, marginality, and heterogeneity' (Best and Kellner, 1991, p. 207).

Research activity needs therefore to recognise the **heterogeneity** of participants in research projects and the fact that our current social conditions are characterised by plurality, difference, ambivalence and contradictions. As a disadvantaged minority group with little say in institutional decision-making and no say at all in political processes affecting their lives (Mayall, 1999, p. 10), children require particular attention as research participants. Mayall (1999) highlights how notions of childhood have also been essentialised: 'Psychological paradigms have focused attention on the character of children's otherness, and their progress towards sameness, that is towards adulthood' (p. 11). Because of the way they are positioned in society, children are rarely offered the opportunity to give their permission for researchers to involve them in research activity, as it is parental permission that is usually attained. Chapters 5 and 11 discuss how to do this effectively and ethically.

Ensuring that research activity reflects the diversity of the particular group being studied is a particularly important equity consideration. Whether children, women, ethnic minorities or aged people are involved in research, the temptation to treat the group as homogeneous needs to be resisted.

DETECTING BIAS IN RESEARCH

When designing research projects, researchers must rely on the resources they have available to them. One such resource is the researcher herself, as 'social researchers are necessarily part of the world they study' (Foster, Gomm and Hammersley, 1995, p. 2). However, to engage in the research process is to draw upon theoretical standpoints and perspectives, either explicit or implicit. Interacting with the world being studied can produce particular effects on the researcher as well as on the participants in the study. Researchers themselves embody particular beliefs, values and interests which are often reflected in the way the problem is formulated, research is designed, data collected and interpreted, and findings displayed.

Locating your own particular values, interests and beliefs that may interfere with justice and fairness in the research endeavour is an important part of researcher responsibility. This means researchers need to foreground their own investments and interests, standpoints and motivations, explicitly stating their theoretical positions and assumptions. Such foregrounding is often referred to as self-reflexivity. Self-reflexivity involves deconstructing the ways in which our desires shape the texts we produce. It also necessitates deconstructing the relations of difference—of gender, class and race—that have been instrumental in the design of the research process. Researchers 'cannot assume they share the world experience of the researched' (Mayall, 1999, p. 14) and so being self-reflexive involves incorporating the views of those researched into the analysis process. Chapter 8 offers further insights on how to design reflexive research.

Self-reflexivity in analysing research

- Check with participants that you have understood what they mean.
- Provide participants with transcripts/field notes/diary entries, etc. to make sure their input is represented accurately.
- Check your interpretations of what participants say with the participants themselves (as an ongoing part of the research).
- Make available the interpretation and analyses to participants and encourage them to respond.

Cultural or gender bias can influence the research at all stages of the process, including initial decisions about the research design, selection of theoretical perspectives, formulation of hypotheses, consideration of variables, selection of participants, analyses and interpretation of data. Quina and Kulberg (1988) discussed these aspects in relation to quantitative research, citing examples of research projects showing bias in specific areas. Much of what they say can also be applied to qualitative approaches. Some of the points they make about detecting bias in relation to hypotheses, theories and variables are included below. Readers are also referred to Chapter 3.

Detecting bias in quantitative research

Hypotheses—watch for:

- Hypotheses, situations and measures that maximise group differences and ignore settings in which differences are not likely to be observed; and
- Individual studies showing gender or race differences that are not shown in multiple studies.

Theories—watch for:

- Deviance and disorder that blames mothers;
- Research on families that implies the nuclear family is the norm against which others are compared;
- Theories that position women and children as inferior to men; and
- Theories that position different racial groups as inferior or as 'other'.

Variables—watch for:

- Use of instruments or measures as universally applicable across groups with little alteration for gender, age or ethnic group;
- Identification of problematic behaviour in one ethnic group that is described as something quite different in another group;
- Confusion of gender and sexuality/sexual orientation;
- Use of 'white' data gatherers in research about ethnic groups; and
- Socioeconomic indicators not being taken into account (Quina and Kulberg, 1988, pp. 72–6).

SUMMARY

Designing research for equity means:
- Being alert to how your research design might position socially disadvantaged groups and groups that have been traditionally 'othered' in research (children, women and ethnic minorities);
- Recognising power relationships in the researcher–researched relationships;
- Analysing how homogeneity is being constructed in the research;
- Rejecting deficit models of research;
- Learning self-reflexivity as a researcher; and

145

- Avoiding bias in the theories, hypothesis, variables, participants and interpretations used during the research process.

QUESTIONS FOR REFLECTION

- What is the goal of the research and how does it relate to issues of equity?
- What are the benefits for the participants, funding bodies and researcher?
- What have I included in the research design to avoid a conflict of interest among these three positions?
- If a 'disadvantaged' group is to be studied, how did I consider the political implications of researching such a group before embarking on the research?
- If a 'disadvantaged' group is to be studied, how will I undertake to make participants aware of this?
- How is diversity within groups (such as children, Spanish-speaking people) reflected in the research design?
- How have I made sure that my research design does not rely on a deficit model?
- How have I understood relations of power between the researcher and participants?
- How is my research design reflexive?

FURTHER READING

Mayall, B. 1999, 'Children and childhood', in S. Hood, B. Mayall and S. Oliver (eds), *Critical Issues on Social Research: Power and Prejudice* (pp. 10–24), Open University Press, Buckingham. Mayall explores power relations involved in research with children, suggesting that sociological methodological approaches can offer ways of researching with children that preserve their integrity and recognise their competence.

Lather, P. 1991, *Getting Smart: Feminist Research and Pedagogy with/in the Postmodern*, Routledge, New York. Lather detailed how she approached research with groups of women and identified several ways of conducting qualitative research effectively in postpositivist times. The book has a focus on methodology and is useful for those interested in refining their understandings of methodological considerations.

Part III

The research process in action

10

Surveys and questionnaires: an evaluative case study

Iram Siraj-Blatchford and John Siraj-Blatchford

When most people think of a survey they imagine the kind of large-scale study carried out for the purposes of market research or the identification of political opinions. The term may even conjure up images of people with clipboards completing questionnaires door to door, or approaching hapless individuals outside supermarkets. Surveys are always carried out to describe some particular characteristic or a range of characteristics of a given population. But not all surveys are large scale, and even small populations, such as the parents and staff of a nursery, can be surveyed. This chapter provides an outline account of a three-year nursery evaluation recently conducted in the UK using interviews and questionnaires. (The design also incorporates other measures but for the purpose of this chapter we only report on the latter.) From this case study, a number of general issues will be explored including sampling, questionnaire construction, the processes of interviewing and the design of small-scale surveys.

WHAT WERE YOUR RESEARCH QUESTIONS?

The nursery involved was a very successful combined centre that integrated preschool child care, education and family support. It has been identified by the UK government as an Early Excellence Centre (EEC) (DfEE, 1997) and was therefore given extra funding to develop its multi-agency approach further and to disseminate good practice. Unsurprisingly, the government was keen to ensure that the additional funding was well spent and to this end instituted a comprehensive national three-year evaluation of the EECs initiative. National evaluators were subsequently appointed, and an elaborate set of 'common indicators' was established to provide the central terms for the annual evaluation of each of the 33 pilot EECs (Pascal et al., 1999). The 72 indicators covered contexts, processes and outcomes. The central research questions were therefore the extent to which each of these indicators was being achieved. If we consider, for example, those indicators most relevant to parental involvement and partnership, P3 of the process indicators included:

- P3a Partnership with parents;
- P3b Responsiveness; and
- P3c Proactive involvement of male family members. (Pascal et al., 1999, p. 52)

In addition, O2 of the Outcome/Impact indicators were:

- O2a Use of services;
- O2b Social and health skills;
- O2c Parenting skills; and
- O2d Employability (Pascal et al., 1999, p. 54).

While some of the data were available through secondary sources such as local employment and social services data, a good deal had to be obtained through primary sources. The head of each early excellence centre was required to appoint a local evaluator to support this process.

All further references to this evaluation (the case study) will be exclusively concerned with the local evaluation, as any additional discussion of the national evaluation is beyond the scope of this chapter. The terms of the evaluation were exceptionally wide so that, again in the interest of brevity, only some aspects of parental partnership (P3/O2) will be reported.

HOW DID YOU ARRIVE AT THE RESEARCH QUESTIONS?

While there was a need to provide the national evaluators with descriptive and reliable summative data, there was clearly an opportunity to work closely with the centre, thus providing a much more formative evaluation. Taking the parent involvement/partnership issue as an example, the centre was aware of the need to continuously monitor and strive to improve practice in these terms. The local evaluator had also been involved in research and development projects concerned with parent partnership for some years (Siraj-Blatchford and Clarke 2000) and therefore brought her own expertise to the area.

As Cronbach (1982) has argued, the design of an evaluative investigation is something of an art. In this case an illuminative perspective was employed where the 'attempted measurement of "educational products" is abandoned for intensive study of the programme as a whole: its rationale and evaluation, its operations, achievements, and difficulties. The innovation is not examined in isolation, but in the . . . context or "learning milieu"' (Parlett and Hamilton, 1987, p. 62)

HOW DID YOU ANSWER IT?

Although most large-scale surveys are aimed at gaining a small amount of information from a large number of people, a good deal of the research carried out in early childhood settings involves relatively small populations. Interviewing was therefore a very practical possibility. It was decided that parents would be interviewed and staff and managers would complete questionnaires to provide triangulation in terms of source. Methodological triangulation was achieved by applying other methods as well, including documentary analysis, focus discussions with staff and the use of standardised rating scales.

The interviews

Interviews can be entirely structured, entirely unstructured or semi-structured (somewhere between the first two). Unstructured interviews, often referred to as a 'conversation with a purpose', are considered to provide the maximum freedom to the respondent in determining their response. In the ideal case, the interviewer will respond to the interviewee to check and elaborate upon their understanding of the chosen subject as they go along. The more structure, the more the interview is 'theory-driven', whether this be in the form of hypotheses to be tested, or through the predetermined terms of an evaluation. The more closely we predefine the range of responses, the greater the opportunity for quantification, and the more we ensure each respondent is asked the same questions in the same way, the more reliable our quantitative data will end up being.

Generally speaking, in any survey there is a trade-off—the greater the structure, the less you find out, but the more reliable the information that you obtain. The less the structure; the more you find out, and the greater the validity this has at the expense of reliability.

All this applies equally to other research instruments such as observation coding schemes and rating scales. From this perspective, ethnography (see Chapter 13) may be considered to offer the least predetermined structure and the greatest validity while rating scales may be employed to give us maximum reliability.

Where the interview has some structure this usually takes the form of a series of predefined questions and a sequence of prompts and probes. Semi-structured interview schedules often include all kinds of strategies employed to encourage the respondent—for instance, a respondent may be reminded of a particular past event to support their recall and/or the interviewer may at times pretend not to fully understand to prompt the respondent to say more. The most highly structured interview schedules are questionnaires; where schedules are in this form there may be no need for an interview at all. The questionnaire would then be referred to as one for 'self-completion', and might be distributed through a simple mailing. In any event prompts and probes can often be used to good effect. A prompt suggests to the interviewee a number of possible answers that the interviewer expects. Probes are used to encourage an expanded response from the interviewee. They may be specific questions such as 'Is there anything else you want to say about that?', they may involve repeating the last thing the interviewer said or they may involve some kind of non-verbal communication (perhaps a raised eyebrow or a period of silence). In the interests of reliability it is usually important to ensure both prompts and probes are applied consistently across interviews.

As far as possible, questions should be short and clear and only one question should ever be asked at a time. Jargon should also be avoided as much as possible. Leading questions can often put words into the interviewee's mouth. For example, the question 'What do you think is the best activity we provide for children of this age group?' presupposes that the interviewee feels positively about some of the activities offered; in fact they might disapprove of all the activities on offer. Perhaps the most important thing of all to avoid is a loaded question using unnecessarily emotionally charged words or phrases—for example, 'Do you approve or disapprove of the abusive practice of teaching basic literacy and numeracy skills in a formal way to under fives?' .

The parent questionnaire that was constructed for the EEC evaluation had a mixture of open and closed questions, prompts and scale items, for a total of 57 questions. The questionnaire began with questions eliciting demographic data such as names/ages. ('How long has your child been at the centre?' etc.) and then asked a series of open questions about the quality/ies of centre buildings and the centre's expectations (for example, with regard to parent involvement). Parents and staff were also asked to provide their responses to these expectations. The parents were asked questions about the main qualities of the staff and about the quality of management; the staff were asked about their own qualities and those of managers. The parents were interviewed by people who were not staff of the centre; the staff self-completed their questionnaire after a half-day training and question and answer session with the researcher. Parent interviews lasted about one hour; self-completion of questionnaires by staff were reported to last 40 minutes to one and a half hours, depending on how detailed the responses to the open questions were.

The following extract illustrates the general pattern.

Short extract from Parent Questionnaire which included over 20 questions on parent involvement.

What kinds of parent involvement does the centre encourage? For example:

24. as helper/volunteer, assistant to a trained adult, centre visits, fund raising
25. to attend workshops or other training—examples?
26. other forms of parent education—examples?
27. parent support for families under stress—examples?
28. What services are you aware of now?

Do you take advantage of any of these?

If yes:

29. How often do you visit . . . ask about their levels of attendance at each/any activity.
30. Do you feel that you have learnt anything from attending centre courses/activities?

If yes: Is there any way that this may have benefitted your child?

31. Do you feel that the centre activities have added anything to your own quality of life?

If yes: Do you think any of this may give you better employment opportunities?

32. Have you made new friends as a result of your involvement?

If yes: Do you find you are you able to help each other?

Prompt: In what ways?

33. If a 'course' referred to:

Was it set at an appropriate level?
Were you satisfied with the course?

Probe: Why?

34. How, if at all, do you feel that you have benefitted from the services provided?

Probe: e.g. confidence?

35. Can you think of any reasons people might not take advantage of any of the services—even when they feel they may be valuable?

Probe: Any gender/socio-economic/moral stigma involved?

Other questions:

36. Is the child's father, or any other male member of your family, involved in bringing up the child?

If yes: Does the centre make a deliberate effort to involve them?

37. To what extent do you think the centre is identifying your child's individual needs?

38. What do you think about the educational provision of the centre? (Siraj-Blatchford, 2000b)

Closed questions set the range of alternative responses and may involve a simple yes or no answer. This was advantageous where we wanted unambiguous data for quantification. Question 28 is therefore closed (there are a limited number of possible responses). Question 30 is another good example of this. Questions 34 and 38, on the other hand, are open-ended and provide a means of collecting more qualitative data. As can be seen, the two questioning strategies were often combined to provide a qualitative check on the interpretation of the quantitative answers. An alternative approach would have been to use scale items, where a question is followed by a range of possible options for the respondent to choose from. For example, 'The staff consider themselves successful in supporting children in developing appropriate social skills. Do you feel that you: strongly agree/agree/aren't sure/disagree/strongly disagree (select one response).'

Instructions for interviewers

A semi-structured questionnaire is incomplete; it leaves you space to 'probe' and 'prompt' and follow-up interesting ideas. To ensure respondents feel comfortable the researcher must emphasize that the information they provide is confidential and will not be used with any names of staff, parents or children. Record these interviews and explain that they are for your purposes only because you want to listen to or read them for analysis. In this case study before beginning the interview a friendly conversation was usually begun about something neutral, e.g. the weather, local traffic or even the price of shoes! Parents were interviewed individually. Where these were mostly 'mums' the researcher tried to probe whether fathers/partners (if present) would hold similar views. Most research on parent involvement seems to be with mothers. (Siraj-Blatchford, 2000b)

Robson (1998) provides a useful five-point model that can be applied in designing your own interview schedule or questionnaire:

- *Introduction:* interviewer introduces herself, explains purpose of the interview, assures of confidentiality, and asks permission to tape and/or make notes.
- *'Warm up':* easy, non-threatening questions at the beginning to settle down both of you.
- *Main body of interview:* covering the main purpose of the interview in what the interviewer considers to be a logical progression. In semi-structured interviewing, this order can be varied, capitalising on the responses made (ensure 'missed' topics are returned to unless this seems inappropriate or unnecessary. Any 'risky' questions should be relatively late in the sequence so that, if the interviewee refuses to continue, less information is lost.
- *'Cool-off':* usually a few straightforward questions at the end to defuse any tension that might have built up.
- *Closure:* thankyou and goodbye. The 'hand on the door' phenomenon, sometimes found at the end of counselling sessions, is also common in interviewing. Interviewees may, when the recorder is switched off or the notebook put away, come out with a lot of interesting material. There are various possible ways of dealing with this (switch on again, reopen the book, forget about it) but in any case you should be consistent, and note how you dealt with it (Robson, 1998).

WHAT SAMPLING ISSUES WERE THERE?

In such small-scale surveys as this example of research in action, you need to obtain the biggest response you possibly can, so that whenever possible you should survey the whole population. Where this is not possible for reasons of time and/or expense you will need to take a random or structured sample. It is worth bearing in mind here that if you wish to carry out any sophisticated form of statistical analysis you will need at least 30 respondents. Remember that your responses need to be representative of the overall population, and that you need to avoid any kind of bias in the selection of (or encouraging participation in) your sample. In the case of the parent survey some of the questions related directly to particular 'user' groups, such as lone parents, ethnic minorities and males, thus it was essential that parents from these categories were interviewed.

A number of alternative sampling strategies could have been employed:

1. *Probability sampling* where the sample is designed to provide an accurate representation of the total population. This includes:
- *Simple random sampling* where each member of the population has an equal chance of being selected.

- *Stratified random sampling* where the total population is first divided into groups considered significant to the area of study. Here the size of the subsamples is often set to reflect their size within the total population. The selection process is designed so that each member of a sub group has an equal chance of being selected.
- *Cluster sampling* is normally applied when the variation among groups is relatively small. In cluster sampling, a random sample of groups is taken and each member within the group has an equal chance of being selected. Again it is important to recognise that group samples will need to be 30 or more if statistical comparisons are to be made.

2. *Non-probability samples* are used where there is a need to over-represent groups with certain characteristics. They are easier to set up and they are cheaper but these are advantages gained at the expense of representation. Non-probability findings cannot be generalised beyond the sample itself. Such samples include:

- *Convenience sampling* where the respondents are selected according to convenience of access. This is entirely legitimate where the population can be reasonably considered heterogeneous in the terms set by the research question.
- *Quota sampling* where representatives from each significant group are selected in proportion to their representation in the total population.
- *Purposive sampling* where members of the sample are selected according to a reasoned case for typicality.

A question every researcher will ask is, 'how large does the sample need to be if it is to be a reliable indicator of the overall population? Unfortunately this is a statistical question that warrants a book in itself, but for a very clear and concise overview of the issues it is worth looking at Anderson (1990, Chapter 18). It is probably enough to note at this point that even in the case of fairly heterogeneous populations, the size of the sample that is required is not proportional to the total population. The sample size of smaller populations needs to be relatively larger. According to Anderson for example, to achieve a 95 per cent level of certainty in a population of 100 you need a sample of at least 79, whereas in a population of 1000 the sample only needs to be around 277 (Anderson, 1990, p. 202).

A recurrent problem in probability samples is non-response. However clever you are in approaching prospective respondents by letter or direct contact, there will be some who will decline the offer of participating in your survey. This can have serious implications for reliability and it is therefore a good idea to do all that you can to reduce the occurrence. Often the reason people choose not to respond will be directly relevant to the subject under study, so that the non-response introduces serious bias. In a postal survey the response rate is often influenced by the length and complexity of the survey, but response rates fewer than 40 per cent are quite common. Follow-up contacts are therefore a necessity to achieve something closer to the 70 to 80 per cent response rate generally considered acceptable. Cohen and Manion (1994) refer to the diminishing return to be expected in following up on non-response (p. 99):

Original dispatch	40%
First follow-up	+20%
Second follow-up	+10%
Third follow-up	+5%
Total	75%

The same general principles apply to the response rates for other forms of research based on random sampling. It is possible to apply statistical strategies that compare the characteristics of first and second choice responders to provide representational justification for a low response, but these methods are controversial. In every case the aim must be to encourage the maximum level of response at the first approach.

In the case of the parent survey, compromises had to be made from the beginning; while we knew the target total population, there were groups within that population that had to be included—yet we didn't know the size of these groups. Many were very small, but as the questions that we were asking related directly to their experiences and concerns it was important to overrepresent them in our sample. This situation, where the conceptual framework of the study must take precedence over representation, is quite common (Cohen and Manion, 1994, p 88). A complete census would have been too expensive (in terms of both time and the budget) and a non-probability stratified random sample was therefore employed. For this reason we were unable to claim to present a comprehensive account of the views of the total population of parents. However, we were able to claim to have identified the range of views held by different groups with some confidence. The self-completed questionnaires by staff, following extensive consultation and the delivery and collection of questionnaires at the centre, yielded a response of over 80 per cent of the total sample.

It is always a good idea to pilot an interview; one very good way of doing this, if there is to be more than one interviewer, is to interview each other. This should also encourage greater uniformity of approach and therefore greater inter-interviewer reliability.

Even if you are interviewing on your own it is important to always keep to the script—if respondents are treated differently, the data that are collected will not be comparable. There are a broad range of factors that can influence responses—most of the published guidance emphasises the importance of considering the way that you dress, the importance of only using standard probes and prompts, of accurate record keeping and a consistently friendly and respectful approach.

As May (1993) argues (citing Gearing and Dant, 1990), effective interviewing involves achieving a balance between maintaining a detached and objective 'distance' and the sort of close engagement that permits intersubjective understanding:

> There is a tension in the biographical interview between, on the one hand, the need of the interviewer to establish and maintain a rapport and a trusting relationship on which the interviewee will disclose significant personal information and, on the other, the practical demands and constraints of any research enquiry . . . what transpires is inevitably something of a balancing act' (Gearing and Dant, 1990, p. 152).

Many novice interviewers tend to talk too much, and it is important to remember that the main object of the exercise is to be *listening*. It is worth considering your interviewing as a kind of dramatic role that you adopt, always showing pleasure in the experience, providing variation in your voice and in your non-verbal expression. Questions must never be threatening or leading, but if the respondent becomes confused or defensive it is important to recognise that your role is to reassure them and make them feel comfortable, regardless of your personal views.

WHAT DID YOU FIND AND HOW DID YOU INTERPRET WHAT YOU FOUND?

Given the open-ended nature of many questions, the amount of data that might be collected can be very great. Some choice and selection is therefore necessary if data are to be manageable. Miles and Huberman (1994, p. 10) provide a useful flow model that illustrates the various components of data analysis. The model shows that analysis is a continuous process that extends throughout the study. It begins, even before you start to collect your data, as you select the particular subject and the analytical framework for your study. In constructing a questionnaire or interview schedule it is inevitable that you will reject some of the many possible questions and forms of data that you might otherwise have collected. Your initial readings, your life experiences and values contribute towards this anticipatory data reduction. They also contribute towards the analysis throughout the study. It is therefore important that you carry out some degree of introspection in order to become aware of your reasons for favouring particular research questions, conceptual frameworks and data collection techniques.

From the earliest stages, the researcher begins to decide what is significant to the question under study and what is not, noting the regularities and patterns, and starting to formulate explanations and possibilities. These formulations need to be very lightly held to begin with—it is important to be sceptical. As the study progresses, you may refer back to your earlier notes, seek corroboration from alternative sources and refer back to documentary evidence. You may even attempt to replicate your initial findings with further data collection. These strategies are employed to test your findings for plausibility, to confirm your assumptions and to demonstrate their validity. This is a process referred to as 'saturation' (Glaser and Strauss, 1967), where our ongoing interpretations of events (hypotheses or intuitions) are repeatedly tested against the data in an attempt to falsify it. Through this continuous testing they may be rejected, modified or elaborated.

In the case of this evaluation, the analytic categories were prescribed by the national evaluation team, who had responded to a government tender specification, but more often we seek to obtain these from the data. A common strategy, if you are engaged in a small study and are not using a computer software package such as SPSS or NU*DIST, is to:

- Make a copy of the data set (the interview transcripts or notes);
- Code each response to distinguish the source;
- Cut the paper so that each response is separated;
- Classify the responses into 'types', and
- Sort all of the responses into these categories.

This takes up a good deal of space (often the floor), and a better way to do it if you have a larger sample is to use the computer software. The best way to learn how to use such packages is to attend a course with some of your pilot material.

The data collected by a survey may be qualitative but they also lend themselves to quantitative analysis. Where responses can be coded and represented as numbers, we can apply statistical tests to describe the data more effectively, to assess the significance of our findings and to test for correlations. A full account of the statistical possibilities lies beyond the scope of this chapter but readers may usefully refer to Clegg (1998). Kinnear, et al.'s (1997) guide to the use of the SPSS for Windows software is also to be strongly recommended (see Further Reading, below).

A common approach to validation through triangulation is to use more than one data collection technique—for example, the validation of observational data through interview. Yet another strategy is to involve a colleague in the process of analysis. Where a group of researchers are able to share the analysis in this way we have a 'critical community', where researchers are able to provide each other with practical support in their 'progressive re-focusing'. In the EEC case study, triangulation was employed as a validation process where the responses of parents, staff and managers were compared and contrasted with each other and with documentary and observational information. Trained volunteers recruited from the governing body carried out the parent interviews. It was the task of a researcher to carry out the analysis and to bring together multiple sources of data.

The following abstracted extracts from the case study findings touch on a small range of issues identified in the analysis. Supplementary data were collected from previous research and from other documentation, such as Social Services Inspection Reports, and in the final presentation a literature review will locate the study within the most relevant theoretical and/or research traditions that have preceded it.

> All the families have a home assessment to establish the type of service required. They are expected to participate in ongoing progress meetings and to work with staff to agree an action plan for their children's development . . .

> The centre had introduced a programme incorporating a range of strategies to develop parents' capacities as educators, encouraging them to take a more active part in their child's learning and progress. In addition to this the centre is offering extensive education activities to the parents, to help with self-awareness, child-rearing, basic skills and more advanced courses. The vast majority of parents who were interviewed experienced success and satisfaction with what the centre offered. For a minority this meant further study and new employment opportunities but the vast majority admitted to better parenting as a result. The work with fathers still had some way to go. This was largely acknowledged in the staff questionnaires rather than the parent responses.

SUMMARY

In this chapter we provide a range of ideas that may be applied in the development of small-scale surveys. The chapter includes the broad outline account of the first part of a three-year nursery evaluation that has recently been conducted in the UK. A particular focus was given to the use of interviews and questionnaires in collecting data on the quality of the parental partnership offered by the centre. Among the technical issues considered was the unavoidable trade-off between reliability and validity; alternative sampling strategies were identified and practical advice was given regarding the effective conduct of interviews.

QUESTIONS FOR REFLECTION

- What might be the key differences between a survey or question-naire developed from your own research interests, and one based upon a commission from some external body, for example, a local authority or a government department?
- What are the main advantages of using one-to-one interviews instead of postal questionnaires?
- List from three to six ideas that might increase the response rate for a postal questionnaire.

FURTHER READING

Blaxter, L., Hughes, C. and Tight, M. 1996, *How to Research*, Open University Press, Buckingham. A very practical and accessible text that avoids unnecessary jargon to provide a valuable guide to small-scale research.

Fitz-Gibbon, C. & Morris, L. 1987, *How to Design a Program Evaluation*, Sage, Newbury Park, CA. Fitz-Gibbon and Morris provide a clear step-by-step guide to the development of the most rigorous form of educational programme evaluation.

Moser, C. & Kalton, G. 1971, *Survey Methods in Social Investigation*, Gower, Aldershot. A classic text on survey design, administration and analysis.

11

Interviewing children

Liz Brooker

This chapter uses an account of two educational research projects, both involving English children just starting school, to illustrate some of the issues to be considered when interviewing young children for research purposes. In both the projects described here, interviews with 4- and 5-year-olds, some of whom had English as an additional language, played an important role. The first project, undertaken while I was still a full-time Early Years teacher, used action research strategies in an effort to foster autonomy and independent, reflective learning among children in their first year of school. The second, undertaken as a full-time postgraduate research project, was an ethnographic study of the home and school learning of children of the same age.

One of the reasons why interviewing children at such an early age has recently become acceptable as a research tool is that the very concept of childhood has changed, particularly in the 'western world'. Over the last few decades in fact we have come to see that the concept itself is culturally and historically constructed, rather than universal and absolute (Nunes, 1994; James and Prout, 1997). Authors such as these identify the following characteristics of childhood, as viewed in the Western world at the end of the twentieth century.

- Childhood is seen as a distinct and intrinsically interesting and important phase in human experience, valued for its own unique qualities rather than for its resemblance to adulthood.

- Children are viewed, therefore, as fully formed and complete individuals with a perspective of their own, rather than as partially-developed, incompletely-formed adults.
- Children are defined as autonomous subjects, rather than as members (or even possessions) of their family: their parents' and family members' interests and views are no longer assumed to be identical to their own.
- Children are recognised as having rights of their own, including the right to protection from harm, and the right to voice opinions and influence decisions in matters relating to their own lives.

In recent years, and in the context of this more respectful view of children, a growing body of early childhood researchers has argued that it is important and appropriate to listen to the voices of children on issues that concern them. They have shown that there are important insights to be gained from inviting children's opinions and experiences, not only about their schooling but also about the most difficult and intractable of social issues (race, sex and class; rights and freedoms; self-esteem and subjection).

Two complementary principles underlie this recent change in attitude: a belief in children's *rights* (including the right to be heard, to participate, to have control of their lives) and a belief in children's *competence* (to understand, to reflect, and to give accurate and appropriate responses). Together, these beliefs imply that it is both ethical and logical to ask children what they think. Nevertheless, many practical questions still arise in carrying out interviews with children. In the case of all such questions it is likely that the younger the children involved, the greater the need for caution. These questions are briefly discussed before the case study accounts.

CHILDREN'S RIGHTS

The recent advocacy of children's *right* to be consulted reflects in part some notable legal judgments and events, which can be seen as markers for a gradual change in public and professional attitudes (Sinclair Taylor, 2000). These include, in the UK:

- An inquiry into alleged child abuse, whose much-publicised final report asserted that professionals should always listen carefully to children, *and* take seriously what they say (Butler-Sloss, 1988);
- A *Children Act 1989* which requires professionals working with children to take account of their 'ascertainable wishes and feelings';

International markers include:

- The 1989 UN Convention on the Rights of the Child, which in Article 12 requires states to 'assure to the child who is capable of forming his or her own views the right to express those views freely', and to give children the opportunity 'to be heard in any judicial or administrative proceedings affecting the child'.

Davie (1996) argues that, although 'listening to children's wishes and feelings is an advancing trend', a residual belief still exists that adults (parents and professionals) do in fact 'know best' what is in a child's interests. Challenging this diehard belief could be an important role for early childhood researchers.

CHILDREN'S COMPETENCE

The view that children, whatever their *right* to be heard, may make inadequate and unreliable research respondents, has proved a methodological obstacle until very recently. As David reports, 'In the past, interviewing children, especially young children, has been seen as a very flawed research method' (1992, p. 208). Standard 'methods' texts on interview techniques list familiar assumptions about children's limitations as respondents: they are prone to an 'acquiescence response bias'; are more inclined to answer 'don't know'; are easily distressed; are over-literal in interpreting the wording of questions; are egocentric; are ignorant of the ground rules underpinning the interview situation— and so on (Powney and Watts, 1987, pp. 48–9; Breakwell, 1995, pp. 236–7).

Nevertheless, recent writers in the field have shown that children can be reliable and informative respondents. Spencer and Flin (1990), reviewing studies which have assessed young children's ability to provide factual evidence in criminal cases, conclude that there is every reason to believe that the youngest children can recall and describe events and situations as accurately as older witnesses. These authors caution that, although there is evidence that very small children's emotional frame of reference is egocentric and that their interpretation of cause and effect is primarily self-centred, this may not constitute the main problem: 'the real danger of egocentrism may be the egocentricity of the adult who is unable to appreciate fully the child's perspective in an interview' (1990, p. 252)

On the whole, researchers agree that the limitations to young children's competence as respondents are generally the limitations of those who interview them. Well-known studies of young children's language (Tizard and Hughes, 1984; Wells, 1985); confirm the commonsense observation of anyone working with the very young, that children's utterances are better in every way (longer, clearer, more complex, more thoughtful) when the children are in a familiar environment, with familiar adults.

> **Research into children's competence shows that:**
> - Children's communicative competence improves when they are given *control* over the content and direction of the conversation (Wood et al., 1981).
> - Direct questions are more likely to make children feel they are being challenged, and tested, than indirect discussions (Wood and Wood, 1983).
> - Children being questioned tend to become monosyllabic (Tizard and Hughes, 1984).
> - Children wish to please adults, and will produce 'answers' to nonsense questions in an effort to please (Hughes and Grieve, 1981).

Piaget, in his clinical interviews with children, observed that the trick was to 'let the child talk freely, without ever checking or side-tracking his utterance' (1929, p. 10, cited in Powney and Watts, 1987). Some strategies for enabling children to 'talk freely', and reveal their own agenda rather than trying to match that of the interviewer, are discussed below.

ETHICAL INTERVIEWING

Ethical issues are especially important in the case of interviews, which are a far greater intrusion into the subject's life than 'passive' research methods such as observation. Children may, as suggested above, respond to the research situation by becoming mute and monosyllabic; they may on the other hand be manipulated into speaking much more freely, and disclosing much more of their personal lives, than the interviewer has anticipated. In such cases, researchers may find themselves the recipients of sensitive information about which difficult decisions have to be made (see Morrow and Richards, 1996).

There are, however, commonsense ethical guidelines for treating children respectfully in interview situations. The sensitive researcher (including the early years professional researching the children in her care) will:

- Plan her questioning to be appropriate and acceptable for her respondents, bearing in mind their emotional and social maturity, and their family and cultural background (see Dwivedi, 1996);
- Terminate any session which she senses is causing distress of any kind to a respondent;

- Conclude the session with debriefing, reassurance, thanks, praise, or whatever is appropriate to sustain the self-esteem of the individual child.

As Cohen and Manion point out, consent involves giving children not only a 'credible and meaningful explanation of their research intentions', but also a 'real and legitimate opportunity to say that they do not want to take part' (1994, p. 353). While other professionals may attempt to cajole children into participating in activities, researchers must be scrupulous in offering children the right to opt out if they choose, before *or* during an interview. Although many researchers (including Pollard, 1996) report children's pleasure in being invited to contribute their views, Hall (1996) warns that children may perceive formal interviews as some kind of reprimand, and need to have their role, and their right to withdraw, made explicit. In a preschool setting, Evans and Fuller (1996) made 'freedom of choice' a priority in devising a research design and interview method (using classroom role-play telephones linked to a taperecorder) into which children only entered voluntarily, as part of their play. Other techniques commonly used in eliciting young children's views are discussed next.

Practicalities, props and prompts

While Davie (1996, p. 6) argues that there is *no* minimum age for 'listening to a child', most researchers agree that the younger the child, the greater the need for special preparation and provision, in order that the child can express himself freely with the minimum stress or disruption. A number of strategies have commonly been used to make the interview process 'child-friendly'.

Much early childhood research has relied on props, prompts and stimuli to engage children's interest, foster thought and reflection, and soften the effects of the high-control, adult-dominant, question-and-answer format ('those infernal direct questions of which our profession seems so fond': David, 1992, p. 210).

Tools commonly used in early childhood research:

- Dolls, soft toys and puppets: Used to help children 'act out' their attitudes and feelings, although it has been suggested that they demonstrate children's feelings towards dolls rather than people (Aboud, 1988).
- Persona dolls: Help children to construct a narrative or scenario about a more 'real' personality (Brown, 1998; Bosisto and Howard, 1999).
- Photographs and drawings: Enable children to sort, group or point to images if they have difficulty communicating verbally.

- 'Smiley faces': enable children to demonstrate without words their degree of liking, or dislike, for a situation or activity.
- Children's *own* drawings and paintings: widely seen as an effective and respectful way of initiating discussion (Ross, 1996; Morrow and Richards, 1996).

In large-scale surveys, where the same standard questions need to be put to a sizeable sample of children, and the researcher is not well known to the children, it is particularly important to fine-tune your research tools. Many studies using young children as respondents, however, are small-scale, in-depth projects where the researcher is a familiar participant observer, or the children's own teacher or carer working within their normal daily setting. In such cases, the researcher's ongoing observations of the children, her familiarity with their background and behaviours, and her alertness to the effects of the research methods upon them, all help to produce good and reliable evidence.

Adult questioning

Not all adult 'direct questioning' is threatening to children, or unproductive for research purposes, as I discuss below. As Hutt and colleagues found, adults who ask lots of questions tend to get answers but little more. In contrast, adults who offer children lots of their own personal views, ideas and observations, tend to receive a more elaborate and less predictable response from the child (Hutt et al., 1989, p. 151).

Far from being 'leading', therefore, adult opinions may be viewed as the stimulus to children's thinking. The reason for this is quite logical: children are used from an early age to adults asking them questions *to which the adults clearly know the answers already*. In other words, children learn that much of adult questioning is 'test' questioning ('I know the answer, but let's see if *you* know'), to which there are right or wrong answers. Hence, in order to produce the required response, much of children's effort consists in working out what is in the adult's mind. This relationship is simply overturned if the adult volunteers information herself; if she indicates that there are things she wonders about herself (the 'outloud thinking', discussed by Hutt et al., 1989; Wood and Attfield, 1996); and suggests that the child may be able to help supply some of the answers.

Parents and professionals who adopt this stance in their day-to-day work with children and carry it over into their research questioning, find children voluble rather than monosyllabic!

One other method of encouraging children to develop as well as articulate their thoughts is the group interview. Lewis (1992) points to the method's well-founded derivation (in the view of children as essentially socially interactive beings, rather than as isolated individuals) as well as its role in enabling children to assist each other to extend their thinking. Both James (1993) and Morrow and Richards (1996) argue that group discussions, when children have the support of their peers, diffuse the normal adult–child power relationship. Early childhood researchers, however, aware of little children's natural egocentricity, may find the process impractical in a 'group' larger than two or three.

Reliability and validity of children's interview evidence

Reliability and validity of evidence needs careful scrutiny in all projects, and should be considered *equally* but *not necessarily more* thoroughly, when the evidence of young children is involved. Reliability (the issue of whether the research findings could be repeated, or replicated, by another researcher or at another point in time) may be difficult to assess when children's development is so rapid that repeating an investigation is not feasible, and exact replication is problematic. Validity (the issue of whether the research instrument—the interview questions—measure what they are intended to measure) is established by piloting, just as it would be for any interview schedule or other instrument. Nevertheless, children's evidence, like all interview data, benefits from triangulation with other evidence, normally from informal or systematic observation or from interviews with others (peers, parents or professionals). Against the concerns over children's 'acquiescence response' (their wish to please) and their egocentrism (interpreting all issues as if they were about themselves), must be set the fact that young children are unlikely deliberately to mislead or conceal. It is probably safe to assume, in fact, that preschool children, to the best of their ability, give 'honest' answers to any questions appropriate to their age and understanding, and that if they do not, the 'fault' is with the researcher rather than with the child.

CASE STUDY

Using child interviews with teacher as researcher

The setting for this study (Brooker, 1996) was an inner urban school in London with a roll of about 300 children aged from 3 to 11 years. Three-year-olds commenced half-day schooling in the school's Nursery class, and transferred to my Reception class for full-time schooling around their fifth birthday; after the Reception year, they would have six further years of increasingly formal study before transferring to their 'secondary school'. I had taught every age group in the school before settling into the Early Years niche where I worked closely with the Nursery teacher on planning a joint curriculum which attempted to offer a smooth transition from preschool to school—one with sufficient familiarity and continuity, *and* sufficient progression, to meet the needs and expectations of 4-year-olds *and* their parents.

What was your research question and how did you arrive at your research question?

The study arose from a concern about the changes in children's behaviour which I observed when they moved from the Nursery into mainstream schooling. Soon after leaving the Nursery, it seemed, the self-confidence and self-direction which had characterised most children's behaviour in that setting began to mutate into obedience and docility, and a wish for teacher-direction and teacher-approval. This dependence and loss of internal motivation struck me as becoming more and more marked as children progressed through the school, with the result that some of the oldest children were extraordinarily passive, while others were seriously disaffected.

My initial questions were:

- What are children's expectations of school (and how are these expectations learned)?
- Can children be helped to recognise and negotiate these expectations, and so to achieve more control of their school experience and learning?

As is the nature of action research, these questions evolved over the year of the study into others arising from the project.

How did you decide how to answer it?

The project as I conceived it aimed to explore children's feelings about school, and possibly to influence them. This meant that the research strategy had a dual function: consulting the children was intended both to inform *me* about the processes which were occurring, and to make *them* conscious participants in these processes, to make them in fact 'consultants' in their own learning. For this to happen, it was important for the children to be aware that their opinions were being sought, and to have the opportunity to reflect on these opinions over time. This meant that formal 'interviews', which drew attention to the children's role as sources of information, and accorded them status as informants, were the most appropriate research method.

As a familiar figure in the setting, I had many privileges as a researcher:

- the trust and confidence of parents and children;
- a shared experience of the settings and activities we were discussing; and
- some prior familiarity with the children's language and point of view.

I was therefore able to ask my 'questions' openly and directly, without recourse to props or prompts.

What sampling issues were there?

For the first sequence of interviews, all twelve prospective Reception children currently attending the Nursery were approached and invited to talk to me during their Nursery session. In the course of the following year, additional groups of respondents were added as they joined the class (in September, January and April). On each occasion, a settling-in period of about six weeks elapsed before I invited the children to come and tell me what they thought about school. By the end of the year, the whole class (27 children) had been recruited, but the fullest information, and most developed thoughts, derived from the initial 'Nursery group', whose communications with me had taken place over a period of more than a year. It is their responses which are reported here.

How did you answer it?

Conducting the interviews

All this group knew that they would be joining my class when they started school full-time and, on my frequent informal visits to the Nursery, many had volunteered to demonstrate their skills and introduce their friends, as well as asking *me* questions ('Why d'you wear them glasses?' 'Where's your dad?'). When I approached them, pen and paper in hand, and politely asked if they would have time to come into the book corner and tell me a bit about school, they readily agreed, even if they needed to 'drive the fire engine back to the fire station' or 'do another painting' first. If a target child was with a friend, I suggested that the friend might come along too, but most children preferred to come on their own: the idea of an adult volunteering to be a captive audience was seen as a treat rather than a threat.

I had already decided, for the sake of flexibility and mobility, to record children's answers in writing rather than to tape them. The method, though apparently low-tech and inefficient, proved to have several advantages. The convention evolved that I would write as fast as I could ('doing your scribble-scrabble writing' as one child patronisingly but sympathetically commented), but would say 'stop' if I needed time to catch up with the child's dictation. The child would then pause until I had finished, which in practice gave her /him time to reconsider or rephrase their last responses.

What did you find?

Without exception, my twelve respondents appeared to relish the opportunities this method offered them: to control the flow of information; to keep me hard at work (but they did admire the speed at which I wrote); to hear their views read back to them; to rethink or modify their first thoughts; and to tell me, in advance of joining my class, what was what. The responses of Cassie (age 4 years 6 months), whose older sister has told her all about school, are typically confident:

Liz: Can you tell me—this is a hard question—why do children go to school?

Cassie: To help you . . . to help you do your work . . .

Liz: And what do you think you'll do at school?

Cassie: I do busy things here: proper writing . . . lovely painting . . .
          I do what my teacher says . . .
          I want to go out to play at playtime!

Liz: What are you specially good at?

Cassie: My writing is easy for me because I do little writing . . .
          reading is easy [*she picks up a book with Punjabi script and tries to tell the story*] I can't read that, that's Property! [Punjabi!] writing (*she 'reads' from the pictures in formal storybook language, studies the illustrations avidly*) . . .
          that's a bit hard . . . numbers are a bit difficult but I can do numbers on my own because I'm learning them: 1, 2, 3, 7, 8 . . .

Liz: So what do you like doing best?

Cassie: I've got good news for you: when I come in your big class I am going to do what you say! (*with emphasis!*) . . . when I go in your big class I am going to be quiet for you, not shout . . . and I like the water . . .

Liz: And do you know what you'd like to be when you grow up?

Cassie: When I grow up I want to be a mummy.

How did you interpret what you found?

While Cassie confidently anticipated being able to set the terms for our relationship, and meet the expected demands of the 'big school' classroom, like most of the respondents she was aware of the dual nature of the Reception experience. Every Nursery child spoke of 'work' or 'learning', and cited literacy and numeracy as examples, but every child also spoke of wanting, or enjoying, play experiences. Even in this first brief encounter, Cassie shows that her expectations of school include 'work', reading (which is 'easy', or 'a bit hard'), writing (which is 'proper' if it is 'little') and 'numbers' (which may be 'difficult'); but that what she really enjoys are playing in the playground and with the water. The consensus in children's responses on the mismatch between their own agenda and the agenda of teachers made it surprising that all of them seemed to be looking forward to school so much, but also indicated how easy it would be for some young children to become demotivated or even disaffected.

Where does that lead you?

Subsequent interview sequences, later in the year, covered similar ground but extended the questioning to include more detailed discussions of the ways we had worked in the classroom, and the relationship of work to play. My respondents became relatively adept at thinking, reflecting and representing their thoughts, verbally or through drawings of themselves 'learning'. Though the findings from the earliest interviews came too late for me to attempt to discover the *sources* of the children's expectations— parents or siblings, nursery staff or the media—they did inform the subsequent course of the inquiry, and prompted classroom interventions which did seem to have an impact on children's attitudes. By July, some children were making their own, less polarised, connections between 'work', 'play', 'learning' and 'fun'.

The final question to each, as we reviewed the year together, was 'Have you worked well, and played well, in this class?'

Harminder: My best playing is bricks and working hard, because working hard is good fun.

Paris: The good playing is that we read, and it's good to learn about and if you don't learn it soon then you're not going to know it.

Cassie: Good playing is doing good work because it's fun doing good work and making good models.

In recording these views I was well aware that the children, whether I wished it or not, had been strongly socialised into the culture of the classroom in the course of the year. Nevertheless, it appeared that the process of reflecting on and representing their experiences and attitudes had aided their metacognition, and perhaps contributed to their positive feelings about school.

CASE STUDY

Using child interviews with researcher as participant observer

The second study discussed here is one in which interviews (with children, parents and teachers) were used as one of many data gathering methods in the course of a year-long ethnographic study of the ways that 4-year-olds are taught, and learn, in their homes and in the Reception class. The first focus of this inquiry was on the fine-grained differences in children's learning experiences in their families which contribute to the large differences in attainment which children demonstrate on entry to school. A second aspect of the inquiry was a study of the contribution made by schools, through their classroom practices, to sustaining such differentials. While parents, especially mothers, were the principal source of data on children's home experience, the children's evidence was important for understanding *their* perceptions of the learning activities of the home and the school, which can be very different from the intentions of both parents and teachers.

What were your research questions?

The research questions for the whole study were concerned with the contribution of the curriculum and pedagogy of children's homes, and their classroom, to their success in 'becoming a pupil' and making academic progress. For the children's interviews, therefore, my aims were similar to those of the earlier project: to learn what their expectations about schooling, and preparation for school, had been; and perhaps to find ways of making these more compatible with the actual experience offered by school.

What sampling issues were there?

The sixteen children in the study were four boys and four girls each from monolingual (English) and bilingual (Bangladeshi) backgrounds. All came from similarly low-income backgrounds, but the two groups were roughly matched on several variables known to influence children's attainments on entry to school, and school progress: ethnicity, sex, age within the year group, family composition and birth order.

All were enrolled at age 4 in a large Reception class organised on a 'liberal-progressive' Early Years model, in which the curriculum was provided largely through freely chosen play activities. Relationships between children and staff in the setting were friendly and informal, and in arranging to have access to the children and the classroom for a whole year, it was understood that I would interact with the children as a normal member of staff (playing, assisting, assessing, observing) when I was not actively engaged in data collection of my own. I was thus familiar to the children (many of whom were also present when I visited their families at home) before I began my 'interviews' in December, towards the end of their first school term.

How did you answer it?

As the spacious setting and informal organisation offered ample opportunities for one-to-one conversations with children, I agreed to the class teacher's request that I conduct the interviews opportunistically within the play areas, rather than removing the children to a quieter location. Nevertheless, I made it clear to each child that our talk was not an everyday casual chat, but an occasion when I would like them to help me by telling me what they thought about school, and how they learned, so that I could write it down and think about it. We therefore selected a relatively quiet and comfortable spot together, such as the book corner, fetched cushions and sat side by side so that the child\ could see what I was writing: despite not being able to read anything I wrote, all seemed charmed to detect that I was writing and underlining their name at the top of the sheet of questions.

The planned questions began with items similar to those of the previous study, but went on to probe more of children's views on *how* they learned, and what they had learned at home. Once again, the children seemed delighted to be invited to give their views, and to be allowed to keep me 'on task' with my writing ('Did you put down where I said I can draw good? where does it say that? what does it say, read it!'). Their response to the first questions, however, quickly brought the process to an untimely end, for the time being. Unlike the children from the earlier study, *and* unlike the same-age, same-background children interviewed in a pilot study in a nearby school, they were unable to respond appropriately to most of my questions. This was for the simple reason that none of the sixteen had the least suspicion that children might go to school to 'learn' or to 'work' (rather than 'to play', 'to have your packed lunch' or 'just because you've got to, my mum says'). This meant that questions about learning, and 'how you learn things' would have been irrelevant to their understanding of school, *and* would have interfered with the development of their thinking about school, and thus with the validity of my study.

Setbacks like this are not, however, real setbacks. Instead they have to be recognised as part of the whole data-set (to be interpreted and understood in the light of all other information about the children), and incorporated into the next phase of data collection. The children's responses were themselves good evidence of their expectations about school (which contrasted interestingly with those of their parents *and* teachers), and also shed light on the behaviour I was observing in the classroom. As my fieldnotes confirmed, the word 'learning' was not used by the adults in school, who instead impressed on children the importance of 'playing'.

What did you find?

Analysis of the children's early responses, together with observation and other evidence, underpinned some of the inquiry strategies used during the next school term, and enabled me to rewrite questions, and continue the interview process, over the following months. By the end of the year, the accumulated responses offered numerous insights into differences and discontinuities in the ways that school was viewed, and learning was understood, by the children (now 5 years old) and their families and educators.

One such outcome was particularly striking, in that it demonstrated the extent to which some children are obliged to *unlearn* what their home culture has taught them, in order to acquire the culture of the classroom. The Bangladeshi children, in keeping with their parents' experience of education, and cultural and religious preferences, had been accustomed to a formal learning style at home: direct instruction and rote memorisation of alphabets and texts were the preferred methods for these families in preparing their children for school. When discussing with children *what they could remember learning at home*, therefore, I expected Bangladeshi children to describe the ABC books and maths books which I had seen on the family dining-tables.

For this to happen, however, the children would need to know that this was what I (to all intents and purposes another of their teachers) referred to as 'learning'. Their experience of the classroom had shown them that this was not the case: we didn't do that kind of thing at school! They offered me instead, in an attempt to foster *my* understanding, as it seemed, the kinds of experiences that *I* would call 'learning'—the kinds of things we did at school:

Tuhura:	I make ice cream.
Liz:	[How did you learn to do that?]
Tuhura:	You put it in the fridge.
Rufia:	Play with dollies.
Liz:	[How did you learn to do that]
Rufia:	My sister Sabina showed me.
Amadur:	Drink a cup of tea with a biscuit.
Liz:	[How did you learn to do that]
Amador:	I learned it by myself: if the tea is too hot you dip the biscuit in and eat the biscuit, then it's not too hot.
Abu Bokkar:	Drawing.
Liz:	[How did you learn to do that]
Abu Bokkar:	My brother Abdul Halim showed me.

Only one of the eight said she had learned reading, from listening to her sister; none mentioned the daily sessions of home tuition which were common in their homes. Yet neither their parents nor their teachers had access to the whole picture of contrasting, or conflicting, beliefs about pedagogy, which the children seemed intuitively to recognise.

CONCLUSION AND SUMMARY

This chapter has suggested that research interviews with young children can not only offer unrivalled information to the researcher wishing to understand children's perceptions, but also be an enjoyable and potentially empowering learning experience for children. The adult–child dialogue which can develop in extended research projects such as those described here can build children's esteem and autonomy, and foster their metacognitive skills—benefits which those working with young children may in the end consider even more worthwhile than their own research results!

In interviewing children you need to consider a number of elements.

- Children's rights when conducting face-to-face research with young children: ideally, the research should be seen as conducted *for*, and *with*, the respondents (rather than *on* them).

- Being honest and open with the children who are our participants: to give them, at an appropriate level of understanding, a truthful account of what we are trying to learn from them.
- The power relations of the interview situation, and be sure we are not abusing our adult role in the way we obtain our information.
- Developmentally appropriate activities for eliciting children's views, to enhance the validity of our findings as well as to avoid stress for our respondents.
- The importance of familiarity: the researcher should have become a trusted adult within the child's setting before attempting to elicit information, particularly of a personal nature, from any child.
- The importance of sensitivity to social class and cultural differences, as well as differences in age and status, between the researcher and her respondents: like all workers in early childhood settings, researchers need to be informed about children's home backgrounds *before* asking their questions!
- Children can offer information which, particularly in combination with other evidence, enables us to see and discover aspects of their lives which no other research method can give.

QUESTIONS FOR REFLECTION

- How should our view of the status of young children in our culture shape the ways we, as researchers, approach them?
- Differences in status frequently exist between early childhood professionals and the families of the children they care for. How should an awareness of such differences influence our research strategies?
- It is not uncommon for young children to disclose evidence of neglect, abuse or criminal activities in their homes while being interviewed for quite other purposes. How should a researcher respond?

FURTHER READING

Davie, R., Upton, G. and Varma, V. (eds) 1996, *The Voice of the Child: A Handbook for Professionals,* Falmer, London. A comprehensive account of 'listening to children' across many professional fields is given by contributors.

Griffiths, M. 1998, *Educational Research for Social Justice: Getting Off the Fence,* Open University Press, Buckingham. A more philosophical but very readable discussion of the ethical and social responsibilities of qualitative researchers is included.

12

Interviewing adults

Leslie Cannold

In this chapter I use my doctoral study of fertile women without children to discuss methodological and ethical issues around interviewing adults on sensitive topics.

WHAT WAS YOUR RESEARCH QUESTION?

For my Ph.D. I studied fertile women, aged 28 to 42, who did not have children. A key area of concern was whether women described their childlessness as 'chosen' and if so, whether that description was a good 'fit' with everyday understandings of choice. The aim was to generate theory (in need of future corroboration by formal hypothesis testing research) about the causes of rising rates of childlessness in western countries like Australia, the United Kingdom and the United States.

HOW DID YOU ARRIVE AT YOUR RESEARCH QUESTION?

I have always been interested in how women make decisions about motherhood. My Master's thesis explored how motherhood figured into women's decisions about unplanned pregnancies. I then became interested in how women without children made decisions about childlessness. The research literature and the popular press tends to see all childless women either as victims of infertility or childless by choice.

I had several childless friends who were not infertile, but would not have described themselves as having chosen childlessness. I wondered whether their experience was isolated, or indicative of a social experience largely ignored by researchers and the mainstream media.

HOW DID YOU ANSWER IT?

Because I was interested in charting the changes in women's reproductive decision-making over time and through this analysis discerning the impact of social structures on such decision-making, I chose to conduct life history interviews, in which I asked participants to recount and to explain their decisions about relationships and motherhood. Such histories provided an 'ideal method for examining the interplay between social constraints, psychological motivation and the developing actor' (Gerson, 1985, p. 38).

Interviews are one of a range of tools researchers use to gather data. For researchers who believe people act on the basis of the meaning they give to people and events, in-depth interviews are a good way to gain an understanding of the meanings that participants give to their lives. These beliefs characterise hermeneutic (interpretive) research approaches, endorsed most prominently by many feminist researchers and researchers working with the symbolic interactionist framework. Recently some early childhood researchers have spoken out in favour of using interview methodologies to capture the voices of teachers, voices they contend are habitually marginalised (Hauser, 1995).

Conducting the interview

There are a variety of types of research interviews. Researchers can arrange an interview to assist a participant to understand and complete a questionnaire. More commonly, however, research interviews are structured 'conversations' between researcher and participant in which the researcher seeks to elicit the participant's subjective point of view on a topic of interest to the researcher. Researchers frequently employ an interview guide to provide the structure necessary to ensure such conversational interviews are concise and productive.

Developing and piloting the interview guide
A literature review, followed by a period in which the aims and objectives of the research and a set of general research questions are developed and refined, should proceed the drawing up of interview questions. The general research questions will determine the structure and content of the interview. If the area is one about which a great deal is known, it may be possible to use a series of **closed-ended questions**

to answer the research question. Closed-ended questions are typically found on questionnaires. They tend to be simple questions with a limited range of answers. 'In what year were you born?' is a closed-ended question, as is 'what is your annual income?' While closed-ended questions are usually used in questionnaires, they may also be used in interviews when, for example, there is only a limited time available to analyse the data and present the findings. The more closed-ended the question, the more the interviewer can restrict the range of issues covered by participants. Providing participants a range of pre-coded answers ('choose A, B or C') can further restrict the complexity of the data collected, and increase its uniformity. The likelihood of obtaining uniform data can also be increased by a more standardised interview approach in which every question is asked, questions are asked in an identical order and a complete and quantifiable answer is obtained for every question. A smaller and more uniform range of answers makes data analysis quicker and easier.

Interviews are more often characterised by **open-ended questions,** which enable a more varied and in-depth participant response and so are more suited to generating (rather than confirming) theory. Open-ended questioning gives participants the freedom to answer questions as they wish, or even to reshape questions that betray a researcher's misunderstanding of previous interview testimony or make unwarranted assumptions. For instance, during interviews conducted for the Women Without Children study I often asked women who were in their late twenties or early thirties to imagine how they might feel about being childless when they were in their late thirties. More often than not, they refused to answer this question. 'It's a bit hypothetical, isn't it?' said one woman. 'I don't think you can know how you're going to feel until you're in the situation,' insisted another, 'Ten years is a long time [and] a hell of a lot of things can happen in ten years.' These responses led me to question my assumption that women could or would engage in this sort of speculation for the purposes of my interview, and to look for other ways to gauge their thoughts and feelings about being childless.

The less controlled and predictable nature of responses to open-ended questioning means these responses are far more likely than data collected from closed-ended questions to challenge the prevailing paradigm or to shed light on something previous researchers have missed altogether. While researchers nearly always carry some notes listing the topics or questions they wish to raise, in roughly the order in which they would like to raise them, this typically serves only as an **interview guide.** The answers participants provide to follow-up questions will make up a large and important part of the data set. Thus, an interview guide is an instrument mid-way between a closed-ended questionnaire with precoded responses, and a completely unstructured interview.

Follow-up questions will assist the researcher to clarify elements of testimony and to encourage participants to further elaborate on areas of interest.

Follow-up questions in the interview

Typical clarification follow-ups include:

- 'Can you give me an example of that?'
- 'What did you mean when you said?'

A typical **mirroring** or **reflective probe** might be:

- 'What I hear you saying is that . . . Have I understood you correctly?'

Encouraging follow-ups, sometimes known as **nudging probes**, include:

- 'Really?'
- 'So what did you do then?'
- 'Was that what you were expecting?'

The outcome of the more free-ranging conversations encouraged open-ended questioning and follow-up questions is that participar are likely to move from subject area to subject area, often answeri questions before the interviewer has had a chance to ask them. F instance, in the following interview conducted for the Women Withc Children study I asked Matilda, 'Would you describe yourself as chil less? Would you describe yourself as childfree?' Her answer to tl question and to follow-ups led her smoothly into the answer to the ne question that was on my interview guide ('Do you intend to have ch dren in the future') without my having to ask it.

Q: Would you describe yourself as childless? Would you descri yourself as childfree? Or would you not use either of those expressio to describe yourself?
Matilda: It's hard to say. Probably, neither of those expressions.
Q: Why not?
Matilda: Because I can still have a child, so that might chang Being childless now might change in a year's time. And childfree, in th sense that I don't see children, or . . .?
Q: Well, if it doesn't mean anything to you, then perhaps it's not good expression to describe you. Some women kind of like it as ; expression because they feel that it is a positive way of describing n having children as opposed to childless, which they feel is a negati way.

Matilda: It's interesting because I don't see either of those as negative. Because it's a choice I think. . . . But at the same time, it's not an issue with me either—if that makes sense.

Q: Well, when you say that you could have a child in a year, is that something you're thinking about?

Matilda: No I'm not. But what I'm saying is that I might be child-less now, but that's not to say that in a year's time or two years' time, I won't have a child.

Q: But at the moment that's not something that's on the agenda?

Matilda: No, definitely not . . . At this point in time, no . . . I haven't really thought about it. So that's why I said, it's always a possibility, but it's not something that I have really thought about seriously . . . Occasionally I think, 'oh well maybe,' but then I think, 'no' . . . I spend a lot of time with children . . . I've got friends with children that I'm close with that run between the age of four . . . to one that's six months . . . Because they're a handful . . . I can handle them for a couple of hours or maybe a day but then . . . It's because I have other things to do that are important to me at the moment than having a child. So that's why it's a fleeting thing.

It is beneficial to pilot the interview guide on somewhere between four and ten participants, during which time critical adjustments may be made to the content, phrasing and order of questions, or even the characteristics of the research sample. For instance, pilot interviews in the Women Without Children study revealed that women in the age range targeted for interview had already made their decision about having children, and were well progressed in understanding their lives as an outcome of this 'choice'. Because the aim of the study was to interview women while they were in the process of making decisions and/or coming to terms with parenting outcomes, the target age range for the remaining interviews was lowered.

Some researchers who begin reading and analysing their data during the interview phase may continually alter their interview guide, as new questions and tentative theories emerge. When circumstance demands, the researcher may decide to leave some questions out, in order to focus a sizeable portion of the approximately one to two hours typically allocated for an individual interview pursuing a particular line of questioning. For instance, near the end of the interview phase for the Women Without Children study, I interviewed a woman who had numerous insights on questions that had arisen in previous interviews. By leaving aside several questions in the interview guide, and altering several others, I was able to spend more time asking her to respond to some of my emerging hypotheses.

Egalitarian or non-exploitative? A realistic approach to researcher capabilities and responsibilities

Feminist researchers are typically concerned with power imbalance in the relationship between the researcher and researched and worry that this imbalance may lead to the exploitation of research participants. In the past, many researchers have seen research 'subjects' as a means to the researchers' ends, often failing to adequately inform them about the risks and benefits of research participation and/or to obtain their voluntary consent to take part. Ethics committees, now an integral part of most institutional research, seek to ensure that potential participants have access to and understand the information they deem necessary to make an informed decision about participation, and can make this decision voluntarily (free from manipulation or coercive influences).

However some researchers, a preponderance of whom would define themselves as feminists, have pursued additional means of democratising the research process. One has been to choose language— 'researcher/participant' rather than 'experimenter/subject'—that suggests the equal importance and standing in the research process of those doing and those being researched. Feminist researchers have also sought to eradicate power differentials between researcher and researched by undercutting the 'one–way hierarchical framework' of traditional interview methodologies (Bloom, 1998, p. 17). Many feminist researchers claim that in-depth woman-to-woman interviews equalise the power relationship between researcher and researched. They argue that democratising the research process in this way provides tangible personal benefits to research participants. These benefits include an egalitarian relationship, friendships and/or intimacy with the researcher, raised consciousness, sympathetic and effective researcher response to difficult or painful interview testimony and—as a consequence of all this—'empowerment' (Kelly, Burton and Regan, 1994; Bloom, 1998). According to such researchers, when investigators listen and respond non-judgementally to a participant's account and provide their personal biographical details to participants in the pre-interview and interview stages, the research process is democratised and the participants empowered. For example, in a study of women's experience of motherhood, the research team ensured that all the women they interviewed were aware of the interviewers' status as mothers of young children (Brown et al., 1994).

However, it is critical for researchers to distinguish between 'not exploiting participants, offering them feedback and more grandiose ambitions' (Kelly et al., 1994, p. 37). Researchers and participants inevitably have a different and unequal relationship to, and interest in, the research project (Glucksmann, 1994). There is no doubt that researchers have an obligation not to exploit participants, to reduce as much as possible any discomfort and/or inconvenience the participant may experience during the research process and to increase wherever possible the participants' comfort and convenience. However, it is both duplicitous and glib for researchers to believe or to contend that such efforts eradicate the unequal relationship researcher and researched have to each other, and to the research.

What this means is that the researcher should provide a non-judgemental interviewing environment because it is least exploitative of participants and most comfortable for them. In addition, and consequently, it is the environment most conducive to the production of high quality research data. Research participants are neither exploited nor made less comfortable when a researcher withholds their personal biographical details until the conclusion of the interview. Thus, if researchers believe such revelations will serve their interests by demonstrating the similarity of their experiences and perspectives and those of their participants, it is ethically permissible for researchers to make them. However, it is also acceptable for researchers to choose not to make such disclosures in the early and middle stages of the research, although I would argue that such disclosures are an essential component of the requisite post-interview **debriefing session**. Wherever possible, I avoided disclosing my status as a mother to participants in the Women Without Children study in order to increase the likelihood that participants would feel free to speak their minds about motherhood, mothers and children. This was not an idle worry. After disclosing my maternal status in the post-interview debriefs, several women clapped their hands to their mouths and exclaimed, 'Oh, I hope I didn't say anything that offended you!'

Other researcher obligations

Informed consent

Plain language statements (PLSs) and consent forms are the primary tools used by institutional ethics committees to ensure researchers are conducting ethical research (see Chapters 2 and 5). A typical PLS provides a brief explanation of the researcher's credentials and/or affiliations, what participation in the research will entail and the researcher's commitment to preserving participant anonymity and confidentiality. The participant's signature on the consent form is often seen as 'proof' that participants have given their free and informed consent to participate.

As many researchers discover, however, the informed consent procedure mandated by their institution is often ill suited to obtaining informed consent from particular research participants. For instance, Phoenix (1994) discovered that several of the participants in her Mothers Under Twenty study had not understood what the study was about, what participation entailed, and why they had been asked to participate, despite having read the handouts and signed the forms. Consequently, they could not be said to have given informed consent. I have found that while the official nature of and language used in the informed consent procedure is often reassuring for educated participants and/or those familiar with research protocol, some less educated and/or less well-informed participants find it extremely disconcerting. Ironically, for these participants, the informed consent procedure can work to convince them that a decision to participate in the research is extremely high risk. This increased suspicion undermines their trust in the researcher, who is seen as having falsely implied early in the recruitment process that participation was relatively straightforward and low-risk. For instance, over my time as a researcher, numerous participants have suggested that it never occurred to them that I would, say, violate their confidentiality, until I gave them the plain language statement approved by the University ethics committee that goes to considerable lengths to assert that I wouldn't. The fact that I am 'protesting too much', in other words, seems to convince many previously unsuspicious participants that I and the entire research enterprise in which I am seeking to engage them is indeed worthy of suspicion. In my experience, it is among samples drawn from populations with little trust for authority figures (homeless youth, for example) that this reaction is more common. I have also encountered it more with prospective male participants than female ones.

One way I have sought to overcome this problem is to verbally walk the participant through the informed consent procedure, not once but twice, before introducing the paperwork. The first time I go through it is on the phone, usually with the PLS in hand to ensure I don't leave out any information essential to their making an informed decision. If and when we meet for the interview, I orally make the necessary disclosures a second time; again with the PLS close at hand to make sure I don't leave anything out. 'So you understand that this research is about . . .' and 'you are aware that I will be endeavoring to protect your anonymity by giving you a false name in anything I publish.' After I have verbally disclosed all the information that is required, answered any questions the participant may have, and feel comfortable that the participant has understood the information necessary to give informed consent, I discuss the formal procedure. I explain that while it may look intimidating and overly formal, it is really designed to ensure I do the right thing by them and make sure they know and understand what is necessary for them to agree to participate. Once they've read it, I ask again if they have any questions. If they have none, I get them to sign the consent form and give them a copy.

The point is that my primary obligation as a researcher is not to disclose information to participants about the research and/or to get them to put their name on the consent form. My responsibility is to ensure the participant makes a decision based on substantial *understanding* (Beauchamps and Childress, 1989). Some participants can make an informed decision by simply reading the PLS and asking a question or two. For others, however, the PLS and other aspects of the formal consent process get in the way of their recognising, requesting and understanding the information necessary for them to give an informed consent to participate. When this happens, researchers are obligated to elicit the participant's concerns, and then adapt the informed consent process to create a climate that facilitates the participant's understanding, and thus their capacity to give their free and informed consent. By doing this, researchers increases the likelihood that when participants sign on the dotted line, their signature indicates that they have understood what participation entails, and have freely consented to participate.

Not wasting the participant's time

There are numerous reasons why researchers should strive to avoid wasting a participant's time, as well as their own. Failing to control the interview and so allowing the interviewee to talk about things in which the researcher is not interested wastes the participant's time; either on the day, or in the long run. If the interviewer extends the interview in order to get the information she actually wants, then the interview takes up more of the participant's time than it should and raises the researcher's transcription and analysis costs. If the interviewer terminates the interview without getting answers to her questions, she will wind up with useless results or no results at all. When the researcher fails to complete her study and/or fails to publish useful results or anything at all, the participant's time has been wasted. She has participated in research that has gone nowhere, and helped no one.

One of the best ways for a researcher to ensure they finish and publish is for them to walk away from every interview with a manageable amount of relevant data. To do this requires interview skill: the skill to draw out information from reticent participants, and the skill to redirect voluble and easily distracted ones. In 'real life' a speaker is responsible for constantly gauging whether the listener is interested in and understanding what she is relating. One of the most common concerns participants have is that they are 'rabbiting on' about things and on topics about which the researcher has little interest. In my experience, participants are always relieved when I promise them that I will redirect them when this happens, and then make good on this promise. This takes the responsibility of gauging whether or not I am interested in and/or understanding what they say from their plate and puts it where it belongs: on mine.

WHAT SAMPLING ISSUES WERE THERE?

Recruiting participants for the Women Without Children study proved difficult because of the social awkwardness many referral sources felt in approaching eligible women, and by so doing indicating their awareness of the woman's age and childless status. Many referral sources also refused to approach eligible women because they knew how unhappy and sensitive they felt about being childless. Consequently, most referrals to the study came from previous participants, with numerous women informing me that it was only their referring friend's report of a 'positive' and 'affirming' interview experience that convinced them to volunteer. This is known as a **snowball sampling** method.

In cases where snowball recruitment has proved difficult because of the stringency of participation criteria and/or the highly charged nature of the research topic, how you conduct your initial interviews can be critical to the success of the research project. In particular, it is important that you use non-judgemental questions and responses in these early interviews.

Non-judgemental questions and responses are a way for the interviewer to establish **rapport** with participants, and to encourage trust. When participants feel their experiences and views are being heard, understood and responded to non-judgementally, they often feel validated.

When participants feel validated two things usually happen that are critical for a successful interview and a successful study. The first is that participants become more forthcoming and honest in their response to questions. The second is that they recommend participation in the study to others.

WHAT DID YOU FIND?

Interview data displays cultural realities and practices (Silverman, 1985). In individualistic western societies, participants tend to understand their lives as 'products created by, and emblematic of the self', in which a 'perception of absolute volitional action' prevails (Alexander, 1992). The retrospective review and evaluation of one's life required by a life history interview may only enhance this culturally specific desire to see oneself as in charge and responsible for one's life, rather than a victim of circumstance.

This means that when participants recount the story of their lives they will seek to understand it as a logical narrative in which earlier choices led inevitably and logically to their current life path.

However, the experiences and understandings common to women that emerge when the data is looked at as a whole and in light of sociological knowledge reveals that women's perception of themselves as choosers is not always mirrored by reality (Gerson, 1985; Gregg, 1995; McMahon, 1995). Taken together, my interviews revealed that women's individual decisions were constrained by common (and therefore socially based) experiences, beliefs and values. How was I to resolve the tension between women's perception of themselves as 'choosers' and the evidence that social attitudes and structures were constraining women's individual freedom to choose? Faced with this problem, McMahon (1995) responded by documenting the contingent and individual nature of the journeys women in her study made to motherhood, while also describing the shared gendered patterns that shaped these journeys.

HOW DID YOU INTERPRET WHAT YOU FOUND?

I chose to adopt a theoretical framework pioneered by Gerson (Gerson, 1985, 1993). Gerson's (1985) approach to this tension was to distinguish between women on the bases of their baseline orientations towards motherhood and work, and the individual way they negotiated the structural constraints they encountered. However, Gerson also recognised the constraints social structures placed on women's choices; reducing the range of options from which they could choose and their freedom to choose between them.

The aim of both these theoretical and methodological approaches was to 'credit women (and others) for their survival skills in the face of real social constraints [while at the same time] move beyond those constrained choices, to try to create situations where women's perceptions of themselves as choosers are mirrored more accurately by the opportunities for real choice within their larger social and political contexts, (Gregg, 1995, p. 144).

Gregg's later point is critical for researchers who want to do research that can contribute to social change. Life history interviews not only 'give voice to experiences that have previously been silenced' (Holland and Ramazanoglu, 1994, p. 131), but indicate the social attitudes and structures constraining the freedom of individuals to choose. Indeed, for some researchers, it is the capacity of their research findings to support or inspire social change that justifies the minimal levels of discomfort or inconvenience some research participants may experience during the interview process. However, as discussed above, researchers can keep such discomfort and inconvenience to a minimum.

HOW DID YOUR PARADIGM INFLUENCE YOUR RESULTS?

My methodological approach draws from insights and practices of researchers working within feminist and symbolic interactionist frameworks (Blumer, 1969; Deegan and Hill, 1987), in particular, the belief that people experience reality through their definition of it and consequently act on the 'basis of meanings that things have for them' (Eyles, 1993, p. 107). Because these meanings are worked out and modified through social interaction in human society, they are tentatively agreed upon but not fixed. The negotiability of such meanings means that the lives of individuals and the social order itself are also subject to reinvention and change. The life history interview, the data collection tool most favoured by researchers working within the symbolic interactionist framework, enables researchers to analyse the change over time of the 'sense of reality that human beings hold about their own worlds' (Minichiello et al., 1990, p. 153).

Safeguarding the subjective point of view (Schutz, 1970) means respecting participants' perceptions that their lives are the outcome of personal and individual choices. However, participants' self-perception as 'choosers' must be reconciled with sociological knowledge about their shared experiences (Gerson, 1985; McMahon, 1995). The agency of participants must not only be respected in the analysis of the data, but during the entire research cycle. It is important that researchers ensure that the interview situation provides a non-judgemental space in which participants feel free to express their ideas. Researchers must also pay strict attention to the informed consent process and should keep in contact with participants until the first results are published. Taken as a whole, the approach I advocate ensures that the highest quality data is obtained, and that participants come away feeling validated—rather than used by—the researcher and the research process.

HOW DID YOUR RESEARCH CONTEXT INFLUENCE YOUR RESULTS?

Circumstantial childlessness is probably not a totally new phenomenon, but it is likely to be on the increase in modern-day Australia. This is because while the vast majority of Australian women continue to want to marry and become mothers, marriage is no longer an economic necessity for many and motherhood not the only means by which women can find a social identity. Much of the explanation for circumstantial childlessness, in other words, is that in Australia at the beginning of the twenty-first century, many women feel they have a choice about who they marry, and about whether they marry at all. Because they can, women are increasingly choosing to delay or forgo marriage unless and until they find a partner willing to 'collaborate' with them in the domestic and child-rearing tasks. The loss of the opportunity to mother for all but the most motivated (who will pursue single motherhood using donor sperm) is an outgrowth of women's choices about relationships (Birrell, 1998; Carlton, 1997, 1999).

WHERE DOES THIS LEAD YOU?

My experience doing research has led me to believe that thinking about the analysis and write-up phases of the research throughout the interview phase results in the collection of better data: it is data better able to answer the questions initially posed by the research and those that have arisen during the research process. Conducting research in this way means the interviewer cannot conduct interviews on 'auto-pilot'. Before each interview, she must think about what she wants that particular interview to achieve—is it, for example, the acquisition of new data to generate theory or confirm theory? During the interview, she must be alert to the particular experiences and insights a participant can offer.

As the Women in Children study progressed, for instance, I became increasingly interested in women's views and experiences of artificial insemination programmes. When I discovered a participant who had experience with these programmes, I tended to spend more interview time exploring the nature of this experience, reducing the number of questions I would ask in an area where that particular participant seemed to have less that was new to offer. Staying alert during the interview phase can also help researchers answer what can often be the most fraught question in interview-based research: how many interviews should I do? If interviewers are constantly asking themselves during an interview whether they have heard most of what a participant is telling them before, they can feel confident—once the answer is 'yes'—that the time has come to conclude the interview phase of the research and proceed to data analysis.

SUMMARY

In this chapter I discussed some theoretical, practical and ethical issues around in-depth interviewing of adults. I focused on the life history interview, the primary tool used by researchers working within a feminist or symbolic interactionist framework. The interview is a good tool for researchers interested in safeguarding the subjective point of view who believe the meaning participants give to things is key to understanding their decisions. Highly structured interviews that ask closed-ended questions and offer precoded answer choices restrict the complexity and range of data collected. This interview approach may be appropriate when investigating a topic about which a great deal is already known, or when there is only a limited time available to analyse the data and present the findings. Less structured 'conversational' interviews are more appropriate when an issue is relatively unexplored and there is more time to analyse the data and present findings. An interview schedule or guide is a good tool to ensure such conversations are concise and focused on the researcher's area of interest. Piloting an interview schedule or guide before beginning interviews may be beneficial, although researchers who begin reading and analysing their data during the interview phase may continually alter the interview guide as new questions and tentative theories emerge. The goal in collecting interview data is to generate theory. It is the social good produced by the dissemination of that theory that largely justifies any minimal discomfort or inconvenience research participants might experience. The relationship between researcher and researched is inherently different and unequal. However, research practices that ensure research participants are not exploited and that decrease their discomfort and inconvenience and increase their comfort and convenience should not be mistaken for practices that democratise the research relationship. Researchers have a range of obligations to their participants. These include not exploiting them, minimising their discomfort and inconvenience and maximising their comfort and convenience, ensuring their consent to participate in the research is voluntary and adequately informed, and not wasting their time by failing to finish the study and/or publish meaningful results.

QUESTIONS FOR REFLECTION

- What is the primary research tool used by researchers in the hermeneutic tradition and why do they favour it?
- What might account for the reason most western research participants see themselves as 'choosers'? Is this perception in tension with reality? What can researchers do to manage this tension?
- When is a more structured interview appropriate, and when is a less structured approach called for? What sort of questions and answers are most suited to each type of approach?
- Why is it beneficial to pilot the interview schedule or guide? Once the interview phase begins, can the interview schedule or guide be changed?
- What methods do some feminist researchers use to undercut the power differential between researcher and researched? Do these methods really democratise the research process? What benefits do they offer to the researcher and the participant and what disadvantages do they pose?
- What are some of the ethical obligations that researchers have to their participants?
- Does the signature of a participant on a consent form necessarily signify that the participant has given their free and informed consent to participate?

FURTHER READING

Bloom, L.R. 1998, *Under the Sign of Hope: Feminist Methodology and Narrative Interpretation*, State University of New York Press,

Albany, NY. Provides a good range of sometimes dissenting views about feminist research methodologies, including questioning long-held beliefs that feminist research should establish egalitarian relationships, friendships and/or intimacy between researcher and research and raise the consciousness of participants, and that the interview is necessarily a way to accomplish this goal.

Minichiello, V., Aroni, R., Timewell, E. and Alexander, L. 1990, *In-Depth Interviewing: Researching Reople,* Longman-Cheshire, Melbourne. An easy to read and understand manual for beginning interviewers. Discusses several types of interviews and the means for deciding which to use in particular circumstances, and practical advice on proceeding.

13

An ethnographic approach to researching young children's learning

Iram Siraj-Blatchford and John Siraj-Blatchford

Ethnographic research has its roots in anthropological and cross-cultural study. In its broadest sense it encompasses any study that aims to describe some aspect of the sociocultural understandings and practices of a group of people. Rather than offering a particular method for data collection, ethnography may be conducted using a wide range of methodologies. It should therefore properly be understood as providing us with a particular perspective on what counts as legitimate knowledge or, to put it in more academic and philosophical terms, as providing us with an **epistemology** for our research. Ethnographies typically aim to provide holistic accounts that include the views and perspectives, beliefs and values of all of those involved in the particular sociocultural practice or institutional context being studied. These broad aims are often difficult to achieve in early childhood studies that are of necessity limited in terms of time and resources. In such circumstances it is more appropriate to refer to the work as contributing towards 'an ethnographic approach' or of providing 'a partial ethnographic account'.

Early childhood researchers have conducted ethnographic research for a wide range of purposes. It has been applied to the study of the educational outcomes for children of early years provision (Sylva, et al., 1999). It has also been applied to identify the different experiences of girls and of young minority ethnic children in institutional settings (Wright, 1986; Davies, 1989; Connolly, 1998), and it has been applied to the study of play (Feitelsen, 1977; Paley, 1983; Dau, 1999).

In the context of preschool improvement and effectiveness studies, ethnographic researchers have often succeeded in getting below the surface of general evaluative characteristics identified in checklists and rating scales looking at quality (Harms, Clifford and Cryer 1998; Sylva, et al., 1999). The best of these studies go a long way towards revealing the processes by which individuals and groups sustain, modify, shape, change and create their working, learning and play environments. Ethnographic forms of analysis can be especially valuable to those engaged in practice and in institutional development. But while an increasing number of quantitative and qualitative studies, and studies employing mixed methodologies, such as the UK Effective Provision of Pre-School Education project, do pay closer attention to the overall contexts and ethos of early childhood education settings than was previously the case, there is clearly a need for more ethnographic research which can paint in the fine-grained reality of educational processes within early childhood settings.

As Dahlberg, Moss and Pence (1999) and James and Prout (1997) have suggested, the qualitative studies that are currently being applied in early childhood education are also important in allowing new voices to be heard—these are the voices of teachers, other carers, families and the children themselves.

It has been suggested that the presentational task of ethnography is to 'paint pictures in words', 'capture a likeness', recreate the 'feel' of an event, 'evoke an image', 'awaken a spirit' or 'reconstruct a mood or atmosphere' (Woods, 1996). Hammersley (1999) provides a useful summary where he refers to ethnography as having the following features:

- People's behaviour is studied in everyday contexts;
- Data are gathered from a range of sources, but observation and/or relatively informal conversations are usually the main sources;
- The approach to data collection is 'unstructured';
- The focus is usually a single setting or group; and
- The analysis of data involves interpretation.

In fact, ethnographic study is by its very nature interpretative, that is, it is concerned to understand the subjective world of human experience. The central aim of the ethnographer is therefore to provide a holistic account that includes the views, perspectives, beliefs, intentions and values of the subjects of the study. To achieve this, we focus upon human actions that are always understood as 'behaviours-with-meaning' (Cohen and Manion, 1994). 'Actions' are only meaningful to us if we can identify the intentions of the actors involved. This is often far from straightforward—a classic example of the difficulty involves considering the difference between a wink and a blink. While there may be no mechanical difference between the two acts, the cultural contexts, and the relationship between individuals that each act suggests, demonstrate that they actually constitute two significantly different actions. As Fetterman (1989) suggests, 'Anyone who has ever mistaken a blink for a wink is fully aware of the significance of cultural interpretation' (p. 28). An account that is capable of discrimination between the two actions involves what Geertz (1993), citing Gilbert Ryle, refers to as 'thick description' (p. 6). A thick description is one that includes everything needed for the reader to understand what is happening. While a thin description would simply describe the rapid closing of an eyelid, a thick description will provide the context, telling the reader whether the movement was a blink caused by a piece of dust, a conspiratorial gesture or a romantic signal transmitted across a crowded room. Again this is a tall order, and it constitutes what has been referred to as the 'paradox of familiarity' for 'insider' researchers such as practitioners conducting ethnographic studies of their own workplace.

The problem is that while we may be able to apply our shared cultural framework of understanding when we *interpret* the behaviour of colleagues, parents and young children in our own 'insider' social group very easily, for precisely the same reasons we find it very much more difficult to isolate and make these cultural principles *explicit*. As Garfinkle's (1963) classic (if problematic) experiments with student volunteers showed, individuals share a whole range of 'background expectancies' upon which social interaction and meaningful communication depend. In one study Garfinkle instructed his students to record the responses of friends or relatives when commonplace remarks and conversation were actively (and unreasonably) pursued to obtain total clarification of their precise meanings. A short passage from one of Garfinkle's transcriptions illustrates the general idea, and a typical response:

(S *waved his hand cheerily*)
S: How are you?
E: How am I in regard to what? My health, my finances, my school work, my peace of mind, my . . .
S: (*red in the face and suddenly out of control*): Look! I was just trying to be polite. Frankly, I don't give a damn how you are.(Garfinkel, 1963, p. 222).

Paley (1984) noted similar, if less dramatic discomfort on the part of a group of 4-year-olds in the following interaction:

Teacher: How do you play house with a Barbie doll?
Charlotte: We pretend they are the sister and the mommy.
Teacher: Then who are you?

Janie: We're the one that acts them out.
Teacher: Oh. You *are* the Barbie doll.
Janie: Right. We *are* the sister or mommy.
Teacher: But you're the sister and mommy even without Barbie.
Jill: This is much more funner. Because you can look at her and see how she looks.
Teacher: By the way, how old is she supposed to be?

The girls blush and giggle as if I have asked an indelicate question. I have never seen them so ill at ease in a discussion.

Charlotte: Maybe a teenager.
Teacher: But sometimes she's a mother?
Charlotte: No.
Janie: Yes. Uh . . . I don't know. Yes, she is.
Teacher: Do you ever pretend she's a mother with a baby?
Charlotte: No! No! She never has a baby. Never!
Jill: Of course not. No babies.
Janie: But we pretend to have babies. Right, Mary Ann? Remember?
There are more side-glances and embarrassed laughter; Barbie is not open to full analysis. By contrast, nothing is covert about superhero dolls. Why is Barbie in this sensitive category of family secrets?'
(Paley, 1984, pp. 11–12).

As Garfinkle argued, the stability and meaningfulness of our day-to-day communications depends upon unstated cultural assumptions about what is said and why we say it. This is as true of young children as it is of adults. If we are to provide an adequate account, it is important that all the significant, unstated assumptions are identified and stated as clearly as possible. Cross-context or cross-cultural comparison can often be useful in this respect. Schieffelin and Ochs (1998), for example, studied the use of simplified registers ('baby talk') by caregivers in different societies and came to the conclusion that these practices may be part of a more general orientation in which situations are adapted to young children's perceived needs. In societies where a simplified register is not applied, children are expected to adapt to the adult world at an early age. In such societies, caregivers direct the children to notice and respond to others, and they frequently model appropriate utterances for the child to repeat to third parties. These features of caregiver speech are therefore neither universal nor necessary for language to be acquired, although this may often be assumed.

This effort to provide an adequate account of the insider perspective provides a central challenge for ethnography. If researchers want to discover how respondents understand and rationalise their practices, they must suspend their own personal values and judgements and identify the hidden assumptions that determine the insider perspectives and approaches. But as we have seen, this is often a special problem for those who study institutional contexts with which they are especially familiar. The task must then be to make the familiar 'strange', to imagine yourself as an 'outsider' and to recognise that even the most common and accepted practices might be questioned or appear questionable from that outsider perspective.

Burgess (1985) cites Howard Becker (1971) who stressed the difficulties that are involved:

> It is not just the survey method of educational testing or any of those things that keeps people from seeing what is going on. I think, instead, that it is first and foremost a matter of it all being so familiar that it becomes impossible to single out events that occur in the classroom as things that have occurred, even when they happen right in front of you. I have not had the experience of observing in elementary and high school classrooms myself, but I have in college classrooms and it takes a tremendous effort of will and imagination to stop seeing the things that are conventionally there to be seen. I have talked to a couple of teams of research people who have sat around in classrooms trying to observe and it is like pulling teeth to get them to see or write anything beyond what 'everyone' knows. (p. 10).

The importance of all this really cannot be overstated—a concrete example may therefore be of value. Consider Connelly's (1998) narrative account of a 4-year-old boy's sexual harassment of Michaela, a 5-year old, in Mr Wallace's classroom at 'East Avenue Primary School':

Hannah and Michaela had just been talking about Michaela's new boyfriend, which appeared to frustrate Sean as he had previously expressed an interest in Michaela as a girlfriend. Hannah was now turning her attention directly to Sean and trying unsuccessfully to engage him in conversation:

Hannah: That's a nice name—'Sean'!
Sean: I hate my name! [*his head remains focused on his work and he slightly turns away from her*] [. . .]
Hannah: [*carries on with her own work for a short while before looking up again and turning her attention to Michaela*]: You're only five and he's six [referring back to Michaela's boyfriend].
Sean: [*looks up and stares at Michaela. Frustratedly*]: He sits on your knee and pulls your clothes off! [*stands up and leans over the table to Michaela, staring her directly in the face*] He sits on your knee and licks your [*whispers the rest—inaudible*].
Michaela: [*appears upset and jumps up, pushes her chair under the table and walks towards Mr Wallace*].
Hannah: [*anxiously sits up straight, folds her arms and momentarily puts one of her fingers over her lips in anticipation of Mr Wallace's attention*].

Michaela: [*as she makes her way towards Mr Wallace, he looks up and asks her to go over and have her turn making a bumble bee with the classroom assistant. She does this, deciding not to tell Mr Wallace*]' (Connolly, 1998, p. 142).

Connolly's account goes on to cite a number of other interactions that showed how the public experiences of the girls at East Avenue were significantly shaped by notions of heterosexuality and the discourse of boyfriends. It isn't difficult in this case to imagine an alternative 'thin' descriptive account that would provide no more than the surface dialogue; such an account would tell us nothing about Sean's possible sense of 'rejection' and do little to show how Michaela considers, but then decides not to complain about, Sean's behaviour to Mr Wallace.

Another example of good practice in terms of **thick description** is taken from Paley's (1984) study of the children playing in her own classroom:

Social action in kindergarten is contained in dramatic plots. Since the characters create the plot, actors must identify themselves. In the doll corner, if a plumber arrives, then a pipe has just broken; the appearance of a school teacher signals that the children are about to receive a lesson. The four girls in the doll corner have announced who they are: Mother, Sister, Baby, Maid. To begin with, then, there will be cooking and eating, crying and cleaning. Charlotte is the mother because, she tells the others, she is wearing the silver shoes. Leadership often goes to the child who is most confident about the meaning of symbols.

Karen: I'm hungry. Wa-a-ah!
Charlotte: Lie down, baby.
Karen: I'm a baby that sits up.
Charlotte: First you lie down and sister covers you and *then* I make your cereal and then you sit up.
Karen: Okay (Paley, 1984, p. 1).

Typically, small-scale studies involve an initial observation phase where various inferences may be made about what has been seen followed by either formal interviews or less structured conversations and documentary analysis. This in turn will be followed with more focused observations to confirm or clarify what is happening. The process is cyclical. Ethnography is concerned with lived experiences and to study this the researcher usually engages in participant observation. That is, they participate in the activities of the group to be studied and simultaneously record what is taking place. Fieldnotes are often written on the spot and subsequently amplified and elaborated while the events remain fresh in the researcher's memory. Increasingly, photographic, audio and video recordings are being used to supplement these accounts and to provide more permanent records. All of these materials may then be drawn upon in writing up the final ethnographic study.

While some readers who plan to research their own working environment may consider that the formality of gaining formal consent is unnecessary, we would argue that, in any form of research, permission should be sought from both the parents and the children. In fact, given the importance of participant observation in ethnography, it should be recognised that the issue of access, and the role of gatekeepers in providing/permitting access, takes on much more *ongoing* significance. Rather than the usual business of gaining formal permission in preparation for a study, in ethnography access becomes a process of continuously establishing and developing relationships with the research participants. Even where the ethnographer is an outsider, the significant gatekeepers may not be the head or manager of the centre you are working in but rather the more vociferous individuals (adults and children) who participate on a day-to-day basis within the setting. For an interesting account of the essentially negotiative and ongoing character, as well as the continuing tensions and problems of participant observation, see Schatzman and Strauss (1973).

We have found that where prior consent is required, initial access is best gained through a mutual contact that can recommend the researcher to the institutional manager. The manager will need to be reassured about confidentiality and will expect to be given assurances that the research will not be disruptive to the normal day-to-day functioning of the establishment. We have found that gatekeepers often have a vested interest in the results of the study—they may be anxious that, however anonymous the study might be, their colleagues, employees and practices are presented in a good light. If they have experience of other non-ethnographic research they may ask you to explain the hypothesis that you intend testing, and to show the interview schedules or questionnaires that you will be using. All of this may take some explaining, and it is wise to arrive at any initial meeting prepared to provide an account of the basic assumptions and philosophy of ethnography to put their minds at rest. Where concerns or suspicions are particularly great it is a good idea to suggest the formation of an advisory committee that you can report to at significant stages of the study. Advisory committees, which may be drawn from user groups (for example, parents as well as administrators/governors, etc.), are often invaluable in providing access to documentary evidence that would otherwise be unavailable. They also provide an additional means of gaining validation through additional triangulation (see below).

Those embarking on their first ethnographic study are often nervous about the prospect of conducting participant observation but we have found most early childhood settings to be extremely friendly and easy-going places. While the participant observation of many of those groups of interest to other social researchers (such as adult and adolescent drug-takers and other social deviants) can be problematic, many researchers find working with young children relatively easy and, as Sluckin (1981) in his research on playground behaviour observed, you can quickly become 'part of the furniture':

> Within a few weeks the children became more and more familiar with my presence and I became part of the furniture of the playground. On one occasion they used me in a game of 'all after that man there' and for fifty seconds I was mobbed, pulled and kicked by a bevy of five-year-olds. Happily, the noise was more alarming than the blows and so I concluded that this was an example of pretend fighting. On another occasion I became incorporated into a piece of rhyming word play, as two five-year-old girls revealed to each other my true identity.

Jane: He's about that big.
Sophie (*to me*): You're about that big.
Jane: He's a dum dum.
Sophie: He's daft, he's a paddy dum dum.
Jane: I know what he is, I know what he is.
Sophie: What?
Jane: He's a lazy bugger; he never gets up in the morning.' (p. 7).

THE PLACE OF THEORY IN ETHNOGRAPHY

Connelly's (1998) study of "East Avenue Primary School' is perhaps especially useful in identifying the place of theory in ethnographic research. Connelly applied theoretical constructs drawn from Gudgeon (1993), Epstein (1997) and Walkerdine (1981), among others, in his analysis of the girls' peer relations. It hardly needs to be said that the children themselves would understand the events quite differently from the academic analysts. Given the need to obtain the world views of those we study, it is important that we should hold back our own interpretations of what is happening to hear the explanations given by those most closely involved in the action. But, just as we have seen in the case of Schieffelin and Ochs' (1998) study, in order to understand the events some theoretical explanations may be required that go beyond the knowledge and experience of our respondents (even when they are adults). While quantitative researchers often begin with a theoretical hypothesis that is to be tested, in ethnography the aim of the researcher is to begin as far as possible with an open mind and to allow the theoretical explanations of the behaviours and statements that are being recorded to emerge from the data. This process, that Glazer and Strauss (1967) referred to as 'grounded theory', is well established and accepted by most practitioners. Ethnographic researchers do need to ground their theory in the data that they collect, but as Fetterman (1989) argues, as a study progresses we should not be too nervous about applying theory from other sources as long as it can be seen to be appropriate and offer useful explanatory power: 'Theories need not be juxtapositions of constructs, assumptions, propositions, and generalisations; they can be midlevel or personal theories about how the world or some small part of it works' (p. 17).

It is important in this context to recognise that it is neither possible nor desirable to deny our personal theories and suppositions, but what we have to do is to declare them and, where appropriate, compare and contrast them to the theories and suppositions of other theorists and our respondents. Throughout the ethnographic enquiry, there should be a continuous interplay between the observations being made and the theories being developed and introduced to explain them. A good deal of flexibility is demanded of the researcher and as the theories become more elaborate, some degree of focused questioning or observation is to be expected. As Burns (2000) has observed, this can be particularly worrying for the novice because they are unable to predict in advance the directions the study may take.

Having selected a suitable subject for study the researcher therefore begins by making broad descriptive observations that provide an overview of the situation being studied. The data collection field is then narrowed down to provide more and more focused observations. The process has often been described as one of 'progressive focusing'; in the process, theories may increasingly be drawn from the researcher's previous knowledge and experience, and they may also be taken off the academic 'shelf'. As previously argued, theory has an important part to play in ethnography, but it should always be recognised that theories are invariably subject specific—they may be applied with great value to some topics but found to be entirely misleading or inappropriate to others.

It is important to capture the meanings and language of the practitioners and a useful analytical (and recording and reporting) technique is to identify 'critical episodes' and to prepare 'vignettes' that illustrate significant behaviours. These episodes may be especially significant in explaining a common behaviour recorded, or to show something characteristic of the setting or, for example, an educational style employed by a particular practitioner. In producing a holistic account the researcher must be aware that the dramas being recorded are set within wider institutional and sociocultural contexts that also have to be accounted for. That said, early childhood professionals themselves recognise that norms are contextual and specific to particular settings, as Waterhouse (1991) shows in this extract from his records of 'staffroom talk': 'I've just found out that the lot I had last time were far below par for this school you know. Not half as good as they're "used to"! Quite! But I didn't realize 'cause I'd always taught in rough schools. They were all pretty good, you know. You forget what the norm is after a while!' (p. 56).

Waterhouse (1991) sought to provide accounts of the day-to-day institutional practices that operated as 'self-fulfilling prophesies' or, perhaps less controversially, as 'self-sustaining prophesies', to the dis-advantage of young working-class children. Following the perspective of Sharp and Green (1973), Waterhouse focused particularly upon the construction of pupil identities, and provides a symbolic interactional-ist study of the processes by which pupils as 'others' are constructed by their teachers in the early years of schooling.

Reflexivity and reflexive abstraction

In terms of learning we all practice what Piaget referred to as 'reflextion', suggesting that this process constituted the very basis of all conceptual learning. Piaget argued that while empirical knowledge might be acquired simply through observation, the learning of explanatory rules and concepts relies upon a process of reflexive abstraction; the self-conscious coordination of the observed with existing cognitive structures of meaning. From this perspective, as an observation is recognised as in some way inconsistent with the individual's cognitive structure of meaning, that structure is reorganised to accommodate it. This elaborated structure of meaning may then, in turn, be applied to explain the observation which is itself transformed in the process. In a word the process is one of equilibration. Piaget's 'reflexive abstraction' is a mechanism of equilibration and it is disequilibrium or cognitive dissonance that provides the motor for the process of learning.

But when we learn about people and about social events, the process is even more complex. Our understanding of any kind of event is conditioned by our prior knowledge, but in this case the object of our interest behaves according to their own under-standing of what it is they are doing. We cannot really understand why they act in a particular way unless we first discover what their intentions are. This process of determining the intentions of the authors of either texts, actions or other cultural products is termed hermeneutics. While the lesson was most clearly learnt in anthropology it is now widely recognised that a hermeneutic process must be applied in all of the social sciences. We now recog-nise that if we wish to describe what someone is doing we must first understand what they think that they are doing. If this wasn't complicated enough, as social scientists we must also recognise the process that Giddens (1975) referred to as the 'double hermenuetic' (p. 12), where our respondent's understanding of events changes as a direct response of our intervention. As James and Prout (1997) have observed, this is nowhere less apparent than in the study of childhood itself (p. 5)

RELIABILITY, REPLICABILITY, VALIDITY AND TRIANGULATION

Reliability, replicability and validity are important in all forms of research but they mean different things, and have different implications, in the case of qualitative research. To a quantitative researcher, reliability is to do with the degree of 'fit' between the data and their theoretical representation of it. In ethnography we attempt to collect multiple representations, to show different definitions, and to present our research in a manner that is open to multiple interpretations. In so far as we are successful in this, reliability becomes more of a concern of the reader than the researcher. The associated problem of replicability—whether another researcher would produce the same results—is solved by providing a clear and explicit account of the research process. The reader should then be able to follow the researcher's footsteps and assess the rationale at every stage. In this context it is important to recognise that while most ethnographies are, by their very nature, case studies, that doesn't mean that sampling isn't an issue. While you are unlikely to be making any strong claims regarding the representative nature of your sample choice, the reasons that you had for choosing that specific case still need to be justified. As Miles and Huberman (1994) argue, your sample in this case is *purposive* and it is your research *purposes* that need to be explained (p. 27).

In Penn's (1997) study, 'ethnographical' observations are used in a comparative study of early childhood educational provision in Italy, Spain and the United Kingdom. Despite recognising the discontinuities between institutional care and education (particularly in the case of 3-year-olds) in the United Kingdom, Penn decided to focus her UK research on day-care centres where the criterion for admission was 'children in need'. We are told that many of these children were at risk of neglect or abuse and that particular attention was given to the 'surveillance and monitoring' of individuals: 'Many of the children who attended the nurseries were depressed and distraught. In one group of 3-year-olds, for instance, not a single child could speak a sentence and some were only monosyllabic'. The Italian and Spanish nurseries, by contrast, apparently had no such criteria for admissions and we are told that they had been influenced by the sophisticated educational practices of Reggio Emilia (Malaguzzi, 1993). Given the apparently unfair comparison, and her failure to demonstrate the representative nature of the sample, Penn's heavy criticisms of UK nurseries are difficult to justify.

To most quantitative researchers 'validity' is all about 'truth conditions', the relationship between what it is that a test measures, and what it will predict (Guildford, 1954). Ethnographic researchers are more interested in what 'seems' to be true than in any objectively defined truth. But ethnographers are attempting to portray the social world as it appears to the people that inhabit it, and something therefore has to be done to ensure that it is the perceptions of the 'inhabitants' and not of the visiting researcher that take precedence. (In discussing validity in these terms it is significant to note that the words 'valid' and 'value' have the same etymological roots). For an idea to have value, or to be valid, is for it to be strong and effective. Our assessments of validity are based upon our perceptions of 'worth' and hence upon our value systems. In clarifying our rationale we are delegating this responsibility to the reader, who may accept or reject our explicit values. Quantitative researchers often present their findings as objective truth and hence *smuggle* their values in (Siraj-Blatchford, 1994). As Penn's (1997) example shows, qualitative researchers can very easily fall into similar traps.

This is where triangulation comes in. The term is borrowed from the contexts of navigation or surveying, where two or more directional markers are used to accurately locate a single geographical feature or position. In qualitative research, to triangulate your data means to confirm their validity by obtaining data from a second or third methodological source. An observation may therefore be backed up by evidence gained in an interview and/or from documentary analysis. Brannen (1992) argues that adequate triangulation (providing multiple sources of information) involves not only methods and data but also investigators and theories. For all of these reasons, mixed method studies are becoming more popular. Pinnell et al, (1994), for example, compared instructional models for the literacy education of 'high-risk' 6-year-olds, using qualitative analyses through videotaped data to support the largely quantitative analyses. This allowed more description and interpretation of teaching and learning processes. They concluded that: 'Solving the problems related to reading failure in the US may ultimately depend on our willingness to examine programmatic outcomes in ways that take into account the multiple, interacting factors that may mean success for our high-risk students' (Pinnell et al., 1991, p. 36).

We believe, like Fetterman (1989), that since the 1990s there has been increasing evidence in the research literature that mixing methods is a valuable strategy for theory development and theory testing.

CONCLUSIONS

The growing popularity of ethnographic methods, as well as 'teacher-research', action and collaborative research may be seen in part as a reaction to a growing dissatisfaction with educational research that was once founded within a naive empiricist tradition. Research at that time was conducted almost exclusively from within the various academic disciplines such as psychology, sociology, philosophy, etc. Much of this research undoubtedly did fail to relate its findings or is problematic to educational practices and concerns. However, the controversy surrounding the academic status of ethnography and other qualitative approaches has never really been resolved. The traditional approaches to research provided at least the illusion of objectivity. Today many ethnographers and quantitative researchers reject the suggestion that any research can be truly value-free. While other writers have embraced poststructuralist and postmodern approaches that reject the very notion of objectivity, many others are still anxious to be persuasive and rigorous in their work. Researchers have responded to this in a variety of ways, and even the psychoanalysis of the researcher has been suggested to provide some legitimising basis for ethnography. An elaboration of our own perspective lies beyond the constraints of this chapter but some of the founding principles may be found in Siraj-Blatchford (1994, 1997).

The funding bodies that have commissioned preschool quality or effectiveness research have tended to favour quantitative measures of children's academic and social development and progress, as these measures have been seen to provide 'reliable' statistical data. The use of large samples and/or the longitudinal nature of many of these studies has determined the use of quantitative methods to ensure greater confidence in terms of the representativeness and the generalisability of findings. But in selecting a particular set of instruments for quantitative study we inevitably limit the possibilities for explanation that are open to us. Even more fundamentally, the research questions that are being asked and the hypotheses that are being tested are drawn from established paradigms and are thus value-loaded in favour of particular explanations. For an increasing number of researchers, this recognition has led to an outright rejection of any form of quantification at all. But while we reject any notion of objective value-neutrality in researchers, we believe that this outright rejection of quantification constitutes an overreaction. While the assumed objectivity of quantitative methods in the past has constituted (and still does constitute) some kind of metaphysical status for its hardened advocates, we feel that this aspect may be rejected without rejecting the underlying discipline. A softer, post-metaphysical, new empiricism offers the possibility of greater rigour, and the continued development of better theoretical models and paradigms. In this it must be recognised that, while quantitative studies provide a means of testing theory, qualitative research has a major role to play in generating and developing theory. The two should be seen as complementary rather than contradictory activities.

Many of the possibilities and limitations of ethnography were actually identified in the debate between Woods and Hammersley in the pages of the *British Educational Research Journal* in 1987. In an earlier paper Woods (1985) had identified three phases in the development of ethnographic research: '1. description; 2. theory formulation; 3. theory testing'.

While to Hammersley (1987a) the notion of 'theory testing' could only mean the use of hypothetical deduction, Woods (1987) clearly accepted a broader definition that would include a wider range of validation strategies that might often fall short of providing any kind of definitive 'proof'. A major difficulty lay in the authors' (Woods, 1985, 1987; Hammersley, 1987a; 1987b) failure to clearly define the difference between individual studies that might include the use of various validation procedures, and the progressive development of an educational paradigm by 'a collaborative research community'. In the circumstances (and perhaps inevitably) the authors were at times 'talking past each other'.

As Sylva (1995) has suggested, we must recognise that in the past twenty years we have seen a major theoretical shift away from the study of the child-as-solitary learner (Piaget) to the child-as-learner-in-social-context (Vygotsky), and narrative and ethnographic research now offer 'an exciting new vein of early years research'. Sylva (1995) therefore suggested that in discriminating between early childhood education studies we might usefully consider their 'fitness for purpose'. But we must also recognise that our evaluation of fitness will ultimately and inevitably depend on our choice of paradigm, and our power to impose our evaluations will depend upon the degree to which our paradigm is established. Early childhood education has traditionally occupied a marginal position in educational debate. The challenge is therefore, as always, to construct paradigms from within the everyday professional and institutional contexts that we study and to develop them, where possible, in collaboration with other researchers, parents, carers and children.

SUMMARY

In this chapter we have argued that ethnography has an important role to play in early childhood and educational research. We have considered the place of theory and argued that the ethnographer should be especially careful to consider explanations and theories other than their own. The challenges and benefits of participant observation was discussed, as well as the nature of the truth claims that may be offered. The central task must always be to provide a reasoned and critical analysis of the data.

QUESTIONS FOR REFLECTION

- What epistemological model do you favour yourself? How will you justify it to your readers?
- If ethnographers reject any claim to (weak or strong) objectivity, what are the implications for the disadvantaged and oppressed groups that they write about?
- Consider the extent to which the study by Penn (1997) represents a fair comparison. If you have time take a closer look at the study and decide on a research design more adequate to the task proposed.

FURTHER READING

Fetterman, D. 1989, *Ethnography: Step by Step, Applied Social Research Methods Series Vol. 17*, Sage, London. An excellent and authoritative introduction written from the perspective of a practising anthropologist. The book provides a very user-friendly introduction to the main issues as well as some valuable references to further reading.

Paley, V. G. 1984, *The Boy who Would be a Helicopter*, Harvard University Press, New York. While any contemporary academic text would be expected to engage more fully in the extant relevant research literature, this text is recommended as an exemplar of good practice.

Woods, P., Boyle, M. and Hubbard, N. 1999, *Multicultural Children in the Early Years: Creative Teaching, Meaningful Learning*, Multilingual Matters, Clevedon. A two year study of children's experiences on their transition to school. Teachers' values and beliefs are explored and a number of practical opportunities and constraints identified.

14

Action research

Glenda Mac Naughton

Action research is about researching with people to create and study change in and through the research process. In early childhood settings it can produce changed ways of doing things and changed ways of understanding why we do what we do. This chapter tells the story of an action research study that attempted to change how early childhood staff understood and practiced gender equity in their services. In this study, known as the Gender Equity Research Group (GERG) study, I drew on **feminist poststructuralist** theoretical perspectives to formulate my research questions, methods and analysis. The chapter traces how I did this and why. My intention is to show how action research works in practice and how to ground it theoretically. While my action research was grounded in feminist poststructuralist theory, it is equally possible to ground action research in other theoretical perspectives. Good action research requires you to know how your theoretical perspectives potentiate and limit your work at each stage of the research.

WHAT WAS YOUR RESEARCH QUESTION?

The broad aim of my research was to further the theoretical and practical development of feminist pedagogies in early childhood education by exploring the question: 'Within which **knowledge–power regimes** are feminist pedagogies in early childhood education created?' Three specific questions flowed from this:

1. How do specific pedagogical and gendering **discourses** enable teachers to intervene in children's play to alter traditional gendering? When adults intervene, how do they deal with particular boys' and girls' resistance? Is there a relationship between their responses to particular boys' and girls' resistance and their view of gendering?
2. What are the discursive and institutional challenges and potentialities of developing practices that enable early childhood educators to work with children's resistance and to empower children to be different?
3. What are the discursive and institutional challenges and potentialities of my practice (as an academic) in assisting teachers who wish to investigate gendering and implement changes in their **praxis**? Is feminist poststructuralism demonstrably and practically useful here?

HOW DID YOU ARRIVE AT THIS RESEARCH QUESTION?

I was led to my research questions through my commitments to, and my concerns and uncertainties about how to create, gender equity in early childhood education. My long-term commitment to feminist pedagogies sat alongside my concerns about how staff and students struggled with, and sometimes rejected, gender equity in their work. It also sat alongside my uncertainties about how to build and disseminate feminist pedagogical knowledge(s) within and without the academy. So, my questions reflected both my feminist commitments and my academic uncertainties and concerns about how to bring these commitments more effectively into my own work.

HOW DID YOU ANSWER IT?

I decided to answer this question using **fourth generation action research.**

While the action research literature is an arena of debate and contestation Carr and Kemmis (1986) identified three 'Minimal Requirements for Action Research'. From their perspective, action research must:

- Have social practice as its subject matter and see the subject matter as open to strategic action and capable of improvement;
- Proceed systematically and self-critically through the action research processes of observing, planning, doing and reflecting (the action research cycle) in a deliberate and ongoing way; and
- Involve those responsible for the practice and be based clearly on principles of collaboration.

These requirements parallel many of the values and concerns of fourth generation action research (McTaggart and Garbutcheon-Singh, 1988). Fourth generation action research assumes research should embody educational transformation and emancipation by working with others to change existing social practices and by using critical reflection and social criticism as key research processes. It is therefore collaborative, change-oriented and overtly political.

Getting started in action research

Action research starts with the desire to change practices and/or to improve your understandings about why and how something happens. In the GERG project I started with the desire to improve gender equity practices in early childhood services. I also wanted to improve my own understandings of how to practise and theorise gender equity using feminist theories. To turn these desires into fourth generation action research I had to take several steps:

- *Find a group of people* involved in working for gender equity in early childhood. In Carr and Kemmis's (1986) terms, I had to involve those responsible for gender equity practices in the research. I found a group of people using several strategies. First, I ran a professional development session about gender equity in early childhood, told participants about the research project, and invited them to join it. Second, I advertised about the project in early child-hood newsletters. Third, I asked colleagues if they knew of early childhood staff who might be interested in participating in the project. After seven months I had a group of twelve people willing to come to a meeting about the project.
- *Initiate a meeting* about the research to explain in detail how action research worked and what people's participation in the project would involve. In all research it is important that participants are clearly informed about what their involvement in the research means. In action research it is especially important for them to understand that the research is change-orientated and political in nature. They need to understand that they are committing to a research process that is deliberately geared to changing their under-standings and their practices.
- *Develop a collaborative research process.* Building collaborative research is difficult. It involves attempting to build an equitable relationship with your co-researchers and trying to ensure that the research questions being explored are of mutual interest and bene-fit. Some of the difficulties in achieving this have been discussed by Campbell and Ryan in Chapter 4. In the GERG project, collabora-tion built slowly as individual group members agreed to initiate several 'gendering projects' in their own centres.

Developing action research

Action research, like all research, has some minimal requirements which must be met in its design and execution for it to be seen as valid research. The requirements in action research centre on the need for action researchers to proceed systematically through the action research processes.

> ### Action research processes
>
> - Observing
> - Planning actions based on these observations
> - Implementing planned actions
> - Reflecting on what happens
> - Sharing with others
> - Collaboratively reflecting on what has been learnt
> - Building theories to guide further action
> - Replanning
> - Implementing
> - Observing
> - Reflecting
> - The cycle then repeats itself.

To start the action research process in GERG I introduced participants to the action research cycle in our first group meeting. I also introduced the group to a set of operational procedures that embedded action research principles into our group meetings (see McTaggart, 1991). Everybody agreed to abide by these principles and to settle on a project that they would like to initiate in their own centres. The projects individual GERG members chose included researching how to: gather gender-inclusive observations, develop processes for challenging sexism, support girls' and boys' non-traditional gendering choices and experiment with gender-inclusive approaches to block play. Each group member agreed during the coming month to observe what was happening in their centre, document this and then to share what they learnt in the group. We then used the group meetings to reflect retrospectively on what had happened in each of the projects and to prospectively plan the next step. This pattern of planning an action, observing, documenting, sharing and reflecting continued for nearly eighteen months.

Action researchers research their practices and understandings using similar methods to other researchers, including case studies, observation, document analysis, policy analysis, interviews and group discussion. They may produce qualitative and quantitative data depending on what they want to find out about in their specific setting.

Thus action research studies are often mixed-method studies. For instance, in GERG, several people used observation schedules to map their interactions with boys and girls and to map where and with whom specific boys and girls played. This produced quantitative data about how many boys and girls played with specific materials, how often they played with them and how long they played with them. These same people also interviewed children about their play preferences and had group discussions with children about gender issues in the centre. This produced qualitative data about how children thought about and understood their relationships with each other. In some instances, the discussions were audiotaped to produce transcript data; in other instances GERG members used journals to record what happened.

Maintaining the integrity of action research

The action research cycle only progresses when you can critically reflect upon and criticise your findings, understandings and practices with others. Critical reflection can be seen as the motor that drives the research process—when it stalls the action research stalls. To maintain the integrity of fourth generation action research, critical reflection needs to be driven collaboratively and be geared towards social criticism. These processes aim to create change by questioning taken-for-granted ways of understanding and doing things. To do this, critical reflection needs to question the status quo and taken-for-granted assumptions, and to be explicitly and deliberately political.

GERG established several processes to facilitate collaborative critical reflection on our work that are common to most action research projects:

- We met regularly as a group to share our individual research findings, understandings and practices.
- We structured our group meetings to allow time for us to retrospectively and prospectively share and talk about the data we gathered in each of the centres.
- We practised asking each other questions about why things happened and how they happened.
- We brought new ideas into the group to help us to answer those questions and to provoke us to think beyond the status quo and our taken-for-granted understandings. We introduced new ideas through sharing and reading research articles and books on gendering in early childhood and articles from the media concerning gender issues.
- We regularly summarised our progress and the issues that were emerging.

Questions to prompt critical reflection

- How do I understand this event/child/group/experience/intervention/issue/practice/theory?
- How have I learnt to understand it?
- What emotional investments have I made in this understanding?
- What are the power effects of my understanding for myself, children, parents and colleagues?
- What would I risk by changing my understanding?
- What other understandings are possible?
- How can I expand the possibilities I see for understanding?
- Which of these understandings challenges unfair and unjust practices and ways of thinking?
- Who would benefit and how if I changed my understanding?
- How might I act differently as a result?

Documenting action research

Critical reflection is the motor of action research, but the fuel needed for the motor to work is data collection and documentation. To drive action research you need to collect two levels of 'data'. First you need to document what happens when you take action. For instance, in GERG we documented what happened when teachers tried to challenge sexism with children.

Documentation tools in GERG

- teacher journals
- observation schedules
- audiotaped conversations between teachers and children
- videotaped observations of children's play
- fieldnotes made by myself as a participant observer.

The data produced through GERG's various documentation techniques were shared in project meetings and formed the basis of our collaboration as the group critically reflected on what was happening and why in each of the projects.

The data generated through this first level of documentation forms the basis for critical reflection and further planning. Your individual and collective reflections and planning decisions also need to be documented. This data constitutes the second level of documentation in action research. In GERG we maintained a written record that individuals agreed to as a fair representation of GERG work, individually and collectively. I took responsibility for this documentation and circulated meeting notes. These notes detailed the actions that individuals had agreed to for the coming month; their experiences and thoughts from the previous month's work; common issues, concerns and questions; and individual and group hypotheses of what was working or not working in their work with children and why. The validity of the notes was commented via the written comments of individuals or in verbal comments at the next meeting. Alterations were then made and circulated. Thus, the meeting notes offered an important point of reflection, and a record of our changing ideas and practices.

HOW DID YOU DECIDE HOW TO ANSWER IT?

I wanted the GERG project to generate historically and culturally specific information about the theory and practice of producing feminist pedagogies in early childhood education. My research questions and the feminist poststructuralist theory driving my research suggested that to achieve these aims and to answer my research questions it needed to:

- critically and consciously theorise change;
- take account of staffs' meaning constructions;
- focus on the relationships between gendering and the children's and adults' subjectivities;
- embody action; and
- uncover constraints to action, including resistance.

Given these research imperatives I decided to answer my question using fourth generation action research because I believed that this kind of research can do several things.

- It enables change to be critically and consciously theorised. It does this because it builds critical reflection and action into research. It is premised on the idea that changed understandings and practices occur as groups work for change. It is, therefore, a research method in which theorising about change becomes possible because change is intended by the method.
- It could account for staff's meaning construction because documentation of critical reflection on changing ideas and understandings is embedded in the research.
- It could uncover the constraints to action, including resistance, because it uses critical reflection and social critique as key research processes.
- It could embody action. The specific focus is on change in action research, in contrast to other research methods.

214

- It enabled a focus on the relationships between gendering and children's and adults' subjectivities as it required me to document our changing discourses and practices as we worked with each other for change.

WHAT SAMPLING ISSUES WERE THERE?

GERG participants were Victorian early childhood educators who had a proclaimed interest in improving their understanding of gender equity in early childhood education; who had an area of their own practice they wished to explore in relation to gender; and who wished to be in an action research group. There were twelve participants, plus myself. All had formal tertiary early childhood education qualifications, three being involved in studying for their Masters in Education on joining the study.

Several formal and informal strategies were used to notify early childhood educators about the study (as discussed above). I quickly learnt, however, that getting action research started can be one of the hardest parts of this type of research. It took me seven months to find ten people prepared to attend an initial meeting to discuss the project. In part this was due to the lack of interest in gender equity issues at that time in early childhood education. However, it was also because the project required people to commit considerable time and energy to it. You need to bear this in mind when choosing to embark on action research—allow time to find a group to work with.

WHAT DID YOU FIND?

The findings from the action research have been fully reported in Mac Naughton (2000). In brief, I found gender inequities alive and well in early childhood centres. I learnt that challenging these inequities was often a very risky and unsupported process for early childhood teachers. I found that the early childhood academy of which I was a part was heavily implicated in silencing the impact of gender on children's lives and that developmentally appropriate practice as understood and practised by GERG participants often got in the way of progressing gender equity. I uncovered a number of gender 'myths' about how gender equity can and should be practised with young children, and discovered how feminist poststructuralist theory could uncover, challenge and reinvent these myths. The myths showed that teachers' practices were heavily regulated through a knowledge–power regime in which developmental and feminist truths of the developing child competed with each other. This competition sometimes worked for gender equity and sometimes worked against it. GERG was part of learning how to make it work for gender equity.

HOW DID YOU INTERPRET WHAT YOU FOUND?

Drawing on feminist poststructuralist theory to interpret what I found, and using Foucauldian understandings of knowledge and power, I argued that the research group sat in an interstice of a shifting knowledge–power regime concerning 'the developing child'. In this interstice feminist and developmentally appropriate pedagogies competed for ascendancy in defining the developing child and in defining the pedagogic implications of particular gendering truths concerning the developing child.

Theoretical and practical imperatives led me to this interpretation and enabled me to detail the particular features of the knowledge–power regime that were implicated in teaching practices, the institutional and discursive challenges within these and the special relationship between the early childhood centre and the academy. In what follows I focus first on the practical imperatives influencing what I chose to interpret and then on the processes I used to create an interpretation of what had happened in GERG.

Practical imperatives driving data selected for interpretation

All action research projects generate an enormous volume of material and GERG was no exception. I had qualitative and quantitative data from group meetings, individual interviews, observations of children's play, discussions with children, interviews with parents, etc. The volume of material produced over the project's eighteen-month life meant I needed to find a way to select data that I thought would help me to answer my questions. This means, like all research, that the final account I told of the project (Mac Naughton, 2000) was highly partial. The impact of this on validity is discussed shortly.

In selecting data for analysis I was influenced by its accessibility and by the length of participation in the project of individual GERG members. Re-accessibility of the particular moments captured by audiorecording (meetings and interviews) meant these moments were privileged over other moments. Many thoughts, conversations and actions that may have been important in how individuals within GERG acted and understood their actions were, therefore, silenced.

The length of individuals' membership and the nature of their involvement were also strong considerations in the selection process. Individuals varied in the time they gave to GERG overall, and to specific projects in their workplace. Most of the information I selected for interpretation derived from the six GERG members who remained for the project's duration. Their time in GERG resulted in a rich and extensive information base from which to explore their changing subjectivities, discourses and practices as they planned work through several action research cycles.

Feminist poststructuralist imperatives about validity in interpreting data

Validity is a highly vexed question in qualitative research (see for example, Cotterill, 1992; Heshusius, 1994; Moss, 1994), but particularly within the specific theoretical approach underpinning the interpretation of the GERG data (Lather, 1993). Poststructuralism is based on an anti-essentialist, anti-foundationalist epistemology or theory of what counts as knowledge (as discussed in Chapter 3). This means that in poststructuralist research there is no essential 'truth' that can be aimed for, and achieved, via your interpretation of the data. Therefore, deciding how to produce a valid/true account of a project is difficult. This difficulty is compounded by how poststructuralists also problematise consensus and, therefore, measures of reliability such as triangulation, used to establish validity within qualitative research (Moss, 1994). This had led to feminist poststructuralist researchers such as Lather (1993) arguing that modernist forms of validity in qualitative research such as triangulation need to be reimagined and repractised in poststructuralist research.

Lather (1993) offered four ways of reimagining validity, and thus repractising it, that could be relevant within poststructuralist research: ironic validity, paralogical validity, rhizomatic validity and voluptuous validity. Each is concerned to disrupt the possibilities of consensus about data. Each is also concerned to make visible the problematics of feminist poststructuralist conceptions of the subject (as non-essential, shifting, multiple) and to make problematic the politics of research so that the researcher constructs open, multiple accounts of the research which do not finally resolve what is to be told. As Lather (1993) talked of the seeming impossibility of establishing poststructuralist validity, the approach taken to validity in reporting GERG was bound to be problematic.

I decided to heed a key suggestion from Lather (1993) and make visible the approach to validity I took. I approached it in three ways:

- By making the process and criteria (theoretical and practical) for my specific selections from the empirical information base as visible as possible;
- By emphasising moments which other GERG participants saw as significant in their gendering praxis, so that the partiality is not mine alone; and
- By seeking feedback/comment/etc. from GERG when selecting material so that I gained more than one perspective on the data, so that more than one account was possible.

These processes do not overcome the partialities of the information I presented about this project in Mac Naughton (2000), nor could they—for instance, while they ensured that the partiality was not mine alone, I powerfully guided it. This was apparent in the consensus that my various accounts of the project produced. Requests for changes to the text by GERG members were minimal; most often they involved additional illustrative material to elaborate or emphasise a point. For me, this raised the question of the extent to which GERG participants felt able to, or had the desire or the resources to, question *my* account. On the other hand, all but two participants wanted their work reported using their own names. This suggests that they were prepared to 'own' the account I have developed.

Hence, the discussion that follows of how I analysed the data needs to be seen within a space that disputes the possibility of validity but where making visible the particular truths that are constructed and sought is seen as important in finding out about our social world.

Selecting and organising the empirical data

I selected and organised the empirical data through a reflexive process of writing and rewriting the original data. Kenway and Willis (1993, p. 5) referred to a process of 'overwriting' case studies of gender and schooling which, in part, captures the process undertaken in this study. Overwriting involved writing a lengthy description of the study from primary data sources, drawing upon this to create a structure and logic for writing up an account of a project, then 'layering interpretation' (p. 5) on the structure to build case studies and snapshots of a research project.

I began the selection process by examining the empirical information generated by GERG for information about how specific discourses, practices and institutions constituted changes in GERG members' gendering praxis. I decided this could best be achieved by selecting information about moments in the project where individuals experienced crisis, or when business-as-usual was disrupted and/or pedagogies were reassembled. Therefore, I traced through all of my data to explore how specific, taken-for-granted aspects of teaching/learning were constructed as problematic, the resultant actions and how these actions were intended to achieve greater equality. Within this, I looked for information about individuals' subjective understandings of their gender equity strategies and how this was constituted in and via practices, discourses and institutions.

The beginnings: a chronological structure

My starting points for overwriting were the audiotaped transcripts of GERG meetings. These were used to build a chronology of the projects, debates and issues that emerged in individuals' work. The chronology detailed our actions and understandings and, through this, identified how specific discourses, practices and institutions were evident in our actions and understandings.

There were two reasons for organising the initial selection chronologically. First, it offered a simple initial organisational framework for representing GERG work to individuals for comment on points of accuracy and fairness and key issues they felt had been silenced or skewed in my summary of our work. Second, a chronology offered a framework through which to identify descriptive information on the three foundational features in the field (discourses, practices and institutions). As such, the chronology provided a starting point for my analysis, but in many ways the initial account was simplistic. It 'lost' individual voices and complexities because it tried to tell GERG's story, not the story of individuals with all our complexities and differences.

Refining selection

The second account was an attempt to add complexities I felt were missing from the initial 'write'. A further exploration of feminist poststructuralist literature helped my thinking about how to conceptually organise an account of the project that permitted the field to be mapped in ways that could answer my research questions.

It was clearly impossible to 'track' *all* the intricacies and complexities of the inter- and intra-discursive relationships between each of the practices, discourses and institutions constitutive of each person's work. In deciding what could and should be included in my second account, my desire to address the research questions more directly, to identify the knowledge–power regime(s) and to focus on issues that had been significant to GERG became paramount. Specifically:

- The study's research questions demanded that I selected information about how staffs' gendering knowledge intersected with their gendering praxis, how they approached children's resistances to their gendering interventions and how the academy and the early childhood service influenced their pedagogical choices.
- Feminist poststructuralist literature (Gore, 1993; Weedon, 1997) concerning knowledge–power regime(s) required me to classify the patterns within and between institutions, between practices and between discourses; expose the dynamics between each of these; and identify the subject positions offered within these discourses from which to understand practice within the field. I also needed to survey the field's topography via relationships between practices and positionings within specific discourses; inter- and intra-discursive relationships and inter- and intra-institutional relationships.
- The initial account had focused on moments in which staff's gender equity interventions challenged their pedagogical 'norms'. Several GERG members vividly recalled these moments, saw them as important in their work for gender equity and felt they were important in an account of GERG's work.

Consequently, I looked for patternings between teachers' gendering and pedagogical discourses, institutions and practices. I decided to concentrate on selecting information about the changing discursive and institutional constitution of gender equity practices in block play as the foundation for the remaining phases in mapping the field.

Refining organisation

With block play's possibilities in mind, I revisited the initial account and the written and verbal comments from individual GERG members searching for information about block play and innovations in gendering praxis. I explored several options for organising this information to permit the field to be mapped via it. After much deliberation I settled on eight vignettes about eight GERG members' work, including my own. I developed them by layering interpretations onto the initial account, including the interpretations of other GERG participants and my own feminist poststructuralist interpretations.

The feminist poststructuralist interpretations rely particularly on Weedon (1997), with additional insights gained from Gore's (1993) examination of the knowledge–power regime of feminist and critical pedagogies. Each vignette:

- sketched our discursive contexts on joining GERG;
- traced transformative moments in our gendering praxis;
- explored outcomes of our gendering interventions; and
- traced how the 'discursive dynamics' and changing subjectivities involved our gendering praxis.

Layering these concepts through the vignettes was theoretically pertinent in four ways. First, they provided very specific understandings of transforming gendering via early childhood pedagogies. Second, they provided intricate and contrasting views of the complexities of constructing feminist pedagogies in early childhood education. Third, they offered an opportunity to 'test the value' of a feminist poststructuralist analysis in tracing, understanding and, therefore, in planning and evaluating transformative moments. Fourth, they illuminated the historical and cultural specificity of how feminist and early childhood pedagogies were structured by institutions and practices and how discourses circulated and competed for meaning.

Consequently, the multi-layered interpretations in the vignettes made it possible to track:

- inter-institutional relationships between the academy and the early childhood service via the seven staffs and myself, with GERG as a specific site;
- inter- and intra-discursive relationships between feminist discourses, DAP discourses and feminist pedagogical discourses; and
- relationships between positionings within feminist pedagogical and DAP discourses and gendering praxis.

The vignettes provided positions from which to explore the specific knowledge–power regime(s) that supported/contested feminist pedagogical innovation in the early childhood service and the academy.

The second account: the vignettes

The vignettes were the outcome of the data selection and organisation process I have just described. They used block play as a focal point from which to tell of contrasting moments in people's attempts to construct feminist pedagogies. The vignettes showed the interconnected pathways through which individuals moved in working for their gender equity vision(s). Each vignette illustrated how early childhood and feminist pedagogical discourses were deconstructed and reassembled as the staff worked for their gender equity vision in and via block play. The vignettes also brought into sharp relief the institutional articulation and circulation of these pedagogical discourses.

Each interpretative layer I used embedded feminist poststructuralist concepts through a series of vignettes to enable a feminist evaluation of the knowledge–power relations constitutive of the project. This enabled the study's specific research questions to be answered and provided the basis for my research conclusions.

HOW DID YOUR PARADIGM INFLUENCE YOUR RESULTS?

My feminist poststructuralist research paradigm directly influenced my results in terms of what I felt it was important to research, the questions I developed, the methods I chose to use and how I analysed my data.

A particular example of this influence was evident in how I approached interpreting GERG's work. I decided that I needed to focus on individual people's local practices as a way to build my analysis. I drew on feminist poststructuralist theory in three ways to justify this. First, Foucault's (1978) argument that: 'No "local center", no "pattern of transformation" could function if, through a series of sequences, it did not eventually enter into an over-all [sic] strategy' (p. 99), suggested that local practices would provide a way into the particular features and patterning of the discursive field by illuminating how the gendering of power operates locally at specific moments through the discourses in circulation. The field could be demonstrated empirically by analysis of pedagogical innovations. For instance, the local pedagogical practices that were implicated in the processes of resistance, challenge and transformation could provide diverse and powerful vantage points through which to survey the discursive field's topography. They could lead to the identification of specific curriculum sites, discourses, practices and institutions that are entwined with the feminist possibilities and challenges of pedagogies in early childhood education.

221

Second, a focus on local practices would address a feminist post-structuralist emphasis on privileging women's subjectivities in and through research. By examining how staff and I were involved in the production of meaning and in negotiation in the curriculum, the real and substantial ways in which gendering was constituted through specific staff's pedagogical practices at specific points in time could be acknowledged. Hence, a focus on local practices offered a way of centring women's/staffs' local and specific experiences.

Third, local practices provide a sense of the intricacies of how early childhood pedagogies were embedded in practices and integrated institutionally in ways that work for and against feminist pedagogies. Analysing specific individuals' local actions could highlight how staffs' material work conditions and early childhood services' specific organisational and political contexts are implicated in feminist pedagogical change. It would also indicate how other institutions such as the academy are involved in the governance and contestation of early childhood and feminist pedagogies. Local practices can, therefore, provide an entry point into analysing power, social relations and discourse in their historical and cultural specificity.

Thus, I felt that an analysis of local practices would contribute to mapping the discursive field's features. It would be possible to identify in historically-specific ways how institutions structure the field, which discourses circulate within it and which subject positions are offered within these discourses. This provided an information base from which to explore the knowledge–power regime(s) as constituted in this study and to explore the feminist potential(s) of feminist poststructuralism's focus on local and specific subjectivities as a means of understanding how staffs' gendering knowledge intersects with their pedagogies (see the first two Research Questions).

HOW DID YOUR RESEARCH CONTEXT INFLUENCE YOUR RESULTS?

The focus in my analysis on the local and the specific meant that my research results are inevitably context-specific. However, I have argued that they also show how wider institutional practices and discourses touch and make some ways of understanding and practicing gender equity in early childhood more possible than others (see Mac Naughton, 2000). So, while the context influenced my results, the wider social, intellectual and political contexts of early childhood education also influenced them.

WHERE DOES THIS LEAD YOU?

Researching the possibilities and challenges of practicing gender equity in early childhood classrooms using action research led me to see the value of researching with practitioners. It also leads me to see the potential of researching for change in classrooms. I see that collaborative action research offers a powerful tool for improving our understandings about how to produce change in early childhood settings. It combines theory and practice in ways that can challenge our existing theories and shows us ways in which we can rethink practice.

SUMMARY

Fourth generation action research:

- is collaborative, change-oriented and overtly political research;
- involves a group of people with shared interests in transforming their practices, knowledges and contexts coming together to critically reflect on what enables and constrains change; and
- generates voluminous data so how you organise and select your data is a key part of the research process.

QUESTIONS FOR REFLECTION

- What practical difficulties do you see with using action research in researching early childhood?
- What are some of the limitations of this research?
- How might these limitations be addressed in a further research study?

FURTHER READING

Cherry, N. 1999, *Action Research: A Pathway to Action, Knowledge and Learning*, RMIT Publications, Melbourne. An excellent introduction to the process of action research for beginners.

MacTaggart, R. 1991, *Action Research: A Short Modern History*, Deakin University, Geelong. This book by a leading theorist of participatory action research provides an in-depth and accessible discussion of the history of the theory and practice of action research. It includes an extensive annotated reading list.

15

Direct observation

Sharne A. Rolfe

Observation is something we all do. We are good at it because our survival, and the survival of those we care for, depends on it. Young children are taught observational skills from an early age: crossing roads safely by careful observation of traffic light signals; avoiding injury by watching out for sharp or hot objects; identifying strangers and so on. Careful observation also underpins skilled communication and promotes learning. We model good communication for our children by eye-to-eye contact and careful listening, we point out aspects of the social environment that are important for empathic responding—'See how sad Sam's face is. Why do you think Sam might be sad?'—and we assist children to focus their attention in learning situations.

Most early childhood students learn about techniques of systematic observation because consistent, careful observation is fundamental to good teaching. The techniques learnt for classroom practice—including running and anecdotal records, checklists, rating scales and time and event sampling—are exactly those we apply in observational research. In this chapter we overview these methods only briefly because they are detailed elsewhere (for example, Bentzen, 1993; Beaty, 1994; Sharman, Cross and Vennis, 1995; Pellegrini, 1996; Nicolson and Shipstead, 1998). Our main focus will be the issues that arise when observational techniques are applied in early childhood research. We will consider why a researcher might choose observation, rather than other methods of data collection; what is needed to achieve reliable observational data; and what considerations guide choice of one observational technique over another.

To illustrate the issues, two observational studies I conducted with my colleague Stella Crossley (Rolfe and Crossley, 1991, 1997) will be considered. Both studies explored, in different ways, the play and social behaviour of preschool children and illustrate some of the strengths and challenges of using observation in early childhood research.

WHAT WERE YOUR RESEARCH QUESTIONS?

As topics for research, preschoolers' play and social behaviour are very broad. In Chapter 2, we discussed how broad topics such as these lend themselves to many possible research questions. Since our interest was predominantly in the factors that influence play and social behaviour, this helped us refine our topic. Searching the literature, we settled on two questions to explore:

- What are the effects of prior experience in early childhood settings on play and social behaviour? and
- How does play environment, specifically inside versus outside, affect play and social behaviour?

HOW DID YOU ARRIVE AT THESE RESEARCH QUESTIONS?

Effects of prior group care experience

When the study began, use of centre-based child-care for infants and toddlers in Australia was uncommon but increasing. Children entered preschool with a range of prior group care experiences, including informal parent-run playgroups (see Rolfe and Crossley, 1991, for a description of types of Australian early childhood services). Some had no group care experiences at all. Reflecting the particular concerns of the time, and based on a thorough review of the literature, we decided to include a range of programmes in our sample, rather than focus as other researchers had done only on children who had experienced centre-based care. We wanted to explore how different care experiences found expression in the behaviour of children once they entered the preschool setting.

Effects of play environment—inside versus outside play

Our interest in play environment grew from informal observations of how differently children played in the two environments. We were interested in the potential of the outside environment to facilitate social interactions, and why this might be so. Although the literature on this question was relatively limited at the time, there were still several studies to guide us.

The Introductions in Rolfe and Crossley (1991, 1997) provide brief overviews of the literature drawn on in formulating these specific research questions and in developing appropriate designs to begin to answer them.

Direct observation

All research data are based on observation. That is, if we define observation broadly as one person's perception or measurement of something about someone else, then data from interviews, surveys, questionnaires, and even physiological recordings, are all in some way based on observation. This chapter focuses specifically on direct observation. As the term implies, this involves researchers recording the data of interest directly from their own observations of the research participants, rather than indirectly via physiological measuring instruments (for example, a heart rate monitor), from a questionnaire that the participant or someone else fills in, or via some other objective test. Most direct observation is of behaviour: children's behaviour, parents' behaviour, the behaviour of early childhood staff. What kinds of behaviour are observed depends on the topic area.

Are you interested in researching children's social behaviour, their emotional behaviour or some aspect of their cognitive behaviour?

- An example of social behaviour that could be observed is the nature of peer interactions, such as instances of quarrelling among peers, or prosocial behaviours such as comforting one another.
- An example of emotional behaviour would be how the young child separates from the parent on entry to the child-care service. Does the child cry or cling to the parent? Does the child separate easily and happily engage with staff, children and activities quickly?
- An example of cognitive behaviour is the child's choice of play activities. Does this child prefer puzzles, painting, reading or block play? Can this child sustain attention to a task or is the child easily distracted?
- Some observations span developmental domains. For example, when we observe how a child reacts to story-book reading, we may record behaviours that relate to aspects of all the developmental domains.

Behavioural observations are not always directed to understanding the children or adults being observed. They may be used in research to assess for example, the quality of an early childhood service, curriculum delivery or effectiveness of intervention programmes.

HOW DID YOU ANSWER THEM?

Because our interest was children's behaviour, direct observation seemed ideal. However, there were a number of techniques to consider and choose between before data collection could begin.

A brief overview of different techniques of direct observation

There are several well-tested methods of direct observation. Note that some writers refer to the same techniques by different names. To avoid confusion, focus on what the technique involves (how it is done) rather than the name given to it.

Probably the technique that practitioners use most, because it is the richest account of ongoing behaviour, is the **running record**, otherwise called a specimen record or descriptive narrative. The observer writes down in longhand everything seen as it occurs, for example, what a child does and says, over a specified period of time. **Anecdotal records** are similar, but are usually written after the event and describe a particular incident in a brief and, ideally, objective way. It is tempting to assume that given enough time and minimal distractions, the observer can record everything using these techniques. This is not so and it is important that observers acknowledge this. According to Martin and Bateson (1986): 'It simply is not possible to record everything that happens, because any stream of behaviour could, in principle, be described in an enormous number of ways. The choice of which particular aspects to measure, and the way in which this is done, should reflect explicit questions' (pp. 12–13).

Another technique is the **checklist**. Checklists are simply lists of behaviours of interest to the researcher. The observer looks for and ticks off the behaviours when and if they occur. The form that a checklist takes is only limited by the interest and ingenuity of the observer. It may be simple, with the behaviours listed down in a column on the left-hand side of the page and boxes to the right in rows that can be ticked when the behaviour is observed. Some checklists leave room for more detailed comments about the behaviour—such as when it occurred, what happened before and after it and in what context it occurred. Checklists can also be used to document characteristics of the curriculum or of the early childhood setting itself.

Rating scales are also relatively simple to use to study people, programmes, settings and environments. They may appear indirect, but are included because the rating scale is completed on the basis of earlier or current direct observations. For example, the observer may spend time watching children in a preschool first, perhaps taking some running or anecdotal records, or keeping checklists, then later complete rating scales from these records. However, the phenomenon of interest is only recorded in terms of where it fits along a continuum. For example, we may prescribe a numerical value—such as 1, 2, 3, 4 or 5 on a 5-point scale—according to the frequency or intensity of a behaviour. Usually scale points are given names, such as 'very high' through 'medium' to 'very low'. There are many rating scales available for use by the early childhood researcher, covering a diverse range of topic areas, and it is not necessary to develop your own, although of course you can.

Two further observational techniques are commonly used. These are **event sampling** and **time sampling**. These are useful when we wish to take a sample of the child's or adult's ongoing behaviour rather than observe all that occurs over a period of time. In event sampling, we wait for a particular event to occur and then we record something about it—for example, what happens, who does what, how long the event lasts. What we try to achieve is a sufficient sample of the individual's behaviour to make generalisations. In event sampling we must record every time the behaviour of interest, sometimes called the target behaviour, occurs within the specified observational period. As Nicolson and Shipstead (1998) write:

> Event sampling permits the observer to collect data about the targeted behaviour in a time efficient manner because it concentrates his or her attention on only that behaviour. Although an observer is not able to see every targeted event of interest over an indefinite period of time, a sample of observations over a limited period should serve to represent the behaviour (p. 175).

In time sampling, occurrences of the behaviour(s) of interest are recorded for set time periods. These can be very short (every 5 seconds) or relatively long (each half hour). Time sampling allows us to measure the relative frequency of the behaviour(s) by counting up the number of time samples in which they occurred.

Qualitative or quantitative?

Techniques of direct observation include both qualitative and quantitative measures. Anecdotal and running records are the most obvious form of qualitative data since they involve narrative (word-based) descriptions. Checklists, rating scales and time-sampling yield quantitative data, that is, numbers.

Having considered the various options, we decided to use a combination of techniques. In Rolfe and Crossley (1991) we primarily used time sampling. In the first study, each child was observed for four 3-minute periods during inside and outside free play. The child's behaviour was classified at 15-second intervals, using four of the categories of social participation developed by Parten (1932): 'unoccupied/onlooker', 'solitary', 'parallel' and 'group'. Other observations, including the involvement of the teacher, were also noted at each sampling time. In the second study we varied this method in response to reflections on the data from the first study. We decided to only sample social participation every 4 minutes during inside and outside play sessions. Each child was observed for 20 seconds to provide a context to the observation, and on the twentieth second the child's behaviour was categorised. We decided on a longer time sample interval (from 15 seconds in the first study to 4 minutes in the second study) on the basis of contingency analysis of data from the first study. The details of this statistical technique are beyond the scope of the current discussion and the interested reader should consult the original publication for more details.

In Rolfe and Crossley (1997) we used a very different approach, based on the method of ethologists, discussed in more detail below. Although still directed to the topic of preschoolers' play and social behaviour, and using direct observation, the focus of this study was on the usefulness or otherwise of this approach in studies of this kind.

HOW DID YOU DECIDE HOW TO ANSWER THEM?

We used direct observation because it was best suited to answer our research questions. It also fitted with the skills, knowledge and research paradigms we brought from our respective academic disciplines. When we are interested in understanding or explaining everyday behaviours as they occur, or data of these kinds will help us understand or explain something else (for example, quality of a service, effectiveness of an intervention), then direct observation is worth considering. Similarly, we choose where we conduct our observations—in a naturalistic or more structured setting—depending on the dictates of our research question. If we want to know how children or adults behave in their normal, everyday environments, it makes little sense to bring them into a structured setting like a university laboratory. Sometimes, however, we want to know how children or adults behave under specific circumstances. Waiting for those specific circumstances to occur in the natural environment would be foolish if they occur only rarely. Sometimes setting up a more structured setting can be used in conjunction with behavioural observations in the natural setting. By combining approaches, a more complete picture or understanding can emerge.

Direct observation can be time consuming but the richness of data achieved, and the insights that come from prolonged periods of sustained attention to the behaviours of interest as they occur in the ongoing behavioural stream, more than compensates.

Which of the following topic areas could be researched using direct observation? Which could not? And which would be better researched using other techniques?

- Children's understanding of death and dying
- Children's response to the birth of a sibling
- The accuracy of children's eyewitness testimony
- Mothers' responses to aggressive behaviour in their children
- TV viewing habits of children in the home
- How early childhood staff respond to distress in young children at sleep time
- Infant response to parental violence
- Young children's understanding of gender.

Choosing among different observational techniques for research data collection

Once the decision is made to use direct observation, the choice of observational technique will again be guided by the specific research question. If your research question calls for detailed description of all the behaviours that occur over a time period in a particular setting, then running records will achieve this richness, or something close to it. Running records or anecdotal records may be particularly useful if you are interested in the minutiae of what occurs at a specific time point, for example, when the child first enters the early childhood service, at sleep time, or on departure. Keeping a detailed account of all the behaviours that occur from when the parent and child first enter the room, to when the parent leaves, can provide a wealth of information missing from a score on a rating scale of separation distress. However, a rating scale score might be quite sufficient, and could be potentially less intrusive and time consuming, for certain research questions. If a single numerical score is all your research question requires, there is no justification for more detailed recording.

Achieving high quality observational data

In deciding how to answer our research questions, another central consideration was how we could achieve observational data of high quality. To do this, we had to address some important, fundamental questions about observational research. I began this chapter by saying that all humans are observers; they have to be. But this does not mean that we all just naturally have the skills to collect high quality observational data. High quality observational data comes from reliable observational records. Behaviour must be recorded in such a way that other observers would produce the same recordings if they, rather than you, did the observations. Also, you must be consistent in your recordings over time. In discussing this topic we need to consider the characteristics of the observer and how these may influence the data obtained, and evaluating and reporting reliability.

Characteristics of the observer

Different observers, watching the same child at the same time, can generate different observational records. Nicolson and Shipstead (1998, pp. 12–13) provide an example of this in terms of two 3-minute running records by different observers of a child playing outside in the sand area. The reason for the differences resides very much in the **subjectivity** of observation, particularly if the observer is attempting to write down all that is seen.

As human observers, it is inevitable that our own feelings and interpretations influence what we see or don't see. The behavioural record reflects, to a greater or lesser extent, our 'biases, preconceptions and emotional responses' (Nicolson and Shipstead, 1998, p. 13). In other words, we see the world around us through a lens; what I see and how I interpret it may not be the same as what you see, or how you interpret it. We may notice different behaviours, focus on certain events or interactions more than others or simply 'miss' certain behaviours because we are distracted or interrupted, even for a brief period of time. Two people may generate different records if behaviours are defined in very general terms, such as 'aggressive' or 'sociable'. How do I decide what behaviour is 'aggressive' and would you and I necessarily agree? The less well defined the target behaviours are, the more likely it is that observer bias will influence the data. If we approach our study with specific hypotheses, there is also the danger that we may 'see what we want to see' in order to support them.

Objectivity is increased when the observer avoids 'evaluations, judgements, impressions, and personal speculations' (Nicolson and Shipstead, 1998, p. 13) about what is seen. There are two main ways to increase objectivity—observer training and careful definition of target behaviours.

Training

It is easy to assume that systematic observation for the purpose of research is quite straightforward. Once we begin the task, however, the difficulties usually become more obvious (Martin and Bateson, 1986). Like most things, we get better at observation the more we do it and the more times we have the opportunity to see the behaviours of interest to us. Training helps us to become better observers.

One way to refine your observational skills is to precede data collection by a 'sit and watch' phase in the setting of your research. Those who study non-human behaviour (ethologists) often do this in order to gain a better understanding of the behaviours of interest and also to develop precise definitions of these behaviours (discussed later). We did this in our studies. By immersing ourselves in the context of interest over a period of months, we became more aware of and sensitive to subtle differences in behaviours that initially looked the same. As we watched, key features of similar behaviours became clearer and were more easily identified.

When you must record, and not just watch, the task becomes even more difficult. Trying to record too much, even when you are an experienced observer, can lead to observer overload. There are limits to our perceptual and attentional capacities. This is one reason some observers prefer to use checklists, rating scales or time and event sampling, because they can in all cases specify very precisely a small number of behaviours of interest and focus exclusively on these.

Gaining observational experience using videotaped records of children's behaviour

Another way to gain observational experience is through videotapes. Most university libraries have child development films and videotapes. Most contain segments of children and adults in early childhood settings. You can play these segments over and over, noting down what you see, how often particular behaviours occur (frequency) and/or how long they last (duration). For many behaviours of interest, a stopwatch provies sufficient accuracy for measuring duration. Other timing devices, like chronoscopes, have the ability to measure duration more precisely.

A problem with this type of training is that you are often working alone, and the subjective biases that we discussed earlier may continue unidentified. Using video clips that have already been coded by skilled observers, and comparing your observational record to theirs, is a better way to train. If you are working with other researchers, they may already have training tapes for you to practise on, or other research teams may be willing to lend their practice tapes. There are also commercial products that include video clips precoded using a variety of the techniques discussed in this chapter. One example is the CD produced by early childhood academics at Queensland University of Technology and published by Prentice-Hall, called 'Observing and analysing young children's behaviour, Version 2.1' (1998). The CD allows you to try out all the different techniques, identify differences between your records and those of skilled observers and keep practising on the same video clips until your records match those of the experts.

Reliability

Martin and Bateson (1986) define reliability as 'the extent to which measurement is repeatable and consistent' (p. 86). The problems already discussed with regard to observer subjectivity mean that in observational studies it is very important to establish the reliability of your observations. Most published observational studies will include a report of the reliability of the data, in either the Method or Results section.

The main way in which reliability is assessed is via inter-observer reliability (IOR) measures. This is a measure of the extent to which two (or more) observers obtain the same results when observing the same behaviours at the same time. It is calculated by dividing the total number of observer 'agreements' (when they both recorded the same behaviour) by the number of agreements and disagreements (when the same behaviours were not recorded by the observers) and is usually represented as a percentage. The closer to 100 per cent that the IOR is, the more reliable the observational data. It is also important to establish that any observer is herself reliable, that is, that she would record the same behaviour if observed on separate occasions in the same way. This is referred to as intra-observer reliability.

Examples of the first kind of reliability assessment or rating is found in Rolfe and Crossley (1991). We achieved coefficients of IOR between 61 and 83 per cent in the first study and between 75 and 100 per cent in the second. Intra-observer reliability is described in Rolfe and Crossley (1997). Average split-half reliability was 75 per cent, which is considered adequate in this sort of research. A more technical description of different ways of assessing the reliability of observational data can be found in Martin and Bateson (1986, pp. 90–6).

WHAT SAMPLING ISSUES WERE THERE?

For the purposes of this discussion of direct observation, two major sampling considerations will be considered—sampling of behaviours and selection of observational settings. Of course, like all those who design research studies, we also had to consider sampling issues to do with our selection of participants. Readers interested in this aspect of our studies should consult the original published articles. As in most studies, practical considerations to do with time constraints and minimal research funding limited the scope and extent of our studies, particularly in terms of sample size. How these and other limitations influenced our conclusions is outlined in the Discussion of each article.

Sampling behaviours: precision of behavioural definition

A lot of what we know about objectivity in behavioural observations has come from the work of researchers interested in the behaviour of non-human species, such as ethologists. The work of ethologists first became well known to developmentalists through the publication of the now classic *Ethological Studies of Child Behaviour* (Blurton Jones, 1978), in which the outcomes of research applying some of the principles of animal ethology to the study of human children were presented. The major impact of this approach was its stress on the importance of precise behavioural definition in observational studies. The advantage of so-called molecular units of behaviour, often described in anatomical terms according to the movements involved, compared to more molar categories of behaviour such as 'aggression', or 'jealousy', was their objectivity, accuracy and the ease with which they could be communicated between observers. While there are limits to the practicality of such precise behavioural units, the approach sensitised researchers to the need for objectivity in studies utilising an observational approach.

The main point to remember in observational research is that behaviour is 'a continuous stream of movements and events' (Martin and Bateson, 1986, p. 39). To measure behaviour, these movements and events must be broken down into categories that should preferably be defined in such a way that different observers viewing the same sequence would produce the same behavioural record. How molecular or molar the behaviour categories should be is determined by the research question.

Different behaviour categories for different research questions

Rolfe and Crossley (1991) and Rolfe and Crossley (1997) used very different behaviour categories for data collection, although the general topic area of the two studies (preschoolers' play and social interaction) was the same. The categories used reflected the particular question each study set out to answer.

In Rolfe and Crossley (1991) the focus was on social participation, that is, how much the children engaged in interaction with their peers. This particular aspect of children's social behaviour was extensively studied by Parten and her colleagues in the 1930s (for example, Parten, 1932) and by others since that time (for example, Barnes, 1971). There is a well-established categorisation of social participation from this work using time sampling techniques. Because each child was observed during both inside and outside play, and had been classified according to their earlier group care experience, the research questions could be answered.

Rolfe and Crossley (1997) set out to examine a different aspect of social play and behaviour. Here the focus was on the usefulness of ethological approaches to studying child behaviour, especially when precisely defined molecular units of behaviour are recorded. To do this, a six-month 'sit and watch' phase preceded data collection, in which 200 molecular units were defined from the ongoing behavioural stream. This is sometimes referred to as an ethogram. These units were then used to record observational data over a three-month period. Eight 5-minute records were made for each child—inside and outside—and the ongoing record marked at 5-second intervals. The frequency of each behaviour for each child was the number of 5-second samples in which the behaviour occurred. Because this was very similar to the methods of other child ethologists, it was then possible to compare the data from this study of Australian children to those reported for children in other countries. The strengths and limitations of such a detailed approach to direct observation could also be identified.

Choosing the setting for observations

Observations can occur in many different contexts or environments. Much early childhood observation occurs in what could be called 'naturalistic environments', such as child-care centres, preschools, homes, parks and shopping centres. Direct observation is also an important tool in laboratory-based research. There are many examples in the early childhood literature of this. One well-known example is the Strange Situation method, used predominantly to assess the quality of attachment relationships between children and their parents (Ainsworth et al., 1978; Main and Solomon, 1990). The laboratory-based method presents the child and caregiver (often the parent) with a series of structured experiences, always presented in the same sequence. The child's reaction to separation and reunion with the parent, sometimes in the presence of a friendly stranger, is carefully observed according to a well-defined set of behavioural criteria and used to classify the children as securely or insecurely attached.

Observational contexts thus vary in terms of the amount of control the observer has over the setting. In naturalistic settings, the observer may have little or no control over the characteristics of the setting and what happens in it. In a laboratory setting the observer may have complete control over at least some parts of the setting. For some research questions this sort of control is very important. For example, in assessing attachment relationships it is critical that the child being observed has a series of relationship-related experiences that last for a set time and occur in a fixed sequence. Any deviation from the procedure will mean that the observations may reflect something other than the quality of the child's attachment relationship. For example, in the reunion episode between mother and child, it is most important that the observer does not talk immediately to the mother when she enters the room, because the crucial observation at this stage is how the child responds to the mother. What occurs in the first few seconds is very telling. If the child or the mother is distracted during this time, the child's response is open to a number of different interpretations that may have little to do with quality of attachment.

In our studies we wished to observe children doing the sorts of things and behaving in the ways they do under the normal day-to-day comings and goings of the preschool. Our questions did not require the constraints and controls of a laboratory room. Of course, while preschools and other educational environments impose constraints on children, these settings are nonetheless 'naturalistic' in the sense of business-as-usual, everyday environments over which the observer, at least, exercises no control.

WHAT DID YOU FIND?

The first study in Rolfe and Crossley (1991) found the play of children who had attended sessions at a similar preschool in the preceding year to be significantly more social during inside play than children with no prior experience in an early childhood programme, although there were no other group differences. Play was significantly more social outside. In the second study, the outcomes in regard to prior experience were not supported and no differences emerged between the groups. However, play outside was again found to be significantly more social.

Rolfe and Crossley (1997) recorded 17 505 behavioural acts over sixteen hours of observation. The approach of ethology was found to be both time consuming and labour intensive, and challenged the attentional capabilities of the observer.

HOW DID YOU INTERPRET WHAT YOU FOUND?

In both studies, the results were interpreted with regard to the limitations of the research process and/or design. In the main, these had to do with the small sample size that limited the likelihood of obtaining statistically significant results. In regard to observational methodologies, we discuss (Rolfe and Crossley, 1991) how use of the molar categories of Parten's (1932) social participation scale may have reduced our ability to detect more subtle differences in behaviour. We also discuss (Rolfe and Crossley, 1997) how the ethological method generates more data, and thus potentially more information, than other methods of direct observation. We discuss how data of these kinds can be used to examine quantity and quality of social behaviour, temporal and sequential organisation and dimensions of individual differences. The method is thus ideal at the preliminary hypothesis generating stage or when doing case study research with individual children.

HOW DID YOUR PARADIGM INFLUENCE YOUR RESULTS?

We sought to explain the behaviour of children according to two variables, prior group care experience and play setting. These questions and the use of quantitative methods of data collection arose from the positivistic paradigm we brought to the research endeavour.

HOW DID YOUR RESEARCH CONTEXT INFLUENCE YOUR RESULTS?

Each researcher contributed different disciplinary perspectives—psychology (Rolfe) and ethology (Crossley)—to these studies. Our aim was to collaborate in such a way that our respective skills and knowledge bases were respected and given voice in the research design. This was at times challenging, as new ways of thinking about and collecting data can be uncomfortable or unsettling.

WHAT DOES THIS LEAD YOU TO?

For us, a major insight from the research was the value of using different observational techniques in order to understand better the phenomenon of interest. It also led us to reflect on a number of practical issues that need to be considered in planning observational research. These include:

- To videotape or not? Videotaping can be a useful way to record observational data which can be coded back at the laboratory. The main advantage is that you can replay behaviour sequences again and again. There are computer packages available to assist in recording video-based observations of this kind such as 'The Observer Video-Pro' (Noldus et al., 2000). However, there are time and resourcing implications in using video. Your project will need to purchase the videotapes and may need to acquire a video camera and playback monitor. It takes a lot more time than recording *in situ*. The camera is highly intrusive and a focus of ongoing interest to the children, well past the time when interest in a human observer fades (see below). In the end we avoided videotaping, and used still photographs to illustrate behaviours as needed (Rolfe and Crossley, 1997).

- The effects of the observer on the participants. How participants behave will be influenced by who is present. Observers are rarely invisible, although the use of one-way mirrors in observational rooms can achieve this. After spending an extended time in an early childhood setting, we found the children showed little interest in us, especially as we rarely engaged in interaction with them. Nonetheless, it is well for those conducting observational research to consider carefully how the presence of the observer may influence the results. With adult participants, and even with children, it is possible to discuss this aspect. Participants should be encouraged to comment on how being observed affected them and how it may have changed their usual behaviours. This can be added to your data and discussed at the point where you interpret your results.

- How much observational data is 'enough'? For us, this was determined by practical considerations like how long we had to complete the study and how much time each week we had to collect our data. If you are doing the study by yourself, and with limited funding, you need also to consider the time required to analyse the data. Observational data, especially of a qualitative type, can take a long time to analyse, particularly if the written records need to be transcribed and recoded, perhaps into some quantitative form.

SUMMARY

This chapter has considered direct, systematic observation as applied in a variety of early childhood settings. Drawing on research in the areas of child social behaviour and play, decision-making around choice of observational method (from anecdotal and running records to category coding using time and event samples) as well as observational setting, were considered. Issues to do with the choice of 'unit' of measurement have been discussed, along with the challenge of operationalising categories, sources of observer bias and error and ways of establishing observer reliability. The relative merits of structured, laboratory-based versus naturalistic observations have been considered, with mention of the contribution of other disciplines such as ethology. Using a combination of methods of direct observation may be a useful way forward in many early childhood studies.

QUESTIONS FOR REFLECTION

- Do you think you are a good observer? Why or why not?
- What are the main differences between systematic observation and

the sort of observation we do as a normal part of everyday living?

- Why is subjectivity in observational data a problem and what can we do about it?
- What topic areas or potential questions of interest to you could be researched using direct observation?

FURTHER READING

Nicolson, S. and Shipstead, S.G. 1998, *Through the Looking Glass: Observations in the Early Childhood Classroom*, Merrill, Upper Saddle River, NJ. This book is written for early childhood students and staff who wish to apply observation in their professional setting. It is useful for students of research because of the detail it provides about each observational technique. It includes discussions of the strengths and weaknesses of each technique.

Pellegrini, A.D. 1996, *Observing Children in Their Natural Worlds: A Methodological Primer*, Erlbaum, Hillsdale, NJ. This book considers observation as a research tool, describing in detail issues such as the setting of the observations, reliability and validity, design of observational research, how to use statistics with observational data and different recording media (pen and paper, audio and video recorders, computer event records).

16

Policy research

Ann Farrell

WHAT WAS YOUR RESEARCH QUESTION?

This chapter explores policy research against the backdrop of an international policy study (conducted in 1992–95) researching the impact of incarceration policies for inmate mothers and their young children in Queensland, New South Wales, Victoria and England (Farrell 1998a, 1998b). Referred to here as the Prison Study, the research included inmate mothers and their young children, both those inmates whose children reside with them in custody and those who are separated from their children. Research sites were nine correctional centres for inmate mothers: Brisbane Women's Correctional Centre (CC), Helena Jones CC (Queensland); Mulawa CC, Norma Parker CC (New South Wales); Her Majesty's Prison (HMP) Fairlea, HMP Tarrengower (Victoria); HMP Holloway, HMP Styal, HMP Askham Grange (United Kingdom). Policy documents analysed in the study were used by policy advisers or senior bureaucrats in corrections, and experienced by prison governors or managers and by inmate mothers and their families. As researcher, therefore, I juxtaposed written and spoken policies in prisons with accounts of the lived experience of those who were their inhabitants.

HOW DID YOU ARRIVE AT THIS RESEARCH QUESTION?

My journey towards the research question involved informal conversations with inmate women in Brisbane and a comprehensive research review of the families of inmate women in the context of my ongoing work in social policy. These early tasks uncovered the invisibility of inmate women and their families in corrections policy and research. Fortuitiously for my research, there was mounting evidence within the early stages of the research that the research question was defensible in a conceptual sense and able to be answered in an operational sense.

HOW DID YOU ANSWER IT?

The study employed a qualitative approach using the research methods of policy document analysis, questionnaire, interview and observation for data gathering and generating with policy players, that is, policy formulators, policy implementers, policy users and those influenced by and influencing the policy phenomenon. It was a process of listening to women, hearing their voices and understanding their lives (Smart 1990) or, in the words of Maxine Green (1995, p. 155), 'Old silences have been shattered; long repressed voices are making themselves heard'.

HOW DID YOU DECIDE TO ANSWER IT?

Notions of policy, **policy contexts** and **policy research** provided a scaffold to decision-making in regard to the design and methods of the study. These are discussed in turn.

Policy

The *Macquarie Dictionary* defines policy as a 'definite course of action adopted as expedient' or 'a course or line of action adopted and pursued by a particular body'. Policy, in this chapter, moves beyond the dictionary definition and is construed as a multi-faceted, multidimensional social and political phenomenon which includes a cycle of strategies bound by time, resources, players and performances within dynamic and often contested political sites. Policy in one field, such as family policy in the criminal justice system, interacts with allied fields such as health and social welfare policy.

A substantial body of policy literature indicates that policy is a state activity insofar as the state initiates legislation and monitors policy to ensure government regulation and control of a particular sector or constituency (Dale, 1989; Taylor et al., 1997). This was clearly the case in the Prison Study and was corroborated by the criminological literature indicating that women's prisons have been built by men for men, sometimes with concessions made for women and their young children (Tomasevski, 1993). Senior policy-makers in the Prison Study were almost exclusively male and male-constructed prisons were antithetical in design and function to the needs of inmate women and their children and enacted by criminal laws which perpetuate the dependence of women on more powerful male others (Farrell, 1998a).

In the Prison Study, policy was deployed to detached implementers whose task was to make policy work. This did not always happen, however. One example of deployed policy not being made to work in everyday practice was prison education. While educational opportunities are mandated in Australian corrections, the research found that the prison culture of surveillance mitigated against the implementation of effective education/rehabilitation policies (Farrell, 1998a). The policy implication is that where children are allowed to reside in custody with their mothers, prisons should make adequate child-care provisions for inmates engaged in educational and employment programmes. Where children are not residing in custody, family support and communication should be promoted in the process of rehabilitation and reentry into society.

Policy is concerned also with control. Ball (1990) suggests that educational policy bureaucrats, in the United Kingdom for example, are primarily concerned with matters of systemic control and efficiency. Not only is policy a public enterprise concerned with control, it is often precipitated by a pervasive crisis or a threat of impending catastrophe (Rivlin, 1987; Silver, 1990). Government and its agencies frequently construct policies reactively in the light of social flux. In some cases policy decisions are mandated first and policy makers trawl *post hoc* for research evidence to support the policy decision. An example of *post hoc* research is the case of government opening new prison facilities to meet custodial demand then seeking research evidence to justify existing policy. Marginson (1997) sees such phenomena as policy market forces spawning policy research which, in turn, supports market-driven decisions.

Policy research is a politically generated process that characteristically involves a critical mass of protagonists such as politicians, interest groups and sections of the media. Bowe et al. (1992) see policy as knowledge, practice and discourse within contested sites of text production. In discussing educational policy, for example, they discuss the context of influence where public policy is usually initiated and where interested parties struggle to influence the definition and social purposes of education. The context of policy text production is usually articulated in the language of general public good with appeal to popular commonsense and political reason. This is clearly the case in my current study of bullying in early childhood centres amid mounting early-intervention crime-prevention agendas (Farrell, in press).

Endemic social and political change is considered by Gee, Hull and Lankshear (1996) as a leading motif of what we now experience as 'new times' which shape and circumscribe: 'human lives, human identities and human possibilities . . . in a world fuelled by fiercer competition than ever before and by unprecedented high technology' (p. xii).

As well as the case of the burgeoning prison sector propelled by law and order agendas (Homel, 1999), you may identify with policy changes in higher education in countries such as Australia. Government now purchases rather than patronises virtual borderless universities (Coaldrake and Stedman 1998; Cunningham et al., 1998). This resonates with the work of Australian education policy theorists (for example, Kemmis 1990; Taylor et al., 1997) who contend that, within the context of economic restructuring and new technologies, broad ideological visions are giving way to politically expedient policies.

This view of policy as dynamic, interactive and negotiable debunks the traditional positivist notion of policy as a fixed, finite document or event that is value-neutral and anchored in essential facts. Proponents of the positivist view (for example, Carley, 1980; Nakamura and Smallwood, 1980) supported the notion that policy is a discrete and rational corpus of blueprint instructions from a defined group of policy-makers to policy-implementers. Policy theorists such as Bowe, Ball and Gold (1992) interrogate the notion of policy as a defined document, event or process as linear in form, whether top-down or bottom-up.

> Given the fragmentation of authority . . . the traditional model of decision making is a highly stylised rendition of reality. The goals of policy are often equally diffuse; which opinions are considered and what set of advantages or disadvantages are assessed, may be impossible to tell in the interactive, multi-participant, diffuse process of formulating policy (Weiss, 1982, p. 26).

Rather than being value-free, policy is value-laden and resides within a defined value stance. The sixteen policy documents analysed in the Prison Study reflected the primacy of transmitted values and received wisdom, such as the older theory of infant–mother attachment as the main criterion for allowing children to reside in custody with their mothers. Ball (1990) contends that policy involves an allocation of values that are embedded in their social context. As Kogan (1985) put it: 'Policy and values interact with the moods of circumstances of their periods . . . social artefacts embodying the aspirations about the good life for the individual and the best arrangement for the whole society' (p. 11).

In theorising policy-making in educational contexts, NcNay and Ozga (1985) emphasise the need to canvass the federation of political and bureaucratic interests, sometimes competing, but sometimes mutually supportive. In the case of women's corrections, these include the needs and interests of inmate women and their families as well as those of the criminal justice system and, ultimately, those of the state. In examining social justice policy, American feminist theorist Iris Marion

Young (1990, p. 37) presents a concept of justice primarily concerned with the degree to which a society supports the institutional conditions that facilitate a good life. The Prison Study found that the culture of containment in which inmate mothers and their young children are embedded, however, thwarts the realisation of such institutional conditions.

In the years that ensued since positivism's hold on policy, various theoretical approaches to policy and policy research have emerged. The most noteworthy of these are: (a) feminism(s); and (b) **poststructuralism**. Feminist theory, which scaffolded the Prison Study, has made divergent theoretical forays into qualitative policy research by making visible women's diverse situations, voices and frames which influence their participation in the policy process (Finch, 1986; Gelf and Palley, 1987; Romalis, 1988; Rittenhouse, 1991; Olesen, 1994).

Feminist criminological theory, espoused by British criminologist Carol Smart (1992), for example, proposes that women's prisons have been built by men, on behalf of the state, to regulate the lives of women. Feminist criminological theorists argue that policy implementation in women's prisons is impaired by a culture of retribution and punishment (Smart, 1990). It is punctuated by a complex ritual from arrival at the prison from court, mandatory body searches using a demeaning form of internal examination, dispatch of prison clothing and written information and rehearsal of prison rules by staff. Once installed in prison, inmates' physical movements are observed, telephone calls are taped and visitors (who may be young children and infants) undergo rigorous security checks (Farrell, 1998a). Along with feminism, another major perspective employed in contemporary policy research is poststructuralism.

Poststructuralism has generated cross-disciplinary insight into the relationship between power and knowledge within a discourse of policy as both text and process (Fulcher 1989; Ball 1994; Taylor et al., 1997). Ball (1994) theorises policy as discourse with policy actors as agents in policy-making, and policy texts with multiple interpretations of agency in the policy cycle. Policy as discourse is a way of indicating the significance of power relationships which frames interpretation of policy texts. Policy goes beyond text to embrace social ideologies that imbue text with meaning and includes processes prior to text formation and those that elapse after text production. Whatever research paradigm is used in policy research, it is necessary to locate the policy under investigation within its policy terrain or the context of practice to which policy refers (Bowe et al., 1992).

Policy contexts

Policy researchers situate policy within its social, cultural and historical contexts, and 'when they are so situated, it becomes clear that they are always and everywhere connected to social identities, that is, to different kinds of people' (Gee et al., 1996, p. xiii). Taylor et al. (1997, p. 45) refer to the policy context as 'the antecedents and pressures leading to the gestation of a specific policy'. This may include the raft of economic, social and political factors that lead to an issue's elevation to the policy agenda and the militancies of social alliances that prompt the state or bureaucracy to take up a policy issue.

Policy researchers realise that policy players bring to policy their values, interests and biographies. Furthermore, '[p]ractitioners do not control policy texts as naive readers, they come with histories, with experience, with values and purposes of their own, they have vested interests in the meaning of policy' (Bowe et al., 1992, p. 22).

When we consider policy research in the context of early childhood, we need to appreciate the pervading social constructions of normative childhood that have come to undergird early childhood policy (Van Krieken, 1991). While there may be social and cultural diversity in early childhood, a core ideology existed that sanctioned particular versions of childhood (James, Jencks and Prout, 1998). An unsettling feature of the landscape of childhood is the historical paradox of children as objects of both protection and exploitation (Farrell, 1999). In addition, Boyden's (1997, p. 190) examination of the ideologies of childhood in the light of human rights debates indicates that universal human rights and welfare policy attempts to secure childhood as a 'carefree, safe, secure and happy phase of human existence'. Boyden (1997, p. 224) argues that children inhabit a universe that is 'phenomenologically distinct' from that of adults, given the situated character of children's understandings and the power imbalance between children and adults. To understand the context of policy research, it is necessary, therefore, to consider the social constructions of the phenomenon under investigation and, in the case of children, to understand the social construction of childhood and the complexity of interconnections between children, families and communities (Bowes and Hayes, 1999).

Policy research

A body of research endeavour known now as policy research has emerged relatively recently within the international research community and, like policy itself, is characterised by a plenitude of definitions and a paucity of exemplary research practice. A decade ago, Ball (1990) argued that the field of policy research had been dominated by commentary and criticism rather than by empirical research and had underemphasised methodological questions such as what policy data are used and how researchers collect and analyse data. Rist (1994) notes that policy research has become centrifugal, spinning off multiple conceptual methodologies and frameworks that, in turn, bring different perspectives to what are difficult and complex policy issues.

Reviews of policy research by both Marginson (1993) and Taylor (1997) concur that we need independent, critical policy research that addresses issues of equity and social justice and contests official wisdom. The Prison Study is an example of independent research that interrogated official policy within a social justice discourse.

Overall, policy research is made possible through knowledge utilisation that ranges from perceptions about the policies to analysis of relevant policy documents, formulation of policy problems and implementation of policy decisions. Anderson (1990) argues that policy research is concerned with:

- the policy-making contexts of the social problem;
- the range of definitions and values held about it; and
- the types of policy recommendations to be documented.

Forms of policy research

Marginson (1993) identified two types of policy research:

- research that is controlled by policy-makers, and
- research that is independent of policy-makers.

Thus, within the historical and sociocultural conditions of policy, policy research might focus on policy processes or policy players.

Policy researchers need also to identify the constituents of the policy research. Along with policy-makers, informers, implementers and recipients (Guba, 1984; Chelimsky, 1985; Rist, 1993), a key constituent is the policy researcher herself, referred to by Denzin and Lincoln (1994, p. 12) as the 'biographically situated researcher'. As an early childhood researcher immersed in a wider discourse on childhood, family studies and human rights, I brought to policy research a suite of dispositions to children. The values, interests and biography that I brought to the Prison Study highlight disparate understandings and differential relationships between myself as researcher and policy protagonists in corrections (Anderson and Biddle, 1991; Postlethwaite, 1991).

A rationale for policy research may be not only to show the generality of effects of policy, but also to generate evidence that will convince particular audiences to take action based on research findings (Krathwohl, 1997). There are usually multiple audiences whose interests may be antagonistic: the staff of a specific programme, its clients, other people or programmes affected by it, policy-makers and legislators. Choice of research methods may depend on the research constituents, their receptiveness to a particular genre of research report and resources available to sustain the research. Krathwohl (1997, p. 623) argues that a key skill of a good researcher is 'the allocation of resources to achieve the goals of the study through proper choice of single or multiple methods to build the strongest possible chain of reasoning within budget limitations'.

This chapter does not attempt to canvass every possible research method used in policy research. Rather I explore a range of pertinent methods used effectively in policy research. It may be illuminating here to refer to Denzin and Lincoln's (1994) notion of the research process. In their terms the research process includes a range of:

- Theoretical paradigms and perspectives such as feminism(s) and poststructuralism;
- Research strategies such as ethnography, case study and participant observation;
- Methods of data collection and analysis such as interview, observation, document, textual analysis and artefact analysis; and
- Interpretation and presentation of research findings to research constituents (Denzin and Lincoln, 1994).

While qualitative research approaches are clearly apposite in unravelling the complexities of the policy process, quantitative research approaches are not antithetical to effective policy research (Taylor et al., 1997).

Also, research questions posed by the policy researcher will determine the type and range of data to be collected in policy research. Research questions addressing the impact of policy on both inmate women and their young children, for example, demanded a combination of theoretical perspectives and data collection techniques in order to understand interpretatively the impact of policy on their lives.

If the research question is concerned with policy text, we might confine our study to textual analysis; if we are interested in its implementation and effects, we might include a case study *in situ* of policy in practice.

Research methods

Given that policy is complex and multi-dimensional, it is feasible to use multiple methods in policy research. Policy researchers share methods of other social researchers and are considered in depth elsewhere in this book. In the ethnographic Prison Study, I used an interpretative research paradigm to generate data from policy documents, interviews and observations. The volume and quality of data varied from system to system and reflected, in part, their respective histories of policy review and development. Her Majesty's Prison Service in the UK, for example, operated an entire policy research unit focusing on inmate mothers and their babies and generated research projects and policy documents in a systemic fashion for their Mother and Baby Units (MBU). In contrast, the Queensland system generated little research and scant written policies. The plenitude or paucity of policy documents that may be subjected to analysis speaks of the values espoused in a particular policy or set of policies within the social and political milieu.

Like all research endeavours, getting started in policy research involves effective planning and preparation. It may require access to key policy players such as politicians, bureaucrats and managers. The position of the researchers in relation to research participants is brought into sharp focus by questions of access to key policy players, and the politics of accessing policy documents, of conducting interviews, of acting as participant observer, of gaining security clearance to enter the research site and of travel to and from the site.

WHAT SAMPLING ISSUES WERE THERE?

Within this qualitative, interpretive study I sampled a range of policy players and policy products to ascertain the nature and scope of policy issues that were relevant to inmate women and their families. Sampling was intended to generate meaningful evidence that would inform both the process of data collection and the types of data collected.

Prior to the fieldwork phases in the Prison Study, I obtained (through written correspondence), statistical data on prisoner populations and facilities, written policies (sixteen official policy documents were collated for analysis) and various documents relating to incarcerated mothers and their children. Early communication was essential for securing the support of the respondents, official approval to conduct the research and availability to participate in the research. Rene Saran (1985, p. 221) contends that such correspondence should be 'carefully drafted to inform the respondent about the researcher's background, the nature of the investigation as well as to indicate broadly the areas on which questions would concentrate, tapping the person's special knowledge'.

WHAT DID YOU FIND AND HOW DID YOU INTERPRET IT?

Policy document analysis

It is crucial that policy document analysis is informed by political and social analysis that seeks to uncover some of the processes that generate policy texts. Gee et al. (1996), along with Bowe et al. (1992), note that texts carry with them possibilities, constraints and contradictions and can be read in multiple ways. In their ethnographic policy study, Bowe et al. (1992) argue that texts, structures and agencies of control need to be considered. The policy researcher sets about to examine what lies beneath the policy discourses, values disputes, points of resistance, accommodation, subterfuge and conformity within and between contending discourses. According to Luke et al. (1993), analysis of policy text focuses on the language and linguistic strategies used to position readers. So too, Bowe et al. (1992) distinguish between 'readerly' and 'writerly' texts, the former limiting possible readings, the latter inviting multiple readings. Gee et al. (1996, p. 3) note: 'Texts are parts of lived, talked, enacted value-laden and belief-laden practices . . . we can never extract just the bits concerned with reading and ignore all the bits concerned with talk, action, interaction, attitudes, values, objects, tools and spaces. All the bits—the print bits and the non-print bits—constitute an integral whole.'

In the Prison Study, I analysed policy documents or texts within a theoretical framework of feminist criminology and with concurrent and continuous cross-referencing of insights via memos from the research literature, the views of participants and my insights as researcher. This was so I could examine the match/mismatch between written policy documents and research literature, what policy-makers and administrators said and what was actually occurring in the field. Theorists such as Plummer (1983) and Wadsworth (1991) concur that written documents can illuminate the mismatch between how things are either planned to be, or alleged to be, and how they are or how people want them to be.

This analytic process was clearly interpretive and 'consistent or compatible with the general underlying philosophy of the research' (Powney and Watts 1987, p. 158). In their treatment of qualitative research approaches of the kind employed in the Prison Study, Glaser and Strauss (1967, p. 3) over three decades ago admitted that 'the researcher does not approach reality as a *tabula rasa*. He [sic] must have a perspective that will help him see relevant data and abstract significant categories from his scrutiny of the data.' I used interpretative description as frames for analysing the sixteen policy documents (such as Queensland's *Corrections Regulations 1988* and *Director-General's Rules 3.9*).

The data management strategy used in the Prison Study involved classification and collation of a large volume of qualitative data on computer and in hard text. Data analysis and management involved what Tesch (1989) described as intertwined routine tasks and creative tasks. Routine tasks of organising raw data involved organisation, classification, storage and extraction of textual data, while creative tasks involved decisions as to how raw data would be organised and interpreted and how conclusions about their significance would be derived.

Documents were read and reread and provisional categories of salient themes and emerging issues were identified under negotiated codes in relation to the conduct of prison life for inmate mothers and their children (Hodder, 1994). Coded data could be extracted and provisionally merged in modified forms. Coding as a conceptualising mechanism is defined by Strauss (1988) as cited in May (1993, p. 105) as 'raising questions and giving provisional answers about categories and about their relations. A code is the term for any product of the analysis whether a category or a relation among two or more categories.' As researcher, I became immersed in their content and intimately aware of their overall tenor. This practice reflected Mostyn's (1985, p. 136) notion that the scripts should be read and re-read until the researcher can 'almost hear the voices' or feel that she is 'getting inside' the participants.

Categories were established, expanded, merged, collapsed or expanded as further data gained admission to the set concurrently from analysed policy texts, transcripted audiotaped interviews and observational memos. Hammersley and Atkinson (1983) advocated that these modified texts allow the researcher to re-analyse data for inconsistencies or contradictions. This practice was particularly useful in the analysis of accounts from different categories of participant, such as those tendered by prison governors, officers and inmates. Scripts were retrieved, treated and then re-entered into the computer, allowing me to audit systematically the frequency and nature of occurrence of coded themes and categories across the four prison systems.

Overall, policy document analysis uncovered the gamut of official and unofficial versions of policy, aroused sensitivities to prison policy and foreshadowed thematic issues that might be addressed in interviews and observations. My immersion in document analysis enculturated me in the bureaucratic culture of corrections, how decisions are made, who makes decisions and on whose behalf. Here I interpreted data using theoretical frameworks around text construction and development to understand the dynamics of sanctioned views of reality.

Interviews with key policy players

Another data source used in conjunction with policy document analysis was interview or the audiorecorded conversation with key policy players in order to make visible what had been hitherto invisible. Schratz (1993) urges researchers to listen to the original voices of the actors in order to get beneath the surface of everyday activities and institutional structures of the social reality. In excess of one hundred interviews in the Prison Study generated extensive descriptive data in the informants' own language, enabling me to understand how informants experienced policy.

Overall, interviews gave voice to policy players, particularly to those women inmates whose voices had been silenced by the experience of incarceration. Interviews exposed issues that were seen as relevant to the lived experience of women and their families in ways that previous research had not allowed. Here I interpreted data using feminist criminological frames in order to understand the sanctioned and non-sanctioned views of reality behind bars.

Participant observations

As well as analysing policy documents and interview transcripts, I experienced the research site as **participant observer** or investigator-participant. In this role, I attempted to enter the social world of the actors (Ball, 1988). This involved naturalistic observations in nine prisons of routine and incidental aspects of what Strauss and Corbin (1990) describe as 'performance sites', where events were occurring and where people are acting. My researcher role was akin to that described by Gans (1982) as investigator-participant, as distinct from total participant or total investigator. As ethnographer, I was positioned as 'marginal native' (Freilich, 1977) or 'peripheral member' (Adler and Adler, 1994), working at the edge of life in the prison and avoiding possible role conflict associated with attempting to be both group member and researcher. Here I waited 'to be impressed by recurrent themes that reappear in various contexts' (Burns, 1990, p. 259). I interacted with prison personnel, inmates and their children in such as way as to establish a participatory relationship, albeit within a frame of 'guarded intimacy' (Glesne and Peshkin, 1992). Data consisting of written memos, or condensed on-the-spot records, gave me first-hand accounts of the world of the participants, from entry through highly fortified barriers to prison hospitals where inmates were reeling from the effects of drug withdrawal. Merriam (1988) contended that when combined with document analysis and interview, such records generate a holistic interpretation of the **policy** phenomenon.

Overall, participant observation gave me entrée to the secret world of the prison and allowed me to participate with players in generating data in ways that document analysis and interview alone could not. Here I interpreted data ethnographically in order to compose accurate versions of reality on the inside.

HOW DID YOUR PARADIGM INFLUENCE YOUR RESULTS, HOW DID YOUR RESEARCH CONTEXT INFLUENCE YOUR RESULTS AND WHAT DOES THIS LEAD YOU TO?

The interpretive paradigms on which the Prison Study was based predisposed the research to a rich array of qualitative data and necessitated the use of multiple analytic tools and processes. As such, the research task was laborious, consuming and deeply satisfying. So too, my understanding of the prison system in which the research was conducted predisposed the study to the data generation techniques that were used. Modes of entry and access to research sites and players were prescribed by the system in ways peculiar to corrections, as were the protocols for conducting research of this kind. A grasp of these predispositions has been useful in the framing of subsequent research and has sensitised me, as a researcher, to the dynamics of prison practice.

Given the multi-dimensional nature of the policy phenomenon, policy research utilises a range of methods to make visible what may be invisible or hidden. Such an approach to policy and policy research may well resonate with the view of policy espoused by John Dewey (1958)—that we can work educatively towards the development of democratic communities in which people can feel free and capable of participation.

SUMMARY

This chapter examines policy research in early childhood with particular emphasis on the methods of policy document analysis and of ethnography to explore the social conditions of policy construction. It shows that:

- Policy is value-laden and context-specific.
- Policy and policy research are value-laden, state activities that regain or maintain social control and regulation in politicised performance sites.
- Policy research requires a combination of theoretical perspectives and research methodologies to better understand in an interpretative way the social phenomenon under investigation.
- The policy-making process involves federations of interest, key players and their espoused values and allocation of resources.
- Policy documents can provide written historical and contextual dimensions to the research record and they can be juxtaposed with other data sources (such as interview and observation) to identify discrepancies between how things are envisaged and how they are experienced.

QUESTIONS FOR REFLECTION

- Identify a specific early childhood policy or set of policies. What historical and contextual factors have led to its development?

- Who are the policy players? What relationship do they have to each other? Who stands to benefit from the policy and who stands to lose?
- What values underlie the policy? Whose opinions are being voiced and in what form? Whose opinions are under-represented or silent?
- How will you as researcher gain access to the policy research sites? What impediments will you encounter and how will you overcome them?

FURTHER READING

Ozga, J. 1999, *Policy Research in Educational Settings*, Open University Press, Buckingham. This book provides practical resources for people interested in doing policy research and deals with some of the problems in doing policy research in education.

17

Developing reciprocity in a multi-method small-scale research study

Mindy Blaise Ochsner

WHAT WERE YOUR RESEARCH QUESTIONS?

This chapter provides readers with a brief overview of how **reciprocity** was developed through the multiple research methods I used to collect data for a small-scale qualitative study. Using a **single case study design**, I conducted a qualitative and feminist poststructuralist study that examined the social construction of gender in an urban preschool classroom.

Single case study design

- A comprehensive research strategy aimed at explaining, describing, illustrating and/or exploring contemporary phenomenon within a real-life context of a single individual, group, event, institution or culture.
- Case studies rely on multiple sources of evidence, such as documents, artefacts, interviews and observations.
- Data collection is usually a direct and personal process.
- A limitation of this research design includes the inability to make generalisations across settings.

The site of this study took place in a preschool classroom of a small, progressive, public elementary school, located in New York City. Two research questions guided my investigation:

- How do discourses of heterosexuality operate in a preschool classroom?
- How do preschool students use their dominant meanings and understandings of heterosexual discourses to regulate the gendered social order of the classroom?

HOW DID YOU ARRIVE AT THEM?

My interest in feminisms influenced the theoretical framework, research design, methods and research questions in my study. The feminist scholarship of Judith Butler (1990), Monique Wittig (1992) and Adrienne Rich (1980) sparked my initial interest in exploring how students used their understandings of gender norms and ideals to discursively constitute themselves through the 'heterosexual matrix', a term created by Judith Butler (1990).

Butler used the heterosexual matrix to help 'designate that grid of cultural intelligibility through which bodies, genders, and desires are naturalized' (p. 151) and how they appeared 'normal'. In order to conceptualise the relational and oppressive nature of heterosexuality and how it constructs femininities and masculinities, I also drew from Monique Wittig's (1992) notion of the 'heterosexual contract' and Adrienne Rich's (1980) ideas of 'compulsory heterosexuality'. These perspectives view heterosexuality as a man-made political institution and a form of sexism. They include the idea that every society has an ideal form of femininity and masculinity constructed through the heterosexual matrix.

With a vague understanding of what these 'theoretically dense' concepts (the heterosexual matrix and compulsory heterosexuality) actually meant or looked like in a classroom, I spent approximately four months conducting a pilot study. During this time, I acted as a participant observer in a preschool classroom, refining my research questions, methods and the overall design of my study. I observed and documented students' talk and actions through fieldnotes, audio-tapings, and videorecordings. I also collected students' drawings and writings. Revisiting feminist theories and ideas enabled me to continuously inform my understandings about gender discourses. At the same time, I was developing a collaborative relationship with the classroom teacher, Isabel.

Participant observation

- Participant observation is a data collection strategy in which the researcher takes part in the activities of the individuals being studied.
- As a participant observer, the researcher has the opportunity to actively gain access to information from the 'inside' rather than passively from the 'outside'.
- The actions of the investigator range along a continuum from complete observer to complete participator.
- The role of a participant observer will fluctuate and change throughout the research process. For example, in the preschool classroom, a researcher might sit with children in the circle for morning meeting, quietly observing and taking fieldnotes. A few moments later, the researcher might be playing and talking with a small group of children at the sand table while audiotaping their conversation.
- While taking on the role of a complete participator, the researcher has opportunities to intervene with students and/or manipulate classroom events.
- Weaknesses of this strategy relate to the personal involvement of the researcher, permitting both bias and distortion to the data collected and the research process.

Slowly, I began noticing and locating the local gender discourses and practices in the classroom. Subsequently, the gendering process began to reveal how femininity and masculinity were socially constructed through the heterosexual matrix and how discourses of heterosexuality regulated the gendered social order of the classroom. I was able to arrive at my research questions by spending time in the classroom, revisiting writings about feminisms and discussing gender events with Isabel.

HOW DID YOU ANSWER THEM?

I attempted to answer my research questions by employing a variety of research methods and a qualitative approach to data collection. I continued my role as a participant observer in the classroom for an additional six months. My relationship with Isabel deepened and together we began uncovering how the practices and discourses of heterosexuality operated within the context of the classroom.

According to Lather (1991), reciprocity is one way of creating a research design that is empowering to both the researcher and researched, as well as encouraging consciousness-raising and transformation. Reciprocity occurred in varying degrees and forms within my study. Although I was the main author and creator of my inquiry, an overarching goal was my attempt to restructure the often oppressive and inequitable relationships that exist between the researcher and the researched in many research projects (Lather, 1991; Burman, 1992; Alldred, 1998;). Instead of a unidirectional process where the researcher goes into the classroom extracting information and data from the research subjects, the methods of my study aimed to encourage a more dialogical process or relationship to occur between those I was researching with and myself. As a result, meanings about gender were negotiated with Isabel and the students through question posing, data collection, and analysis (Wilkinson, 1986; Lather, 1991; Gitlin and Russell, 1994).

Reciprocity with the researched was built into the design in three ways. First, informal, reflective teacher interviews included Isabel helping to decide such issues as the best data collection methods to use, the identification of certain students to observe and interview, and the identification of classroom events worth investigating further. These reflective, ongoing conversations were originally planned to occur through scheduled monthly meetings. However, I believe that they are more accurately described as informal, ongoing and continuous 'research talks'. Every time that I entered the classroom, research talks transpired with Isabel.

Our research talks occurred daily and in various ways. Sometimes they happened while we were walking up three flights of stairs escorting the class to art or music, when students were playing at learning centres during choice time, or while having lunch. Although most of our talks were short and quite informal, the information we exchanged was vital and important. These research talks influenced the entire research process and project. Since gender events and issues happen daily in the classroom, it was more practical and necessary to talk about them with Isabel as they transpired, rather than waiting to talk about them once every month. Although reflective meetings took place once a month, our research talks made the research process more meaningful and attentive to the daily interactions and happenings in classroom life. These talks strengthened our collaborative relationship and helped to maintain reciprocity throughout the duration of the research project.

A second way that reciprocity was incorporated into the research design was through monthly, scheduled reflective interviews with selected students, and having a small group of students analyse episodes of video data. Again, the immediate and continuous developments of gender events and issues emerging in the classroom encouraged informal talks with students on a daily basis. Reflective interviews or talks with students transpired as a result of data being collected and reflected upon with Isabel during our research talks. Each month a few students viewed and analysed video data. Students asked to participate in data analysis of videotaped episodes selected by Isabel and me were part of the episodes being viewed.

A third way that I included reciprocity in the design of this study was by sharing data with the entire class. Participating in classroom routines, such as show-and-tell or work-share, did this. After centre time, a part of the day when children chose from ten learning centres to play in, there was usually a work-share period, which included the teacher selecting a few students to share the work they did during centre time. Sometimes work-share would include students sharing block constructions or easel paintings, at other times a group of students would be asked to report to the class about what they played at dramatic play or discovered at the science centre. By actively taking part in these classroom routines, I had the opportunity to share my research and initial findings with the class, as well as obtaining and documenting students' analysis and interpretations. Although I originally proposed to participate in show-and-tell once a month, data was shared with the class in a variety of ways. Again, because of research talks, Isabel would often raise research and gender issues with the class as a large group.

Though several of these informal conversations, research talks and data sharing sessions were audiotaped and transcribed, most of my quick research talks with Isabel and conversations with students were immediately documented into my fieldnotes or a researcher journal. The purpose of this journal was twofold. Not only was my journal utilised as a way to document reflective and analytic notes after participant observations in the classroom, but I also used it to reflect on the process of negotiating meanings with the students and Isabel. Finally, although the research methods employed were qualitative in nature, my deliberate attempts to develop reciprocity between Isabel, the students and myself had a strong feminist intent.

HOW DID YOU DECIDE HOW TO ANSWER THE QUESTIONS?

Reciprocity influenced who, what, where, when and how I looked at classroom events and therefore how I answered my research questions. For example, Isabel collected and saved students' self-portraits done during art class, with the intention of sharing them with me because of their gendered themes. After looking through students' self-portraits with Isabel during lunch, we talked about them and raised several questions together. For instance, we noticed how Valerie's long hair literally went off the page, and how an Asian-American girl named Kim made a collage of herself with blonde hair, huge red lips and blue eyes. Isabel suggested that I interview these two students about their self-portraits. Later that morning during choice time, I sat out in the hall with Valerie and Kim talking about their self-portraits. In the afternoon during work-share, Isabel deliberately chose to highlight the research that the three of us were engaged in during choice time. Subsequently, Valerie, Kim and I shared with the class our conversations in the hall, disclosing the importance of looking and being beautiful (Ochsner, 1999). Isabel's suggestions and actions influenced several of my research decisions.

WHAT SAMPLING ISSUES WERE THERE?

The most obvious sampling issue, and a limitation of my study, involved the uneven ratio of girls (18) to boys (8). Although case study research is not sampling research, I was sensitive to the contextual features of the gender make-up of the class and was aware of the possible effects it might have on the research process. When looking for a classroom to conduct my study, I was more interested in finding a teacher who did not mind having a researcher in her classroom for the entire school year, rather than worrying about equal numbers of girls and boys. It was the potential for developing a collaborative relationship with Isabel that I valued, not the students' gender.

WHAT DID YOU FIND?

I found that students in this classroom were practising a range of femininities and masculinities. Six gendered themes, including wearing femininity, body movements, make-up, beauty, fashion talk and the public/private spheres were located in the classroom. Analysing how students were talking about and performing gender in the classroom enabled me to then construct three case studies of two girls and one boy. Through these case studies, I highlight how each student maintained and resisted heterosexual gender norms.

HOW DID YOU INTERPRET WHAT YOU FOUND?

I used **critical discourse analysis** to interpret how broader forms of gender discourse and power were manifested in every day texts (Hicks, 1995; Luke, 1995; Gavey, 1997; Mac Naughton, 1998). The particular form of critical discourse analysis that I employed was influenced by feminist poststructuralist ideas, stressing the thoroughly discursive and textual nature of gendered life (Gill, 1995). Since discourse analysis views discourse as constructive and as a social practice, I began by first identifying critical gender incidents and then analysing them as discourses of heterosexuality available to and used by the students.

From a feminist poststructuralist viewpoint, identifying these discourses is vital in understanding how the power–knowledge regimes of heterosexuality provide students with subject positions, constituting their subjectivities and reproducing or challenging the existing gendered social order (Holloway, 1984; Walkerdine, 1986).

Feminist poststructuralism informed the critical discourse analysis in four ways. First, close attention was given to the social context of language and its relations to structures of power, such as heterosexuality. Second, all social texts were approached in their own right and viewed as an action-oriented medium, rather than a transparent information channel. Third, analysis involved a careful reading of texts, with awareness of discursive patterns of meanings, contradictions and inconsistencies. Feminist poststructuralist critical discourse analysis is an approach that identifies how people use language and action to constitute their own and others' subjectivities. These processes are related to the regulation of the gendered social order. Fourth, my critical discourse analysis proceeded with the assumption that these processes are neither static nor fixed, but rather unstable, fragmented and inconsistent (Gavey, 1997).

HOW DID YOUR PARADIGM INFLUENCE YOUR RESULTS?

Since feminist poststructuralism influenced my research questions, design, methods and analysis, it undoubtedly affected my results. An example of how feminist poststructuralism shaped my three case studies begins with the ways in which I noticed gender events in the classroom. Instead of concentrating on gender differences of girls and boys, I attended to the relationships between students, documenting their talk and actions. When analysing data, I specifically coded relationships between students, using concepts such as gender relations and power relations. For this study, power relations were understood as being relational, fluid, shifting and changing. Instead of only including relationships existing between boys and girls, I also attended to other gender relations, such as interactions among groups of boys or between two girls. Focusing on a range of gender relationships allowed me to locate six gender discourses and uncover the heterosexual matrix. Additionally, three case studies of two girls and one boy were constructed, highlighting their gendered relationships within the heterosexual matrix.

HOW DID YOUR RESEARCH CONTEXT INFLUENCE YOUR RESULTS?

A teacher for over twenty years, Isabel was involved in the American women's movement of the late 1960s; she believes that good teaching requires a proactive and political stance on the part of the teacher. Isabel's background in feminism and her beliefs about teaching influenced the curriculum, her interests in gender and my study. Subsequently, both gender and my research became a part of classroom life and were purposefully discussed with students. Not only did the context of the classroom influence my study, but my research also informed the curriculum.

WHAT DOES THIS LEAD YOU TO?

Current feminist analyses of traditional research methods have analysed and reconceptualised the relationship between feminist researchers and those they collaborate with in research (Roberts, 1981; Nielson, 1990; Stanley and Wise, 1993; Ribbens and Edwards, 1998). Roman and Apple (1990) assert that feminist research must move beyond arguing the validity of women's subjectivities towards recognising the transformative potential of critical inquiries. They claim that recognising power relationships between the researcher and researched (students and teacher) is essential to understanding how social understandings are constituted in and through the research process. Therefore, to do feminist research means not just taking a female's perspective or documenting the experiences of girls in classrooms, but also includes engaging in the research process to provide understandings that enable women and girls to transform their own world and become conscious of oppression. In other words, theory, praxis and method become inseparable from each other within feminist research and my study (Fay, 1987; Nielson, 1990).

By conducting this multi-method small scale research study, I have come to realise that there is no single feminist, poststructural or feminist poststructuralist 'method' of doing research. Rather, as a methodology, feminist poststructuralism draws from a variety of **post-positivist paradigms** of inquiry, each offering a different approach to generating and legitimating knowledge, but each focusing on the constructed rather than found worlds of knowledge. As a feminist poststructuralist research design, my study placed the social construction of gender at the center of its inquiry (Lather, 1992). As praxis-oriented work or an act of consciousness-raising, this study was purposefully designed to turn critical thought into social action. That is, multiple methods, including reciprocity, were developed with the intent of influencing Isabel's classroom practices, students' understandings about gender and my practices as a researcher, thereby opening up the possibility of transforming the current gendered social order (Cook and Fonow, 1990; Nielson, 1990; Lather, 1991; Fine, 1994).

261

SUMMARY

Feminist poststructuralism informed the research design and methods created in a qualitative and multi-method small-scale study of gender in a preschool classroom. As a participant observer in the classroom I observed and documented children's play and talk through fieldnotes, audiotapings and videorecordings and collecting student artefacts. Because of my commitment to enacting a research project that was empowering to all those involved, I built reciprocity into the research design using three processes:

- Informal, reflective teacher interviews and informal, ongoing and continuous 'research talks';
- Monthly, scheduled reflective interviews with selected students, and having a small group of students analyse episodes of video data; and
- Data sharing with the entire class.

The multiple methods employed in this qualitative study allowed the teacher and me to uncover the practices and discourses of heterosexuality and how they operated within the context of the preschool classroom, encouraging us to rethink gender and gender equity strategies in our lives as women teachers and researchers.

QUESTIONS FOR REFLECTION

- How do a researcher's values and beliefs influence the research process?
- Can researchers and the research process really be objective?
- In what ways does a researcher's gender influence the research process?
- How would you develop reciprocity into your research design?

FURTHER READING

Boldt, G. M. 1996, 'Sexist and heterosexist responses to gender bending in an elementary classroom', *Curriculum Inquiry*, vol. 26, no. 2, pp. 113–31. This study documents third-grade students' responses to gender performances in the classroom. Queer theory is used to inform analysis and understand how incidents in the early childhood classroom were forms of heterosexism. This study sheds light onto the complicated and often abstract ideas of gender being socially constructed and performed through sexist and heterosexist power matrices.

Lather, P. 1991, *Getting Smart: Feminist Research and Pedagogy with/in the Postmodern*, Routledge, New York. This book explores the ways in which feminist research designs and methods can potentially be an empowering approach to generating knowledge. Not only are new theories of pedagogy presented, but how this theory is enacted, taught and learned is also presented. Research as praxis and the role of reciprocity and reflexivity within feminist research are discussed.

Appendix

Getting the terms right

The language used in the research literature can sometimes be confusing for the novice researcher. Discussions can feature uncommon, specialist terms, such as 'methodology' and 'paradigm', which are used commonly by academics but might be new to practitioners. Sometimes researchers use terms such as 'method' and 'technique' that are common in everyday language but give them specialist meanings. To add to the confusion, different researchers sometimes use the same term to mean different things. For example, one researcher may use 'paradigm' to refer to what another researcher may call a 'theory' and another may call a 'frame'.

The table sets out how some key terms in the research literature have been used in this book. It lists these key terms roughly in the order in which a researcher would use them when discussing the research process or planning a research project. Thus, the researcher's first task is to choose the paradigm within which to work; their choice effectively shapes the sort of theory they set out to investigate and methodology through which to do so. From that base, the researcher then designs the project, specifying its approach, the methods to be used and the techniques of using them. Finally, a researcher will describe how the data will be analysed, reflecting the project's paradigm, methodology and approach.

Term	Definition in this book	Examples	Chapters that feature this term
Paradigm (also known as frame or—erroneously—as theoretical framework)	A way to 'see' the world and organise it into a coherent whole. Each paradigm has three elements: • a belief about the nature of knowledge—what it means to say that we know something; • a methodology—what to investigate, how to investigate it, what to measure or assess and how to do so; • criteria of validity—how to judge someone's claim to know something. Any research project always happens within a particular paradigm that will be more or less overtly acknowledged by the researcher.	Positivism Interpretivism Structuralism Poststructuralism	Chapter 3 Chapter 13
Theory (also known as theoretical perspective or theoretical framework)	An abstract explanation of something (e.g. an event, a behaviour a relationship) that can be either proved or disproved.	Feminist theories seek to explain relations within and between genders. Developmental psychology theories seek to explain how children's skills, understandings and cognitions change over time.	Chapter 3

Term	Definition in this book	Examples	Chapters that feature this term
Methodology (also known as methodological approach)	The rules governing how to produce knowledge within a specific paradigm. The rules concern what to investigate, how to investigate it, what to measure or assess and how to do so. More complex than 'method' and, therefore, not synonymous with 'method'.	Induction Deduction	Chapter 2 Chapter 3 Chapter 13
Design (also known as plan)	A statement of how a research project will be conducted. It specifies what will be researched, how, when and where the research will occur, the participants, what data will be collected and how they will be analysed.	Experimental, quasi-experimental or non-experimental Retrospective or prospective Longitudinal or cross-sectional	Chapter 6 Chapter 7 Chapter 8 Chapter 9 Chapter 10 Chapter 13
Approach	The type or form of knowledge produced and how it is collected, presented, analysed and interpreted.	Qualitative Quantitative	Chapter 3 Chapter 6 Chapter 7 Chapter 8

Term	Definition in this book	Examples	Chapters that feature this term
Method	A way to investigate, examine or otherwise collect information about something (e.g. an event or behaviour).	Interviews Observations Surveys Experiments Database searches	Each case study chapter uses a particular method
Technique (also known as tool or procedure)	The practicalities of a method.	Interviews: open questions, closed questions, internal cross-checking, funnelling. Observations: running records, anecdotal records, checklists, time sampling, event sampling, rating scales.	Each case study chapter discusses the techniques of its featured method.

Glossary

Analytic memos   Written records of interpretations of the evidence collected, usually one or two pages in length. They should be written regularly, and used as signposts to indicate the developing analysis of the evidence. They contain notes on how to interpret evidence using the theoretical frameworks of the study, new questions that arise, cross-references to evidence already gathered, reminders about the focus to be taken in future data collection.

Bias   Occurs when researchers make prejudiced judgements about any aspect of the research process.

Causation   The principle behind cause and effect relationships. Causation is established when there is a sufficient degree of association between the cause (the independent variable) and the effect (the dependent variable), when the cause is shown to precede the effect, and when there can be no other reasonable cause to explain the outcome.

Closed-ended questions   Questions that ask the respondent to choose between responses determined by the interviewer. For instance, "Did you feel happy or sad when that happened?"

Cluster random sampling   Random selection of groups rather than individuals.

Content analysis   A method of data analysis used by qualitative researchers who want to explore and label patterns of behaviour or text. Researchers decide on a unit of analysis such as a behaviour, a grouping of words or a broad stream of conversation, and the descriptors that might be applied to each unit of analysis. The descriptors (labels) may be derived from previous research or a specific theoretical framework.

Control group   A group that does not receive the independent variable (or treatment) in an experiment, but is treated 'as usual'.

Critical discourse analysis A research strategy for understanding how discourse and power are manifested in everyday texts.

Critical reflection A process of questioning our understandings and practices that empowers those practising it and produces social criticism of the status quo.

Cross-sectional designs Comparison of different age groups at a single time.

Cultural inventions Artefacts, technologies, knowledge and concepts that are created by a particular group of people.

Debriefing session A session in which a researcher tells participants about the research aims and objectives, any working hypotheses, the researcher's interest in the areas and answers any questions the participants might have.

Deductive research methodology The researcher develops clear statements about the expected outcomes of the study (hypotheses), based on theory and prior research, and designs the research study to test these hypotheses in a controlled and systematic way. Data are generally not analysed until data collection is complete.

Deficit model Comparisons (often implicit) of groups of people with white middle-class norms and identification of those groups as deficient.

Degrees of freedom (df) A value that represents the extent to which data are 'restrained' by the analysis and/or the total number of subjects. Calculated in different ways, depending on the method of analysis being used, the principle is to calculate df as $N-1$, where N represents the number of subjects or the number of groups.

Dependent relationship A relationship between researcher and subject where the researcher has some power over, or can supply some benefit to, the subject, e.g. teacher/student, parent/child, professional/client and manager of child-care centre/parent.

Dependent variable A characteristic of subjects that is measured to determine the effect on them of the variable manipulated by the experimenter (the independent variable).

Direct observation Involves the researcher recording the data of interest directly from her own observations rather than indirectly (e.g. via questionnaire or other objective test). Most direct observation is of behaviour: children's, parents', or that of early childhood staff.

Discourses The emotional, social and institutional frameworks through which we make sense of our desires, practices and understandings.

Epistemology Any philosophical theory of knowledge that provides an account of what counts as legitimate knowledge.

Equity Used in a sense of justice and fairness, and therefore often requires moving beyond making things equal.

Essentialism Belief in possession of intrinsic or characteristic properties that constitute the true nature of something.

Ethics In research, refers to a consideration of the effects of the research on the rights and well-being of all those who may be affected by the research.

Ethograms Inventories of observed behaviours (defined in terms of the anatomical movements involved) for particular groups in particular contexts; originally developed by ethologists to study the behaviour of non-human species in natural environments.

Eurocentric Research based on the 'use of the White middle class (male) as the standard and its adherence to the comparative approach in conducting research' (Padilla and Lindholm, 1995, p. 110). (*See also* Deficit model).

Experiment Data collection under conditions that control as many relevant variables as possible, while manipulating a treatment variable (the independent variable) and measuring its effect or outcome (the dependent variable). Experiments involve random assignment to groups.

External validity The extent to which the results of a study can be generalised to the wider population. It requires attention to sample representativeness, replication of test conditions, replication of results, sample sensitisation to the research procedures, and bias in the sample or the research process.

Feminism(s) A range of theories critiquing patriarchal structures and highlighting the inability of existing social texts to represent lived experience.

Feminist criminological theory Theorises how the lives of women are regulated by men on behalf of the state and seeks to make visible their experience.

Feminist poststructuralist theory Theorises the mechanisms of power and how meaning and power are organised, enacted and opposed in society, and places the social construction of gender at the centre of its inquiry.

Fourth generation action research Collaborative research that aims for empowerment of those involved by using critical reflection to drive the research process. The research process involves observing, planning, doing and reflecting (the action research cycle) in a deliberate and ongoing way.

Generalisability The extent to which results from a research study apply to and/or can explain the phenomenon in general, for the population as a whole, and under real world conditions.

Grand narratives 'Big pictures' about humanity's 'progress' on its 'journey'.

Heterogeneity When people/groups are characterised by diversity, as containing variety and difference.

Homogeneity When aspects or characteristics of people/groups are the same, or are seen to be the same.

Hypotheses Predictive statements containing a possible explanation of some phenomenon and its likely causation.

Illumination Research as illumination; allows researchers and practitioners to interpret and respond to aspects of the field with gazes informed by the insights of previous research.

Independent variable Something that is manipulated by the experimenter to determine its effect on the subjects. Subjects are grouped according to the level of the independent variable that they receive/experience.

Inductive research methodology The researcher does not commence the study with clear expectations of what will be found and avoids fixed preconceptions and hypotheses. Data are analysed 'as they come in' and are used to generate a range of ideas, understandings, meanings and/or relationships.

Internal validity Refers to the extent to which an assessment tool correctly represents a phenomenon of interest, that is, how well the construct is defined by the measure. Internal validity requires attention to the content of a measure.

Interpretivist A belief that we continually create and re-create our social world as a dynamic system of meanings by continually negotiating with others the meanings of our actions and circumstances and theirs, and the meanings of social and cultural institutions and products.

Knowledge–power regimes Institutionally articulated systems of meaning (knowledge) that regulate what we think are the normal, right and desirable ways to think, feel and act in a particular situation and that enable particular groups of people to exercise power in ways that benefit them.

Lifestory Data usually collected through a series of several in depth interviews which encourage detailed recall of previous and current events, and current interpretations of these events, and how these identities shape the beliefs and behaviours of the person whose lifestory is being described.

Longitudinal research A design that allows investigation of naturally occurring changes on repeated occasions over a substantial period of time.

Mandated Required by law to fulfil particular requirements.

Mirroring or reflective probe A follow up question that reflects the participant's testimony back to them; used by an interviewer to clarify or verify participant testimony.

Non-judgemental questions and responses Interviewer questions and responses that do not, either in tone or content, seek to estimate or decide the merits of things.

Non-parametric (statistics) Used when the assumption of normal distribution cannot be met. In most cases, this occurs when variables are not quantified but are based on nominal or ordinal groupings.

Objectivity In observational research refers to the extent to which observer bias is minimised, mainly through observer training and careful definition of behaviour categories.

Open-ended questions Interviewer questions that have no predetermined responses and seek to avoid directing the participant to answer in a particular way. For instance, 'How did you feel when that happened?'

Operational definition A specification of a construct or variable in measurable terms that gives meaning to a variable by identifying how it is to be measured.

Paradigm A way to 'see' the world and organise it into a coherent framework. Each paradigm is a specific collection of beliefs about what constitutes knowledge and about our relationships with it, together with practices based upon those beliefs.

Parametric (statistics) Used when variables are measured as a quantity, that is, as a parameter. Measures must be based on interval scales. Parametric tests assume that the sample scores are normally distributed, that is, are symmetrical about the mean.

Participant observer Data collection strategy in which the researcher takes part in the activities of the individuals being studied. As a participant observer, the researcher has the opportunity to actively gain access to information from the 'inside' rather than passively from the 'outside'.

Policy Multi-dimensional, value-laden, social and political phenomena comprising policy texts and processes.

Policy contexts The situation of policy players in complex and often contested social, cultural and historical sites.

Policy research The process of understanding policy-making contexts, policy players, policy texts, policy processes and policy outcomes.

Positivists Researchers who try to explain and predict their surroundings in terms of cause-and-effect relationships between apparently random events and appearances and an underlying order of universal laws.

Postmodernism Theories used by researchers who 'see' human societies as fundamentally incoherent and discontinuous, rather than regarding each society as at a particular stage of 'development' or 'progress'.

Postpositivist paradigms Assume that only partially objective accounts of the world can be produced.

Poststructuralism Refers to a set of theories that assume language, meaning and subjectivity are never fixed and therefore can never be fully revealed or understood by the research process.

Poststructuralists Researchers who 'see' the individual and her/his circumstances as fundamentally incoherent and discontinuous and try to explain this constant instability without attempting to 'capture' or stabilise it.

Praxis Practice informed by theory and vice versa.

Qualitative approaches Involve collection of data that are non-numerical in form, usually text-based. These methods are favoured (but not necessarily used exclusively) by researchers following an inductive research process that seeks understanding rather than explanation and encourages diversity and complexity in the data rather than experimental control.

Quantitative approaches Involve collection of data that are numerical in form. These methods are favoured (but not necessarily used exclusively) by researchers following a deductive research process based on careful experimental design and control to determine and/or explain relationships between independent and dependent (outcome) variables.

Random sample A sample selected in a manner that ensures that every member of a population has an equal chance of selection.

Rapport A positive interpersonal climate between interviewer and participant necessary for the fruitful conduct of the interview.

Reciprocity A data-gathering technique where meaning and power are negotiated between the researcher and researched and between data and theory.

Reflexivity Responsiveness to the evidence gathered in the field.

Reliability In a positivistic paradigm, reliability usually refers to the consistency, accuracy and stability of the measurements used or observations collected in the study. The more reliable the measurement or observation the more 'error-free' it is considered to be. There are various ways in which reliability can be assessed by calculation of so-called 'reliability coefficients'.

Replication The process of repeating an experiment, ideally with different researchers, in different laboratories.

Research diaries Useful tools for both action researchers and those working with qualitative data more generally. Diaries allow researchers to keep track of the development of ideas as a study progresses, through their written reflections on the research process.

Retrospective research The collection of historical data related to the participants.

Sampling Process of selecting a portion of a defined category—usually people, but can be applied to other aspects of the research design such as settings or events—that is in some ways representative of the defined category as a whole (the 'population').

Single case study design Research strategy aimed at explaining, describing, illustrating, and/or exploring contemporary phenomena within a real-life context of a single individual, group, event, institution or culture.

Snowball sampling A method of assembling a research sample that relies on referrals to the study by those who have already participated.

Stratified random sampling Sampling technique that selects individuals from subgroups in the proportion that they are represented in the population.

Structuralism Theoretical approach used by researchers who believe that meaning doesn't lie *within* something, waiting to be discovered through careful observation. Instead, meaning lies in the non-observable system of relationships *between* that 'something' and something else.

Subjectivity Used in positivist research to refer to the extent that the observer's own feelings, biases and interpretations influence what they observe and record, or don't observe and record. Used in post-structuralist theory to describe an individual's conscious and unconscious thoughts, sense of self, and understandings of one's relation to the world. One's subjectivity is a process that is socially constructed through discourses and language.

Systematic observation A process of collecting observational data, usually about the behaviour of children and/or adults, using prede-fined behaviour categories and standard observational techniques by observers trained to an acceptable criterion of observational reliability. Systematic observations in natural settings (e.g. homes, preschools or parks) are referred to as naturalistic observations; those in observer-controlled settings (e.g. laboratories) are called structured observations.

Telos A 'journey' by humanity towards some ill-defined 'goal' or 'endpoint'.

Theory building In qualitative research, relates closely to the mod-ernist 'moment' outlined in Chapter 8. In this sense it is the process of constructing coherent patterns from analyses of evidence from the field, using these patterns to form the basis of a grounded theory which can be generalised across other similar settings and events.

Thick description A description that includes everything needed for the reader to understand what is happening.

Treatment group A group that receives the independent variable (or treatment) in an experiment.

Triangulation Research practice of comparing and combining differ-ent forms, or different sources, of information in order to reach a better understanding of processes or perspectives. An example would be using the views of both teachers and pupils to gain an informed view of school processes; or using classroom obser-vations as well as teacher interviews to learn about teachers' practices.

Trustworthiness Judgements about the quality and credibility of the research design, enactment, analysis, findings and conclusions.

Validity The process of establishing the 'truth' of the research outcomes. Each paradigm has its own validity processes, as summarised in Chapter 3.

References

CHAPTER 1 RESEARCH AS A TOOL

Achenbach, T. 1978, *Research in Developmental Psychology: Concepts, Strategies and Methods*, The Free Press, New York.

Bell, S. M. and Ainsworth, M. D. S. 1972, 'Infant crying and maternal responsiveness', *Child Development*, vol. 43, pp. 1171–90.

Cannella, G. S. and Bailey, C. 1999, 'Postmodern research in early childhood education', in S. Reifel (ed.), *Advances in Early Childhood Education and Day Care. Volume 10: Foundations, Adult Dynamics, Teacher Education and Play*, JAI Press, Stamford, Conn.

Curtiss, S. 1977, *Genie: A Psycholinguistic Study of a Modern-Day 'Wild Child'*, Academic Press, New York.

Dallape, F. 1996, 'Urban children: a challenge and an opportunity', *Childhood: A Global Journal of Child Research*, vol. 3, no. 3, pp. 279–93.

Elliot, J. 1991, *Action Research for Educational Change*, Open University Press, Milton Keynes.

Flake, C., Kuhs, T., Donnelly, A. and Ebert, C. 1995, 'Teacher as researcher: reinventing the role of teacher', *Phi Delta Kappan*, vol. 76, pp. 405–7.

Gewirtz, J. L. and Boyd, E. F. 1977, 'Does maternal responding imply reduced infant crying? A critique of the 1972 Bell and Ainsworth report', *Child Development*, vol. 48, pp. 1200–7.

Goodwin, W. L. and Goodwin, L. D. 1996, *Understanding*

Quantitative and Qualitative Research in Early Childhood Education, Teachers College Press, New York.

Hubbard, F. O. A and van IJzendoorn, M. H. 1991, 'Maternal unresponsiveness and infant crying across the first nine months: A naturalistic longitudinal study', *Infant Behaviour and Development*, vol. 14, pp. 299–312.

Wadsworth, Y. 1984, *Do It Yourself Social Research*, Victorian Council of Social Service and Melbourne Family Care Organisation, Melbourne.

Werner, E. E. 1993, 'Risk, resilience and recovery: Perspectives from the Kauai Longitudinal Study', *Development and Psychopathology*, vol. 5, pp. 503–15.

Wiersma, W. 2000, *Research Methods in Education*, (7th edn), Allyn & Bacon, Boston.

CHAPTER 2   THE RESEARCH PROCESS

Berg, B. 1995, *Qualitative Research Methods for the Social Sciences* (2nd edn), Allyn & Bacon, London.

Charles, C. 1998, *Introduction to Educational Research* (3rd edn), Addison Wesley Longman, New York.

Goodwin, W. L. and Goodwin, L. D. 1996, *Understanding Quantitative and Qualitative Research in Early Childhood Education*, Teachers College Press, New York.

Kumar, R. 1996, *Research Methodology: A Step-by-Step Guide for Beginners*, Longman, Melbourne.

Wadsworth, Y. 1991, *Do It Yourself Social Research*, Victorian Council of Social Service and Melbourne Family Care Organisation, Melbourne.

Wiersma, W. 2000, *Research Methods in Education* (7th edn), Allyn & Bacon, Boston.

CHAPTER 3   PARADIGMS, METHODS AND KNOWLEDGE

Davies, B. 1989, *Frogs and Snails and Feminist Tales: Preschool Children and Gender*, Allen & Unwin, Sydney.

Godelier, M. 1974, *Rationality and Irrationality in Economics*, New Left Books, London.

Harland, R. 1987, *Superstructuralism*, Routledge, London.

Kenway, J. and Willis, S. 1997, *Answering Back: Girls, Boys and Feminism in Schools*, Allen & Unwin, Sydney.

Kuhn, T. S. 1970, *The Structure of Scientific Revolutions* (2nd edn.), University of Chicago Press, Chicago.

MacBeth, T. M. 1996, 'Indirect Effects of Television: Creativity, Persistence, School Achievement, and Participation in Other Activities', in T. M. MacBeth (ed.), *Tuning in to Young Viewers:*

Social Science Perspectives on Television, Sage, Thousand Oaks, CA (*ED422130*).

Massey, D. 1998, 'The Spacial Construction of Youth Cultures', in T. Skelton and G. Valentine (eds), *Cool Places: Geographies of Youth Cultures*, Routledge, London.

O'Sullivan, T., Hartley, J., Saunders, D. and Fiske, J. 1983, *Key Concepts in Communication*, Methuen, London.

Palmerton, P. R. and Judas, J. 1994, 'Selling Violence: Television Commercials Targeted to Children'. Paper presented at the 44th Annual Meeting of the International Communication Association, Sydney, July 11–15 (*ED371425*).

Sarup, M. 1988, *An Introductory Guide to Post-structuralism and Postmodernism*, Harvester Wheatsheaf, New York.

de Saussure, F. 1959, *A Course in General Linguistics*, McGraw-Hill, New York.

Winch, P. 1958, *The Idea of Social Science and its Relation to Philosophy*, Routledge & Kegan Paul, London.

CHAPTER 4   DOING RESEARCH FOR THE FIRST TIME

Blair, M. 1995, 'Race, class and gender in school research', in J. Holland, M. Blair and S. Sheldon (eds), *Debates and Issues in Feminist Research and Pedagogy*, The Open University, Milton Keynes, pp. 248–61.

Bredekamp, S. and Copple, C. (eds) 1997, *Developmentally Appropriate Practice in Early Childhood Programs* (rev. edn), National Association for the Education of Young Children, Washington, DC.

Bloch, M. 1992, 'Critical perspectives on the historical relationship between child development and early childhood education research', in S. Kessler and B. B. Swadener (eds), *Reconceptualising the early childhood curriculum: Beginning the dialogue*, Teachers College Press, New York, pp. 21–42.

Campbell, S. (forthcoming), 'The Definition and Description of a Justice Disposition in Young Children', unpublished doctoral dissertation, University of Melbourne.

Carr, M. 1997, 'Persistence when it's difficult: A disposition to learn for early childhood', *Early Childhood Folio Number 3: A Collection of Recent Research*, New Zealand Council for Educational Research, Wellington, pp. 9–12.

Cannella, G. S. 1997, *Deconstructing Early Childhood Education: Social Justice and Revolution*, Peter Lang, New York.

Davies, B. 1993, *Shards of Glass: Children Reading and Writing Beyond Gendered Identities*, Allen & Unwin, Sydney.

Derman-Sparks, L. 1993–94, 'Empowering children to create a caring culture in a world of differences', *Childhood Education: Infancy*

Through Adolescence, vol. 70, no. 2, pp. 66–71.

Kessler, S. and Swadener, B. B. (eds) 1994, *Reconceptualizing the Early Childhood Curriculum: Beginning the Dialogue*, Teachers College Press, New York.

Lather, P. 1991, *Getting Smart: Feminist Research and Pedagogy with/in the Postmodern*, Routledge, New York.

Lubeck, S. 1994, 'The politics of developmentally appropriate practice: Exploring issues of culture, class and curriculum', in B. L. Mallory and R. S. New (eds), *Diversity and Developmentally Appropriate Practices*, Teachers College Press, New York, pp. 17–39.

Mac Naughton, G. 1995, 'A post-structuralist analysis of learning in early childhood settings', in M. Fleer (ed.), *DAP Centrism: Challenging developmentally appropriate practice*, AECA, Canberra, pp. 35–54.

Marshall, J. 1990, 'Foucault and educational research', in S. Ball (ed.) *Foucault and Education: Disciplines and Knowledge*, Routledge, London, pp. 11–28.

McTaggart, R. and Garbutcheon-Singh, M. 1988, 'A fourth generation of action research: Notes on the Deakin seminar', in *The Action Research Reader* (3rd edn), Deakin University Press, Geelong, pp. 409–427.

New, R. S. and Mallory, B. L. 1994, 'Introduction: The ethic of inclusion', in B. L. Mallory, and R. S. New, (eds), *Diversity and Developmentally Appropriate Practices: Challenges for Early Childhood Education*, Teachers College Press, New York, pp. 1–13.

Ryan, S. K. 1998, 'Freedom to choose: A post–structural study of child-centered pedagogy in a kindergarten classroom', unpublished doctoral dissertation, Columbia University, New York.

Silin, J. 1995, *Sex, Death, and the Education of Children: Our Passion for Ignorance in the Age of AIDS*, Teachers College Press, New York.

Tobin, J. 1997, *Making a Place for Pleasure in Early Childhood Education*, Yale University Press, New York.

CHAPTER 5   ETHICS IN EARLY CHILDHOOD RESEARCH

Bronfenbrenner, U. 1952, 'Principles of professional ethics: Cornell studies in social growth', *American Psychologist*, vol. 7, pp. 452–519.

Grodin, M. and Glantz, L. (eds) 1994, *Children as Research Subjects*, Oxford University Press, New York.

Hoagwood, K., Jensen, P. S. and Fisher, Celia B. (eds) 1996, *Ethical Issues in Mental Health Research with Children and Adolescents*, L. Erlbaum, NJ.

Leach, A., Hilton, S., Greenwood, B. M., Manneh, E., Dibba, B., Wilkins, A. and Mulholland, E. K. 1999, 'An evaluation of the informed consent procedure used during a trial of a *Haemophilus influenzae* type B conjugate vaccine undertaken in The Gambia, West Africa, *Social Science and Medicine*, vol. 48, pp. 139–48.

Lederer, S. and Grodin, M. 1994, 'Historical overview: pediatric experimentation', in M. Grodin and L. Glantz (eds), *Children as Research Subjects*, Oxford University Press, New York.

McNeill, P. 1993, *The Ethics and Politics of Human Experimentation*, Cambridge University Press, Cambridge.

Rymer, R. 1994, *Genie: A Scientific Tragedy*, Penguin, London.

Southall, D., Plunkett, M., Banks, M., Falkov, A. and Samuels, M. 1997, 'Covert video-recordings of life-threatening child abuse: Lessons for child protection', *Pediatrics*, vol. 100, no. 5, pp. 735–60.

CHAPTER 6   DESIGN ISSUES

Baltes, P. B. and Schaie, K. W. 1974, 'The myth of the twilight years', *Psychology Today*, vol. 7, pp. 35–40.

—— 1976, 'On the plasticity of intelligence in adulthood and old age: where Horn and Donaldson fail?' *American Psychologist*, vol. 31, pp. 720–25.

Bell, J. 1993, *Doing your Research Project: A Guide for First-time Researchers in Education and Social Science* (2nd edn), Open University Press, Buckingham.

Bergman, L. R., Eklund, G. and Magnusson, D. 1991, 'Studying individual development: problems and methods', in D. Magnusson, L. R. Bergman, G. Rudinger, and B. Törestad (eds), *Problems and Methods in Longitudinal Research: Stability and Change*, Cambridge University Press, Cambridge, pp.1–27.

Bogdan, R. C. and Biklen, S. K. 1998, *Qualitative Research for Education: An Introduction to Theory and Methods*, Allyn & Bacon, Boston.

Booth, W. C., Williams, G. G. and Williams, J. M. 1995, *The Craft of Research*, University of Chicago Press, Chicago.

Cattell, R. 1934, *Your Mind and Mine: An Account of Psychology for the Inquiring Layman and the Prospective Student*, George G. Harrap, London.

Cook, T. D. and Campbell, D. T. 1979, *Quasi-experimentation: Design and Analysis Issues for Field Settings*, Houghton Mifflin, Boston.

Cynader, M. and Frost, B. J. 1999, 'Mechanisms of brain development: neuronal sculpting by the physical and social environment', in D. P. Keating, and C. Hertzman (eds), *Developmental Health and the Wealth of Nations: Social, Biological, and Educational Dynamics*, The Guilford Press, New York, pp.153–84.

Fraenkel, J. R. and Wallen, N. E. 1996, *How to Design and Evaluate*

Research in Education, McGraw-Hill, New York.

Gall, M. D. and Borg, W. R. 1996, *Educational Research: An Introduction* (6th edn), Longman, New York.

Gay, L. R. 1996, *Educational Research: Competencies for Analysis and Application.* (6th edn), Prentice-Hall, New Jersey.

Gesell, A. 1952, *Infant Development: The Embryology of Early Human Development*, Hamish Hamilton, London.

Gilmore, L. and Hayes, A. 1996, 'Asperger's Syndrome: A case diagnosed in late adolescence', *Clinical Child Psychology and Psychiatry*, vol. 1, pp. 431–9.

Goodwin, W. L. and Goodwin, L. D. 1996, *Understanding Quantitative and Qualitative Research in Early Childhood Education*, Teachers College Press, New York.

Hayes, A. 1980, 'Visual regard and vocalization in mother–infant dyads', unpublished doctoral thesis, Macquarie University, Sydney.

Hersen, M.,and Barlow, D. H. 1976, *Single-case Experimental Designs: Strategies for Studying Behavior Change*, Pergamon Press, New York.

Hopkins, K. D., Stanley, J. C. and Hopkins, B. R. 1990, *Educational and Psychological Measurement and Evaluation* (7th edn), Allyn & Bacon, Boston.

Hubbard, R. S. and Power, B. M. 1993, *The Art of Classroom Inquiry: A Handbook for Teacher-researchers*, Heinemann, Portsmith, NH.

Hubel, D.H. and Weisel, T.N. 1962, 'Receptive fields, binocular interaction, and functional architecture in the cat's visual cortex', *Journal of Physiology*, vol. 160, pp. 106–56.

Kumar, R. 1996, *Research Methodology*, Longman, Melbourne.

Mauch, J. E. and Birch, J. W. 1998, *Guide to the Successful Thesis and Dissertation: A Handbook for Students and Faculty.* (4th edn), Marcel Dekker, New York.

Miller, S. A. 1987, *Developmental Research Methods*, Prentice-Hall, Englewood Cliffs, NJ.

O'Brien, C. and Hayes, A. 1995, *Normal and Impaired Motor Development: Theory into Practice*, Chapman & Hall, London.

Olweus, D., and Alsaker, F. D. 1991, 'Assessing change in a cohort-longitudinal study with hierarchical data', in D. Magnusson, L. R. Bergman, G. Rudinger and B. Törestad (eds), *Problems and Methods in Longitudinal Research: Stability and Change*, Cambridge University Press, Cambridge, pp.107–32.

Patterson, L., Santa, C. M., Short, K. G. and Smith, K. (eds) 1993, *Teachers are Researchers: Reflection and Action*, International Reading Association, Delaware.

Pedhazur, E. J. and Schmelkin, L. P. 1991, *Measurement, Design, and Analysis: An Integrated Approach*, Lawrence Erlbaum, Hillsdale, NJ.

Pickles, A. and Rutter, M. 1991, 'Statistical and conceptual models of "turning points" in developmental processes', in D. Magnusson, L. R. Bergman, G. Rudinger, and B. Törestad (eds), *Problems and Methods in Longitudinal Research: Stability and Change,* Cambridge University Press, Cambridge, pp.133–65.

Sameroff, A. and Chandler, M. J. 1975, 'Reproductive risk and the continuum of caretaking casualty', in F. D. Horowitz, M. Heatherington, S. Scarr-Salapatek and G. Siegel (eds) *Review of Child Development Research* vol. 4, University of Chicago Press, Chicago, pp 187–244.

Senapati, R. 1989, 'Sibling relationships of disabled children: A study of play, prosocial and conflict behaviour, and teaching between siblings', unpublished doctoral thesis, University of Queensland, Brisbane.

Strauss, A. and Corbin, J. 1990, *Basics of Qualitative Research: Grounded Theory Procedure and Techniques,* Sage, Newbury Park, CA.

Tawney, J. W. and Gast, D. L. 1984, *Single Subject Research in Special Education,* Charles E. Merrill, Columbus.

Tilley, A. 1996, *An Introduction to Psychological Research and Statistics* (3rd edn), Pineapple Press, Brisbane.

Tuckman, B. W. 1994, *Conducting Educational Research* (4th edn), Harcourt Brace, Forth Worth, TX.

Weatherburn, D. and Lind, B. 1997, *Social and Economic Stress, Child Neglect and Juvenile Delinquency,* NSW Bureau of Crime Statistics and Research, Sydney.

White, B. L. 1971, *Human Infants: Experience and Psychological Development,* Prentice-Hall, Englewood Cliffs, NJ.

CHAPTER 7   QUANTITATIVE DESIGNS AND STATISTICAL ANALYSIS

Ainsworth, M., Blehar, M., Waters, E. and Wall, S. 1978, *Patterns of Attachment,* Erlbaum, Hillsdale, NJ.

Baron, R. and Kenny, D. 1986, 'The moderator-mediator variable distinction in social psychological research: Conceptual, strategic, and statistical considerations', *Journal of Personality and Social Psychology,* vol. 51, pp. 1173–82.

Belsky, J. 1988, 'The "effects" of infant day care reconsidered', *Early Childhood Research Quarterly,* vol. 3, pp. 235–72.

Belsky, J. and Isabella, R. 1988, 'Maternal, infant, and social-contextual determinants of attachment security', in J. Belsky & T. Nezworski (eds), *Clinical Implications of Attachment,* Erlbaum, Hillsdale, NJ, pp. 41–94.

Belsky, J., Rosenberger, K. and Crnic, K. 1995, 'The origins of attachment security: "Classical" and contextual determinants', in S. Goldberg, R. Muir, and J. Kerr (eds), *Attachment Theory: Social,*

Developmental and Clinical Perspectives, Analytic Press, Hillsdale, NJ, pp. 153–83.

Burns, R. B. 2000, *Introduction to Research Methods*, (4th edn), Addison Wesley Longman, Melbourne.

Cohen, L. and Manion, L. 1985, *Research Methods in Education* (2nd edn), Croom Helm, London.

Cook, D. T. and Campbell, D. T. 1979, *Quasi-experimentation: Design and Analysis Issues for Field Settings*, Houghton Mifflin, Boston.

Cramer, D. 1998, *Fundamental Statistics for Social Research: Using SPSS for Windows*, Routledge, London.

Daniel, A. 1983, *Power, Privilege and Prestige: Occupations in Australia*, Longman-Cheshire, Melbourne.

Edwards, A. 1976, *An Introduction to Linear Regression and Correlation*, W. H. Freeman, San Francisco.

Foster, J. 1998, *Data Analysis Using SPSS for Windows: A Beginner's Guide*, Sage, London.

Goodwin, W. L. and Goodwin, L. D. 1996, *Understanding Quantitative and Qualitative Research in Early Childhood Education*, Teachers College Press, New York.

Hair, J. F., Anderson, R. E., Tatham, R. L. and Black, W. C. 1998, *Multivariate Data Analysis*, (5th edn), Prentice-Hall International, New Jersey.

Harrison, L. J. 1999, 'Predictors of attachment security and social competence: A longitudinal study of the first three years', unpublished doctoral dissertation, Macquarie University, Sydney.

Harrison, L. J. and Ungerer, J. A. 1997, 'Child care predictors of infant–mother attachment security at age 12 months', *Early Child Development and Care*, vol. 137, pp. 31–46.

—— 1999, 'The Sydney Family Development Project: Longitudinal predictors of children's socioemotional development', in *Children at the Top: Darwin Conference Papers*. Available Online: http://www.aeca.org.au/darconfharr.html

—— 2000, 'Children and child care: A longitudinal study of the relationships between developmental outcomes and use of non-parental care from birth to six'. Invited paper presented at the Commonwealth Family and Community Services Panel Data and Policy Conference, Canberra, May 2000. Available Online: http//:www.csu.edu.au/educat/teached/harr.html

Hollingshead, A. 1975, 'Four factor index of social status', unpublished manuscript, Yale University.

Hosmer, D. and Lemeshow, S. 1989, *Applied Logistic Regression*, Wiley, New York.

Howes, C. 1980, 'Peer Play Scale as an index of complexity of peer interaction', *Developmental Psychology*, vol. 16, pp. 371–2.

Howes, C., Phillips, D. and Whitebook, M. 1992, 'Thresholds of quality: Implications for the social development of children in center-based child care', *Child Development*, vol. 63, pp. 449–60.

Huck, S. W., Cormier, W. H. and Bounds, W. G. 1974, *Reading Statistics and Research*, Harper & Row, New York.

Kerlinger, F. N. 1986, *Foundations of Behavioral Research*, Holt, Rinehart & Winston, New York.

Kumar, R. 1996, *Research Methodology: A Step-by-Step Guide for Beginners*, Addison Wesley Longman, Melbourne.

NICHD Early Child Care Research Network 1997, 'The effects of infant child care on infant–mother attachment security: Results of the NICHD study on early child care', *Child Development*, vol. 68, pp. 860–79.

Tuckman, B. W. 1999, *Conducting Educational Research* (5th edn), Harcourt Brace, Fort Worth, TX.

Ungerer, J.A., Waters, B., Barnett, B. and Dolby, R. 1997, 'Defense style and adjustment in interpersonal relationships', *Journal of Research in Personality*, vol. 31, pp. 375–84.

Wangmann, J. 1995, *Towards Integration and Quality Assurance in Children's Services*, Australian Institute of Family Studies, Melbourne.

White, B. L. and Watts, J. C. 1973, *Experience and Environment, Vol.1*, Prentice-Hall, Englewood Cliffs, NJ.

Wright, M. 1983, *Compensatory Education in the Preschool*, High/Scope Press, Ypsilanti, MI.

CHAPTER 8   QUALITATIVE DESIGNS AND ANALYSIS

Anning, A. and Edwards, A. 1999, *Promoting Learning from Birth to Five: Developing the New Early Years Professional*, Open University Press, Buckingham.

Atkinson, P. and Delamont, S. 1985, 'Bread and dreams or bread and circuses? A critique of case study in educational research', in M. Shipman (ed.), *Educational Research: Principles, Policies and Practices*, Falmer, London, pp. 26–45.

Bromley, D. 1986, *The Case Study Method in Psychology and Related Disciplines*, Wiley, New York.

Campbell, S. 1999, 'Making the political pedagogical in early childhood education', *Australian Journal of Early Childhood*, vol. 24, no. 4, pp. 21–6.

Chaiklin, S. 1993, 'Understanding the social scientific practice of understanding practice', in S. Chaiklin and J. Lave (eds), *Understanding Practice: Perspectives on Activity and Context*, Cambridge University Press, Cambridge, pp. 377–401.

Clark, C. 1990, 'What you can learn from applesauce: a case of qualitative inquiry in use', in E. Eisner and A. Peshkin (eds), *Qualitative Inquiry in Education: The Continuing Debate*, Teachers College Press, New York.

Denzin, N. 1978, *The Research Act* (2nd edn), McGraw-Hill, New York.

Denzin, N. and Lincoln, Y. (eds) 1994, *Handbook of Qualitative Research*, Sage, London.

Dey, I. 1993, *Qualitative Data Analysis*, Routledge, London.

Dunn, J. 1988, *The Beginnings of Social Understanding*, Blackwell, Oxford.

Edwards, A. 1997, 'Guests bearing gifts: the position of student teachers in primary school classrooms', *British Educational Research Journal*, vol. 23, no. 91, pp. 27–37.

Edwards, A. (in press), 'Investigating the complexities of teaching and mentoring', in I. Abbott and L. Evans (eds), *The Future of Educational Research*, Falmer, London.

Edwards, A. and Talbot, R. 1999, *The Hardpressed Researcher: A Research Handbook for Health Education and Social Care* (2nd edn), Longman, London.

Geertz, C. 1983, Local *Knowledge: Further Essays in Interpretative Anthropology*, Basic Books, New York.

Hammersley, M. 1997, 'Educational research and teaching: response to David Hargreaves' TTA lecture', *British Educational Research Journal*, vol. 23, no. 2, pp. 141–61.

Lather, P. 1993, 'Fertile obsession: validity after poststructuralism', *Sociological Quarterly*, vol. 34, no. 4, pp. 673–93.

Munn, P. and Schaffer, H. R. 1993, 'Literacy and numeracy events in social interactive contexts', *International Journal of Early Years Education*, vol. 1, no. 3, pp. 61–80.

Saxe, G., Guberman, G. and Gearhart, M. 1987, *Social Processes in Early Number Development*, Monographs of the Society for Research in Child Development, Serial No. 216, vol. 52, no. 2.

Schaffer, H. R. 1977, *Mothering*, Fontana, London.

Stake, R. 1994, 'Case studies', in N. Denzin and Y. Lincoln (eds), *Handbook of Qualitative Research*, Sage, London, pp. 236–47.

—— 1995, *The Art of Case Study Research*, Sage, London.

Sylva, K., Roy, C. and Painter, M. 1980, *Childwatching at Playgroup and Nursery School*, Grant McIntyre, London.

Tizard, B. and Hughes, M. 1984, *Young Children Learning: Talking and Thinking at Home and School*, Fontana, London.

Wells, G. 1986, *The Meaning Makers*, Hodder & Stoughton, London.

Wertsch, J. 1991, *Voices of the Mind*, Harvard University Press, Cambridge, MA.

Yin, R. K. 1998, 'The abridged version of case study research: design and method', in L. Bickman and D. Rog (eds), *Handbook of Applied Social Research Methods*, Sage, London, pp. 229–59.

CHAPTER 9   EQUITY ISSUES IN RESEARCH DESIGN

Alarcon, O., Erkut, S., Coll, C. G. and Varquez Garcia, H. A. 1994, 'An approach to engaging in culturally-sensitive research on Puerto Rican youth', *ERIC ED 408 398*.

Atweh, B. and Burton, L. 1995, 'Students as researchers: Rationale and critique', *British Educational Research Journal*, vol. 21, no 5, pp. 561–75.

Best, S. and Kellner, D. 1991, *Postmodern Theory: Critical Interrogations*, Macmillan, Hampshire.

Bredekamp, S. (ed.) 1987, *Developmentally Appropriate Practice in Early Childhood Programs Serving Children From Birth Through Age 8* (exp. edn.), National Association for the Education of Young Children, Washington, DC.

Bredekamp, S. and Copple, C. 1997, *Developmentally Appropriate Practice in Early Childhood Programs Serving Children From Birth Through Age 8* (rev. edn), National Association for the Education of Young Children, Washington, DC.

Brennan, D. 1994, *The Politics of Australian Child Care: From Philanthropy to Feminism*, Cambridge University Press, Cambridge.

Burman, E. 1994, *Deconstructing Developmental Psychology*, Routledge, London.

Cannella, G. S. 1997, *Deconstructing Early Childhood Education: Social Justice and Revolution*, Peter Lang, New York.

Drew, C. J. and Hardman, M. L. 1985, *Designing and Conducting Behavioral Research*, Pergamon Press, New York.

Foster, P., Gomm, R., and Hammersley, M. 1995, *Constructing Educational Equality: An Assessment of Research on School Processes*, Falmer, London.

Hatch, J. A. 1995, 'Studying childhood as a cultural invention', in J. A. Hatch (ed.), *Qualitative Research in Early Childhood Settings*, Praeger, Westport, CT, pp. 117–33.

Harris, O. 1991, 'Time and difference in anthropological writing', in L. Nencel and P. Pels (eds), *Constructing Knowledge: Authority and Critique in Social Science*, Sage, London, pp. 145–61.

Huizer, G. 1991, 'Participatory research and healing witchcraft: an essay in the anthropology of crisis', in L. Nencel and P. Pels (eds), *Constructing Knowledge: Authority and Critique in Social Science*, Sage, London, pp. 40–58.

Kessen, W. 1979, 'The American child and other cultural inventions', *American Psychologist*, vol. 34, no. 10, pp. 815–20.

Lather, P. 1986, 'Research as praxis', *Harvard Educational Review*, vol. 56, no. 3, pp. 257–77.

—— 1991, *Getting Smart: Feminist Research and Pedagogy with/in the Postmodern*, Routledge, New York.

Lubeck, S. 1994, 'The politics of developmentally appropriate practice,' in B. L. Mallory and R. S. New (eds), *Diversity and Developmentally Appropriate Practices: Challenges for Early Childhood Education*, Teachers College Press, New York, pp. 17–43.

Mayall, B. 1999, 'Children and childhood', in S. Hood, B. Mayall and S. Oliver (eds.), *Critical Issues on Social Research: Power and Prejudice*, Open University Press, Buckingham, pp. 10–24.

Mayall, B., Hood, S. and Oliver, S. 1999, 'Introduction', in S. Hood, B. Mayall and S. Oliver (eds), *Critical Issues on Social Research: Power and Prejudice*, Open University Press, Buckingham, pp. 1–9.

Oakley, A. 1999, 'People's ways of knowing: gender and methodology' in S. Hood, B. Mayall and S. Oliver (eds), *Critical Issues on Social Research: Power and Prejudice*, Open University Press, Buckingham, pp. 154–70.

Padilla, A. and Lindholm, K. J. 1995, 'Quantitative research with ethnic minorities', in J. A. Banks and C. A. Banks (eds), *Handbook of Research on Multicultural Education*, Macmillan, New York, pp. 97–113.

Pels, P. and Nencel, L. (1991), 'Introduction: critique and deconstruction of anthropological authority', in L. Nencel and P. Pels (eds), *Constructing Knowledge: Authority and Critique in Social Science*, Sage, London, pp. 1–21.

Quina, K. and Kulberg, J. M. (1988), 'The experimental psychology course', in P. Bronstein and K. Quina (eds), *Teaching a Psychology of People: Resources for Gender and Sociocultural Awareness*, American Psychological Association, Washington, DC, pp. 69–79.

Schrijvers, J. 1991, 'Dialectics of a dialogical ideal: studying down, studying sideways and studying up', in L. Nencel and P. Pels (eds), *Constructing Knowledge: Authority and Critique in Social Science*, Sage, London, pp. 162–79.

Smithmier, A. 1996, 'The "Double Bind" of re-presentation in qualitative research methods'. Paper presented at the *Qualitative Research in Education Conference*, University of St Thomas, St Paul, Minnesota, June 28, *ERIC ED 410 648*.

Utley, C. A. and Obiakor, F. E. 1995, 'Scientific and methodological concerns in research: Perspectives for multicultural learners'. Portions of paper presented at the Office of Special Education Programs Project Directors' Conference, Washington, DC, July 1995, *ERIC ED 393 251*.

Weber, E. 1984, *Ideas Influencing Early Childhood Education: A Theoretical Analysis*, Teachers College Press, New York.

Williams, S. and Stewart, I. (1992), 'Community control and self-determination in Aboriginal educational research: The changed roles, relationships and responsibilities of Aboriginal and non-Aboriginal researchers and Aboriginal communities'. Paper presented to the National Aboriginal and Torres Strait Islander Higher Education Conference, Hervey Bay, Queensland, December 6–11, *ERIC ED 388 461*.

CHAPTER 10 SURVEYS AND QUESTIONNAIRES

Anderson, G. 1990, *Fundamentals of Educational Research*, Falmer, London.

Adelman, C. and Alexander, R. J. 1982, *The Self-Evaluating Institution: Practices and Principles in the Management of Educational Change*, Methuen, London.

Clegg, F. 1998, *Simple Statistics: A Course Book for the Social Sciences*, Cambridge University Press, Cambridge.

Cohen, L. and Manion, L. 1994, *Research Methods in Education* (4th edn), Routledge, London.

Cronbach, L. 1982, *Designing Evaluations of Educational and Social Programs*, Jossey-Bass, San Francisco.

Department of Education and Employment (DfEE) 1997, *Excellence in Schools, White Paper*, DfEE, London.

Gearing, B. and Dant, T. 1990, 'Doing Biographical Research', in S. Peace, (ed.), *Researching Social Gerontology: Concepts, Methods and Issues*, Sage, London.

Glaser, B. and Strauss, A. 1967, *The Discovery of Grounded Theory*, Aldine, Chicago.

May, T. 1993, *Social Research: Issues, Methods and Process*, Open University Press, Buckingham.

Miles, M. and Huberman, A. 1994, *Qualitative Data Analysis* (2nd edn), Sage, London.

Parlett, M. and Hamilton, D. 1987, 'Evaluation as Illumination', in R. Murphy and H. Torrance, *Evaluating Education: Issues and Methods*, Harper & Row, London.

Pascal, C., Bertram, T., Gasper, M., Mould, C., Ramsden, F. and Saunders, M. 1999, *Research to Inform the Evaluation of the Early Excellence Centres Pilot Programme*, Centre for Research in Early Childhood, University College, Worcester.

Robson, C. 1998, *Real World Research*, Blackwell, Oxford.

Siraj-Blatchford, I. 2000, *Parent and Staff Questionnaires to Evaluate Early Excellence*, Institute of Education, London.

Siraj-Blatchford, I. and Clarke, P. 2000, *Supporting Identity, Diversity and Language in the Early Years*, Open University Press, Buckingham.

CHAPTER 11 INTERVIEWING CHILDREN

Aboud, F. 1988, *Children and Prejudice*, Blackwell, Oxford.

Bosisto, K. & Howard, A. 1999, 'Persona dolls: the effects on attitudes and play', in E. Dau (ed.), *Child's Play: Revisiting Play in Early Childhood Settings*, Maclennan & Petty, Sydney, pp. 164–80.

Breakwell, G. 1995, 'Interviewing', in G. Breakwell, S. Hammond and C. Fife-Shaw (eds), *Research Methods in Psychology*, Sage, London.

Brooker, L. 1996, '"Why do children go to school?" Consulting children in the Reception class', *Early Years*, vol. 17, no. 1.

Brown, B. 1998, *Unlearning Discrimination in the Early Years*, Trentham, Stoke, UK.

Butler-Sloss, E. 1988, *Report of the Inquiry into Child Abuse in Cleveland in 1987*, HMSO, London.

Cohen, L. and Manion, L. 1994, *Research Methods in Education*, Routledge, London.

David, T. 1992, '"Do we have to do this?", The Children Act 1989 and Obtaining Children's Views in Early Childhood Settings', *Children and Society*, vol. 6, no. 3, pp. 204–11.

Davie, R. and Galloway, D. (eds) 1996, *Listening to Children in Education*, David Fulton, London.

Davie, R., Upton, G. and Varma, V. (eds) 1996, *The Voice of the Child: A Handbook for Professionals*, Falmer, London.

Dwivedi, K. 1996, 'Race and the children's perspective', in R. Davie, G. Upton and V. Varma (eds), 1996, *The Voice of the Child: A Handbook for Professionals*, Falmer, London.

Evans, P. and Fuller, M. 1996, '"Hello, Who am I speaking to?" Communicating with pre-school children in educational research settings', *Early Years*, vol. 17, no. 1, pp. 17–20.

Hall, N. 1996, 'Eliciting children's views: The contribution of psychologists', in R. Davie, G. Upton and V. Varma (eds), 1996, *The Voice of the Child: A Handbook for Professionals*, Falmer, London.

Hughes, M. and Grieve, R. 1980, 'On asking children bizarre questions', *First Language*, vol. 1, pp. 149–60.

Hutt, S., Tyler, S., Hutt, C. and Christopherson, H. 1989, *Play, Exploration and Learning: A Natural History of the Pre-school*, Routledge, London.

James, A. 1993, *Childhood Identities: Self and Social Relationships in the Experience of the Child*, Edinburgh University Press, Edinburgh.

James, A. and Prout, A. 1997, *Constructing and Reconstructing Childhood*, Falmer, London.

Lewis, A. 1992, 'Group child interviews as a research tool', *British Educational Research Journal*, vol. 18, no. 4, pp. 413–21.

Morrow, V. and Richards, M. 1996, 'The ethics of social research with children: an overview', *Children and Society*, vol. 10, no. 2, pp. 90–105.

Nunes, T. 1994, *The Environment of the Child*, Bernard van Leer Foundation, Hague.

Pollard, A. 1996, *The Social World of Children's Learning*, Cassell, London.

Powney, J. and Watts, M. 1987, *Interviewing in Educational Research*, Routledge, London.

Ross, E. 1996, 'Learning to listen to children', in R. Davie, G. Upton and V. Varma (eds), 1996, *The Voice of the Child: A Handbook for Professionals*, Falmer, London.

Sinclair Taylor, A. 2000, 'The UN Convention on the Rights of the Child: giving children a voice,' in A. Lewis and G. Lindsay (eds), *Researching Children's Perspectives*, Open University Press, Buckingham.

Spencer, J. and Flin, R. 1990, *The Evidence of Children*, Blackstone, London.

Tizard, B. and Hughes, M. 1984, *Young Children Learning*, Fontana, London.

Wells, G. 1985, *The Meaning Makers*, Hodder & Stoughton, London.

Wood, E. and Attfield, J. 1996, *Play, Learning and the Early Childhood Curriculum*, Paul Chapman, London.

Wood, D., MacMahon, L. and Cranstoun, Y. 1980, *Working with Under-Fives*, Grant McIntyre, London.

Wood, H. and Wood, D. 1983, 'Questioning the pre-school child', *Educational Review*, vol. 35, no. 2, pp. 149–62.

CHAPTER 12   INTERVIEWING ADULTS

Beauchamps, T. and Childress, J. 1989, *Principles of Biomedical Ethics* (3rd edn), Oxford University Press, New York.

Birrell, B. and Ripson, V. 1998, 'The Great Separation', *The Age*, 22 October, p. 15.

Bloom, L.R. 1998, *Under the Sign of Hope: Feminist Methodology and Narrative Interpretation*, State University of New York Press, Albany, NY.

Blumer, H. 1969, *Symbolic Interactionism*, Prentice-Hall, Englewood Cliffs, NJ.

Brown, S., Lumley, J., Small, R. and Astbury, J. 1994, *Missing Voices: The Experience of Motherhood*, Oxford University Press, Melbourne.

Cannold, L. 1998, *The Abortion Myth: Feminism, Morality and the Hard Choices Women Make*. Allen & Unwin, Sydney.

Carlton, T. 1997, 1999, 'Fertility Issues', personal communication.

Deegan, M. J. and Hill, M. (eds). 1987, *Women and Symbolic Interaction*, Allen & Unwin, Boston.

Eyles, J. and Eugenio, P. 1993, 'Life history as method: an Italian––Canadian family in an industrial city', *The Canadian Geographer*, vol. 37(2), pp. 104–19.

Gerson, K. 1985, *Hard Choices: How Women Decide about Work, Career, and Motherhood*, University of California Press, Berkeley CA.

—— 1993, *No Man's Land: Men's Changing Commitments to Family and Work*, Basic Books, New York.

Glucksmann, M. 1994, 'The work of knowledge and the knowledge of women's work', in M. Maynard and J. Purvis (eds), *Researching Women's Lives from a Feminist Perspective*, Taylor & Francis, London, PA, pp. 149–65.

Gregg, R. 1995, *Pregnancy in a High-Tech Age*, New York University Press, New York.

Holland, J., and Ramazanoglu, C. 1999, 'Power and interpretation in researching young women's sexuality', in M. Maynard and J. Purvis (eds), *Researching Women's Lives from a Feminist Perspective*, Taylor & Francis, London, PA, pp. 125–48.

Kelly, L., Burton, S. and Regan, L. 1994, 'Researching women's lives or studying women's oppression?' in M. Maynard and J. Purvis (eds), *Researching Women's Lives from a Feminist Perspective*, Taylor & Francis, London, PA, pp. 27–48.

McMahon, M. 1995, *Engendering Motherhood: Identity and Self-Transformation in Women's Lives*, The Guilford Press, New York.

Minichiello, V., Aroni, R., Timewell, E. and Alexander, L. 1990, *In-Depth Interviewing: Researching People*, Longman-Cheshire, Melbourne.

Silverman, D. 1985, *Qualitative Methodology and Sociology*, Gower, Aldershot.

CHAPTER 13   AN ETHNOGRAPHIC APPROACH TO RESEARCHING YOUNG CHILDREN'S LEARNING

Becker, H. 1971, 'Footnote', in M. Wax, et al. (eds), *Anthropological Perspectives in Education*, Basic Books, New York.

Brannen, J. (ed.) 1992, *Mixing Methods: Qualitative and Quantitative Research*, Avebury, Aldershot.

Burgess, R. 1988, *Field Methods in the Study of Education*, Falmer, London.

Burns, R. 2000, *Introduction to Research Methods*, Sage, London.

Cohen, L. and Manion, L. 1994, *Research Methods in Education*, Routledge, London.

Connelly, P. 1998, *Racism, Gender Identities and Young Children*, Routledge, London.

Dahlberg, G., Moss, P. and Pence, A. 1999, *Beyond Quality in Early Childhood Education and Care: Postmodern Perspectives*, Falmer, London.

Dau, E. 1999, *Child's Play: Revisiting Play in Early Childhood Settings*, MacLennan & Petty, Sydney.

Davies, B. 1989, *Frogs and Snails and Feminist Tails: Preschool Children and Gender*, Allen & Unwin, Sydney.

Epstein, D. 1997, 'Cultures of schooling/cultures of sexuality', *International Journal of Inclusive Education*, vol. 1, no, 1, pp. 37–53.

Feitelson, D. 1977, 'Cross-cultural studies of representational play', in B. Tizard and D. Harvey (eds) *Biology of Play*, Heinemann Medical.

Fetterman, D. 1989, *Ethnography: Step by Step, Applied Social Research Methods Series Vol. 17*, Sage, London

Garfinkle, H. 1963, 'A conception of, and experiments with, "trust" as a condition of stable social actions', in O. Harvey (ed.) *Motivation and Social Interaction*, Ronald Press, New York.

Geertz, C. 1993, *The Interpretation of Cultures*, Fontana, London.

Glazer, B. and Strauss, A. 1967, *The Discovery of Grounded Theory*, Aldine, Chicago.

Guildford, J. 1954, *Psychometric Methods*, McGraw Hill, New York.

Gudgeon, E. 1993, 'Gender implications of children's playground culture', in P. Woods and M. Hammersley (eds) *Gender and Ethnicity in Schools: Ethnographic Accounts*, Routledge, London, pp. 00–00.

Hammersley, M. 1987a, 'Ethnography and the cumulative development of theory: a discussion of Woods' proposal for "phase two" research', *British Education Research Journal*, vol. 13, no, 3, pp. 283–86.

—— 1987b, 'Ethnography for Survival?: a reply to Woods', *British Education Research Journal*, vol.13, no. 3, pp. 309–17.

—— 1992 *What's Wrong with Ethnography?: Methodological Explorations*, Routledge in association with The Open University, London.

—— (ed.) 1999, *Researching School Experience: Ethnographic Studies of Teaching and Learning*, Falmer, London.

Harms, T., Clifford, R. and Cryer, D. 1998, *Early Childhood Environment Rating Scale: Revised Edition*, Teachers College Press, New York.

James, A. and Prout, A. (eds) 1997, *Constructing and Reconstructing Childhood*, Falmer, London.

Malaguzzi, L. 1993, 'History, ideas and basic philosophy', in C. Edwards, L. Gandini and G. Forman (eds) *The Hundred Languages of Children: The Reggio Emilia Approach to Early Childhood*, Ablex, Norwood, NJ.

Miles, M. and Huberman, A. 1994, *Qualitative Data Analysis*, Sage, London.

Paley, V. G. 1984, *Boys and Girls : Superheroes in the Doll Corner* (with a foreword by Philip W. Jackson), University of Chicago Press, Chicago.

Penn, H. 1997, *Comparing Nurseries: Staff and Children in Italy, Spain and the UK*, Paul Chapman, London.

Pinnell, G. S. 1990, *Studying the Effectiveness of Early Intervention Approaches for First Grade Children having Difficulty in Reading*, Martha L. King Language and Literacy Center, Ohio State University, Columbus.

Sharp, R. and Green, A. 1973, *Education and Social Control*, Routledge & Kegan Paul, London.

Schatzman & Strauss 1973, *Field Research*, Prentice-Hall, Englewood Cliffs, NJ.

Schieffelin, B. and Ochs, E. 1998, 'A cultural perspective on the transition from prelinguistic to linguistic communication,' in M. Wood, D. Faulkner and K. Littleton. (eds) *Cultural Worlds of Early Childhood*, Routledge, London.

Sluckin, A. 1981, *Growing Up in the Playground: The Social Development of Children*, Routledge & Kegan Paul, London.

Smith, P. and Connolly, K. 1980, *The Ecology of Preschool Behaviour*, Cambridge University Press, Cambridge.

Siraj-Blatchford, I. 1994, *Praxis Makes Perfect: Critical Educational Research for Social Justice*, Education Now Books, Nottingham.

—— 1997, 'Postmodernism', in R. Meighan and I. Siraj-Blatchford, (eds), *A Sociology of Educating*, Cassell, London.

Siraj-Blatchford, J., Ashcroft, K. and Jones, M. 1997, *Researching into Student Learning and Support in Colleges and Universities*, David Fulton, London.

Stenhouse, L. 1975, *An Introduction to Curriculum Research and Development*, Heinemann, London.

Sylva, K. 1995, 'Research as a mediaeval banquet—barons, troubadours and minstrels'. Paper presented at the RSA 'Start Right' Conference, September 1995, London.

Sylva, K., Sammons, P. Melhuish, E., Siraj-Blatchford, I. and Taggart, B. 1999, *An Introduction to the EPPE Project, Technical Paper 1*, Institute of Education and DfEE, London.

—— 1999b, *Characteristics of the Centres in the EPPE Sample: Observational Profiles, Technical Paper 6*, Institute of Education and DfEE, London.

Walkerdine, V. 1981, 'Sex, power and pedagogy', *Screen Education*, vol. 38, pp. 14–24.

Waterhouse, S. 1991, *First Episodes: Pupil Careers in the Early Years of School*, Falmer, London.

Woods, P. 1985, 'Ethnography and theory construction in educational research, in R. Burgess (ed.), *Field Methods in the Study of Education*, Falmer, London.

—— 1987, 'Ethnography at the crossroads: a reply to Hammersley', *British Education Research Journal*, vol. 13, no. 3, pp. 291–307.

—— 1996, *Researching the Art of Teaching: Ethnography for Educational Use*, Routledge, London.

Wright, C. 1986, 'School processes: an ethnographic study', in J. Eggleston, D. Dunn and M. Anjali (eds) *Education for Some*, Trentham Books, Stoke-on-Trent.

CHAPTER 14   ACTION RESEARCH

Carr, W. and Kemmis, S. 1986, *Becoming Critical: Knowing through Action Research*, Deakin University, Geelong.

Cotterill, P. 1992, 'Interviewing women: issues of friendship, vulnerability, and power', *Women's Studies International Forum*, vol. 15, no. 5/6, pp. 593–606.

Foucault, M. 1978, *The History of Sexuality. Volume 1: An Introduction*, Vintage Books, New York.

Gore, J. 1993, *The Struggle for Pedagogies: Critical and Feminist Discourses as Regimes of Truth*, Routledge, London.

Heshusius, L. 1994, 'Freeing ourselves from objectivity: managing subjectivity or turning toward a participatory mode of consciousness?', *Educational Researcher*, vol. 2, no. 3, pp. 15–22.

Kenway, J. and Willis, S. 1993, *Telling Tales: Girls and Schools and Changing their Ways*, Department of Employment, Training and Education, Canberra.

Lather, P. 1993, 'Fertile obsession: validity after poststructuralism', *The Sociological Quarterly*, vol. 34, no. 4, pp. 673–93.

Mac Naughton, G. 2000, *Rethinking Gender in Early Childhood Education*, Allen & Unwin, Sydney.

McTaggart, R. 1991, 'Principles for participatory action research', *Adult Education Quarterly*, vol. 41, no. 3, pp. 168–87.

McTaggart, R. and Garbutcheon-Singh, M. (1988), 'A fourth generation of action research: notes on the Deakin seminar', in S. Kemmis and R. McTaggart (eds), *The Action Research Reader* (3rd edn), Deakin University, Geelong, pp. 409–28.

Moss, P. 1994, 'Can there be validity without reliability?', *Educational Researcher*, vol. 23, no. 2, pp. 5–12.

Weedon, C. 1997, *Feminist Practice and Poststructualist Theory* (2nd edn), Blackwell, Oxford.

CHAPTER 15   DIRECT OBSERVATION

Ainsworth, M.D.S., Blehar, M., Waters, E. and Wall, S. 1978, *Patterns of Attachment*, Erlbaum, Hillsdale, NJ.

Barnes, K. E. 1971, 'Preschool play norms: a replication', *Developmental Psychology*, vol. 5, pp. 99–103.

Beaty, J. 1994, *Observing the Development of the Young Child* (3rd edn), Merrill, New York.

Bentzen, W. 1993, *Seeing Young Children: A Guide to Observing and Recording Behaviour*, Delmar, Albany, NY.

Blurton Jones, N. G. 1972, *Ethological Studies of Child Behaviour*, Cambridge University Press, Cambridge.

Main, M. and Solomon, J. 1990, 'Procedures for identifying infants as disorganised/disoriented during the Ainsworth Strange Situation', in M. Greenberg, D. Cicchetti and M. Cummings (eds), *Attachment in the Preschool Years: Theory, Research and Intervention*, University of Chicago Press, Chicago, pp. 121–60.

Martin, P. and Bateson, P. 1986, *Measuring Behaviour: An*

Introductory Guide, Cambridge University Press, Cambridge.

Nicolson, S. and Shipstead, S.G. 1998, *Through the Looking Glass: Observations in the Early Childhood Classroom*, Merrill, Upper Saddle River, NJ.

Noldus, L. P. J. J., Trienes, R. J. H., Hendrikson, A. H. M., Jansen, H. and Jansen R. G. 2000, 'The Observer Video-Pro: New software for the collection, management, and presentation of timestructured data from videotapes and digital media files', *Behaviour Research Methods, Instruments and Computers*, vol. 32, no. 1, pp. 197–206.

Parten, M. B. 1932, 'Social participation among preschool children', *Journal of Abnormal and Social Psychology*, vol. 27, pp. 243–69.

Pellegrini, A. D. 1996, *Observing Children in their Natural Worlds: A Methodological Primer*, Erlbaum, Hillsdale, NJ.

Rolfe, S. A. and Crossley, S. A. 1991, 'The effects of prior experience in early childhood programs and play setting on social behaviour and play in preschoolers', *Early Child Development and Care*, vol. 72, pp. 23–37.

—— 1997, 'Using the method of ethology to study Australian preschool children's play and social behaviour', *Australian Journal of Early Childhood*, vol. 22, pp. 6–11.

Sharman, C., Cross, W. and Vennis, D. 1995, *Observing Children: A Practical Guide*, Cassell, London.

CHAPTER 16   POLICY RESEARCH

Adler, P. A. and Adler, P. 1994, 'Observation techniques', in N. K. Denzin and Y. S. Lincoln (eds), *Handbook of Qualitative Research*, Sage, Thousand Oaks, CA, pp. 337–92.

Anderson, G. 1990, *Fundamentals of Educational Research*, Falmer, London.

Ball, S. J. 1987, *The Micro-politics of the School*, Methuen, London.

—— 1990, *Politics and Policy Making in Education: Explorations in Policy Sociology*, Routledge, London.

—— 1994, *Education Reform: A Critical and Poststructural Approach*, Open University Press, Buckingham.

Bowe, R., Ball, S. J. and Gold, A. 1992, *Reforming Education and Changing Schools: Case Studies in Policy Sociology*, Routledge, London.

Bowes, J. and Hayes, A. (eds), 1999, *Children, Families and Communities: Contexts and Consequences*, Oxford University Press, Melbourne.

Boyden, J. 1997, 'Childhood and the policy makers: a comparative perspective on the globalisation of childhood', in A. James and A. Prout (eds), *Constructing and Reconstructing Childhood: Contemporary Issues in the Sociological Study of Childhood*, Falmer, Washington, DC, pp. 190–229.

Burns, R. B. 1994, *Introduction to Research Methods*, Longman-Cheshire, Melbourne.

Carley, M. 1980, *Rational Techniques in Policy Analysis*, Gower, Aldershot.

Coaldrake, P. and Stedman, L. 1998, *On the Brink: Australia's Universities Confronting their Future*, University of Queensland Press, St Lucia.

Cunningham, S., Tapsall, S., Ryan, Y., Stedman, L., Bagdon, K. and Flew, T. 1998, *New Media and Borderless Education: A Review of the Convergence between Global Media Networks and Higher Education Provision*, Department of Employment, Education, Training and Youth Affairs, Canberra.

Dale, R. 1989, *The State and Education Policy*, Open University Press, Milton Keynes.

Denzin, N. K. and Lincoln, Y. S. (eds), 1994, *Handbook of Qualitative Research*, Sage, London.

Dewey, J. 1958, *Experience and Nature*, Dover, New York.

Farrell, M. A. 1998a, 'Educating on the inside: Inmate mothers in Australian corrections', *Australia and New Zealand Journal of Law and Education*, vol. 3.2, pp. 16–28.

—— 1998b, 'Mothers offending against their role: An Australian experience', *Women and Criminal Justice*, vol. 9.4, pp. 47–68.

—— 1998c, 'Gendered settings and human rights in early childhood', in N. Yelland (ed.), *Gender in Early Childhood*, Routledge, London, pp. 98–112.

—— 1999a 'A study of bullying in early childhood centres', *Australia and New Zealand Journal of Law and Education*, vol. 4.1, pp. 40–46.

—— 1999b, 'Children in a consumer society: Early childhood policies on children's rights', in H. K. Chiam (ed.), *Excellence in Early Childhood*, Pelanduk Publications, Selangor, pp. 252–60.

Finch, J. 1986, *Research and Policy: The Uses of Qualitative Research in Social and Educational Research*, Falmer, London.

Freilich, M. 1977, *Marginal Natives: Anthropologist at Work*, Harper & Row, New York.

Fulcher, G. 1989, *Disabling Policies? A Comparative Approach to Education Policy and Disability*, Falmer, London.

Gee, J. P., Hull, G. and Lankshear, C. 1996, *The New Work Order: Behind the Language of the New Capitalism*, Allen & Unwin, Sydney.

Gelf, J. and Palley, M. L. 1987, *Women and Public Policies*, Princeton University Press, Princeton, NJ.

Glaser, B. and Strauss, A. 1967, *The Discovery of Grounded Theory: Strategies for Qualitative Research*, Aldine, Chicago.

Glesne, C. and Peshkin, A. 1992, *Becoming Qualitative Researchers: An Introduction*, Longman, New York.

Green, M. 1995, *Releasing the Imagination: Essays on Education, the Arts and Social Change*, Jossey-Bass, San Francisco.

Guba, E. G. 1984, 'The effect of definitions of policy on the nature and outcomes of policy analysis', *Educational Leadership*, vol. 42, p. 2.

Hammersley, M. and Atkinson, P. 1983, *Ethnography: Principles in Practice*, Tavistock, New York.

Hodder, I. 1994, 'The interpretation of documents and material culture', in N. K. Denzin and Y. S. Lincoln (eds), *Handbook of Qualitative Research*, Sage, Thousand Oaks, CA, pp. 393–402.

Homel, R. 1998, *A Report for the National Campaign Against Violence and Crime and the National Crime Strategy*, Developmental Crime Prevention Consortium, Canberra.

James, A., Jenks, C. and Prout, A. 1998, *Theorising Childhood*, Polity Press, Cambridge, UK.

Kemmis, S. 1990, *Curriculum, Contestation and Change*, Deakin University, Geelong.

Kogon, M. 1985, 'Education policy and values', in I. McNay and J. Ozga, (eds), *Policy Making in Education: The Breakdown of Consensus*, Pergamon, Oxford, pp. 11–24.

Krathwohl, D.R. 1997, *Methods of Educational and Social Science Research*, Longman, New York.

Luke, A., Nakata, M., Singh, M. and Smith, R. 1993, 'Policy and the politics of representation: Torres Strait Islanders and Aborigines at the margins', in B. Lingard, J. Knight and P. Porter (eds), *Schooling Reform in Hard Times*, Falmer, London, pp. 139–52.

Marginson, S. 1993, 'Educational policy development and implementation', in J. Walker (ed.), *Educational Policy Development and Implementation*, Australian Association for Research in Education, Canberra, pp. 15–28.

—— 1997, 'Markets in education: Policy effects and policy research', *VIER Bulletin*, vol. 78, pp. 3–24.

May, T. 1993, *Social Research: Issues, Methods and Process*, Open University Press, Buckingham, UK.

McNay, I. and Ozga, J. 1985, 'Perspectives on policy', in I. McNay and J. Ozga (eds), *Policy-making in Education: The Breakdown of Consensus*, Pergamon, Oxford, pp. 1–7.

Merriam, S. 1988, *Case Study Research in Education: A Qualitative Approach*, Jossey-Bass, San Francisco.

Mostyn, B. 1985, 'Content analysis of qualitative research data: A dynamic approach', in M. Brenner, J. Brown and D. Canter (eds), *The Research Interview: Uses and Approaches*, Academic Press, London, pp. 115–45.

Nakamura, R. and Smallwood, T. 1980, *The Politics of Policy Implementation*, St Martins, New York.

Olesen, V. 1998, 'Feminism and models of qualitative research', in N. Denzin and Y. Lincoln (eds), *The Landscape of Qualitative*

Research: Theories and Issues, Sage, London, pp. 300–32.

Plummer, K. 1983, *Documents of Life: An Introduction to the Problems and Literature of Humanistic Method*, Allen & Unwin, London.

Postlethwaite, T. N. 1991, 'Research and policy making in education: Some possible links', in D. Anderson and B. J. Biddle (eds), *Knowledge for Policy: Improving Education through Research*, Falmer, London, pp. 200–13.

Rist, R.C. 1994, 'Influencing the policy process with qualitative research', in N. K. Denzin and Y. S. Lincoln (eds), *Handbook of Qualitative Research*, Sage, London, pp. 545–58.

Rittenhouse, C. A. 1991, 'The emergence of pre-menstrual syndrome as a social problem', *Social Problems*, vol. 38, pp. 15–25.

Rivlin, A. M. 1987, 'Reflections on 20 years of higher education policy', *Educational Access and Achievement in America*, College Entrance Examination Board, New York.

Rizvi, F. and Kemmis, S. 1987, *Dilemmas of Reform*, Deakin Institute for Studies in Education, Geelong.

Romalis, S. 1985, 'Struggle between providers and recipient: The case of birth practices', in E. Lewin and V. Olesen (eds), *Women, Health and Healing: Toward a New Perspective*, Tavistock, London, pp. 174–200.

Saran, R. 1985, 'The use of archives and interviews in research on educational policy', in R. G. Burgess (ed.), *Strategies of Educational Research*, Falmer, London.

Schratz, M. (ed.), 1993, *Qualitative Voices in Educational Research*, Falmer, London.

Silver, J. 1990, *Education, Change and the Policy Process*, Falmer, London.

Smart, C. 1990, *Feminism and the Power of the Law*, Routledge, London.

—— 1992, 'Regulating womanhood', in C. Smart (ed.), *Regulating Womanhood: Historical Essays on Marriage, Motherhood and Sexuality*, Routledge, London, pp. 1–6.

Sommerville, J. 1982, *The Rise and Fall of Childhood*, Sage, London.

Strauss, A. 1987, *Qualitative Analysis for Social Scientists*, Cambridge University Press, Cambridge.

Strauss, A. and Corbin, J. 1990, *Basics of Qualitative Research*, Sage, London.

Taylor, S. 1997, 'Critical policy analysis: Exploring contexts, texts and consequences', *Discourse*, vol. 18, pp. 23–35.

Taylor, S., Rizvi, F., Lingard, B. and Henry, M. 1997, *Educational Policy and the Politics of Change*, Routledge, London.

Tomasevski, K. 1993, *Women and Human Rights*, Zed Books, London.

Van Krieken, R. 1991, *Children and the State: Social Control and the Formation of Australian Child Welfare*, Allen & Unwin, Sydney.

Wadsworth, Y. 1991, *Do It Yourself Social Research*, Allen & Unwin, Sydney.

Young, I. 1990, *Justice and the Politics of Difference*, Princeton University Press, Princeton, NJ.

CHAPTER 17   DEVELOPING RECIPROCITY

Alldred, P. 1998, 'Ethnography and discourse analysis: Dilemmas in representing the voices of children', in J. Ribbens and R. Edwards (eds), *Feminist Dilemmas in Qualitative Research: Public Knowledge and Private Lives*, Sage, Thousand Oaks, CA, pp. 147–70.

Burman, E. 1992, 'Feminism and discourse in developmental psychology: Power, subjectivity, and interpretation', *Feminism and Psychology*, vol. 2, no. 1, pp. 45–60.

Butler, J. 1990, *Gender Trouble: Feminisms and the Subversion of Identity*, Routledge, New York.

Cook, J.A. and Fonow, M.M. 1990, 'Knowledge and women's interests: issues of epistemology and methodology in feminist sociological research', in J. M. Nielson (ed.), *Feminist Research Methods: Exemplary Readings in the Social Sciences*, Westview Press, San Francisco, pp. 69–93.

Fay, B. 1987, *Critical Social Science*, Cornell University Press, Ithaca, NY.

Fine, M. 1994, 'Dis-stance and other stances: negotiations of power inside feminist research,' in A. Gitlin (ed.), *Power and Method: Political Activism and Educational Research*, Routledge, New York, pp. 13–35.

Gavey, N. 1997, 'Feminist poststructuralism and discourse analysis', in M.M. Gergen and S.N. Davis (eds.), *Toward a New Psychology of Gender: A Reader*, Routledge, New York, pp. 49–64.

Gill, R. 1995, 'Relativism, reflexivity, and politics: interrogating discourse analysis from a feminist perspective', in S. Wilkinson and C. Kitzinger (eds), *Feminism and Discourse: Psychological Perspectives*, Sage, Thousand Oaks, CA, pp. 165–86.

Hicks, D. 1995, 'Discourse, learning, and teaching', *Review of Research in Education*, vol. 21, pp. 49–93.

Holloway, W. 1984, 'Gender difference and the production of subjectivity', in J. Henriques, W. Hollway, C. Urwin, C. Venn and V. Walkerdine (eds), *Changing the Subject: Psychology, Social Regulation, and Subjectivity*, London, pp. 227–63.

Gitlin, A. and Russell, R. 1994, 'Alternative methodologies and the research context', in A. Gitlin (ed.), *Power and Method: Political Activism and Educational Research*, Routledge, New York, pp. 181–202.

Lather, P. 1991, *Getting Smart: Feminist Research and Pedagogy with/in the Postmodern*, Routledge, New York.

—— 1992, 'Critical frames in educational research: Feminist and poststructural perspectives', *Theory into Practice*, vol. 31, no. 2, pp. 87–99.

Luke, A. 1995, 'Text and discourse in education: An introduction to critical discourse analysis', *Review of Research in Education*, vol. 21, pp. 3–48.

Mac Naughton, G. 1998, 'Improving our gender equity "tools": A case for discourse analysis', in N. Yelland (ed.), *Gender in Early Childhood*, Routledge, New York, pp. 149–74.

Nielson, J. M. 1990, 'Introduction', in J. M. Nielson (ed.) *Feminist Research Methods: Exemplary Readings in the Social Sciences*, Westview Press, San Francisco, pp. 1–34.

Ochsner, M. B. 1999, 'Something rad and risqué: A feminist post-structuralist study of gender in an urban kindergarten classroom', unpublished doctoral dissertation, Columbia University Teachers College, New York.

Ribbens, J. and Edwards, R. 1998, *Feminist Dilemmas in Qualitative Research: Public Knowledge and Private Lives*, Sage, Thousand Oaks, CA.

Rich, A. 1980, 'Compulsory heterosexuality and the lesbian existence', *Signs: Journal of Women in Culture and Society*, vol. 5, pp. 631–60.

Roberts, H. 1981, *Doing Feminist Research*, Routledge & Kegan Paul, Boston.

Roman, L. and Apple, M. 1990, 'Is naturalism a move away from positivism? Materialist and feminist approaches to subjectivity in ethnographic research', in E. Eisner and A. Peshkin (eds), *Qualitative Inquiry in Education*, Teachers College Press, New York, pp. 38–73.

Stanley, L. and Wise, S. 1993, *Breaking Out Again: Feminist Ontology and Epistemology* (new edn), Routledge, New York.

Walkerdine, V. 1986, 'Poststructuralist theory and everyday social practices: The family and the school', in S. Wilkinson (ed.), *Feminist Social Psychology: Developing Theory and Practice*, Open University Press, Philadelphia, pp. 57–76.

Wilkinson, S. 1986, *Feminist Social Psychology: Developing Theory and Practice*, Open University Press, Philadelphia.

Wittig, M. 1992, *The Straight Mind*, Beacon, Boston.

Index

Aboriginal communities, research in 139–40
Aboriginal and Torres Strait Islander health research guidelines 70
abstracts, research 29; on databases 16
Achenbach, T. 8
acknowledgments, research 29
action research 8, 59, 139; documenting 213–14; fourth generation 59, 139, 209, 214–15; processes 211–12; see also Gender Equity Research Group (GERG) study
adults, interviewing Chapter 12 (Women Without Children research); analysis/interpretation of findings 187–8; influence of paradigm and research context 188–9; and informed consent 184–6, see also consent; interview guide 179–82, 190–1; and non-exploitation 182–4; pilot interviews 182; and post-interview debriefing 184; research/interview questions 178–81; researcher obligations 184–6; and researcher/participant relationship 183–4; sampling issues 186–7
age groups 84–5
Ainsworth, M.D.S. 5, 7–8
analysis, see data/information analysis; statistical, see statistical analysis

Anderson, G. 156
appendices, research 29
approaches, see methodologies
Atkinson, P. 127, 250
Atweh, B. 139, 140

Ball, S.J. 242, 243, 244, 245
Becker, Howard 197
Bell, S.M. 5, 7–8
Belsky, J. 93
benefits, research 4; see also risk/benefit equation
bias in research, detecting 10, 144–5
Bowe, R. et al 242, 243, 248–9
Boyden, J. 245
Brannen, J. 204
Bronfenbrenner, U. 64
Brooker, E. ix
Buckingham, D. et al 42, 43, 45
Burgess, R. 197
Burman, E. 137
Burns, R. 201
Burton, L. 139, 140
Butler, J. 255

Campbell, D.T. 98
Campbell, S. ix, xvi, Chapter 4, 210
Cannold, L. ix–x, 24

Carr, W. 209, 210
case study research 8; in child interviews
168-76; in children and the media
Chapter 3; data collection 128–31;
designing 126; exemplary 127–8;
nursery evaluation, *see* evaluative
(nursery) case study; observation in
129–31; theory building 127; types of
126–8
causation, concept of 75, 85; criteria 98
Chandler, M.J. 85
child abuse issues 66–7, 68, 163
child-care research, statistical analysis in 4,
Chapter 7; *see also* statistical analysis of
quantitative research
child-centred education, research in 57–62
childhood, characteristics of 162–3
children, interviewing Chapter 11; adult
questioning in 167–8, 177; and age of
child 166; analysis/interpretation of
findings 172, 175–6; and children's
competence 163, 164–5; choice of
research questions 169–70; ethical
guidelines 165–8; reliability and validity
of evidence 168; with researcher as
participant observer (Case Study) 173–6;
and rights of the child 66, 163–4, 166,
176; with teacher as researcher (Case
Study) 168–73; tools, prompts and
probes 166–7
children as research victims 4, 64–5
Children Act, 1989 (UK) 163
children's learning, *see* ethnographic
approach to young children's learning;
classroom-based research
Clarke, P. 151
classroom-based research Chapters 4 and
17; collaborative relationships in 60–2
cluster random sampling 90
Coady, M. M. x, 4
codes/numbers in quantitative research 99
Cohen, L. 166
collaborative research/approaches 60–2,
139, 210–13
competence of children 163, 164–5
computer software for research analysis 94,
159
conclusions, research 5, 13, 28
confidentiality 67–8, 122
Connelly, P. 197, 200
consent, participant 26–7, 65–6, 122, 166,
184–6, 199; and culture difference
69–70; requirements 65
controls, statistical 95
Cook, D.T. 98

Corbin, J. 251
correlation analysis/study 82, 102
critical reflection 212–13
Cronbach, L. 151
cross-sectional design 75, 84–5, 86
Crossley, S.A. 225, 226, 233, 234, 235
cultural assumptions/interpretations 195–8
cultural bias 144–5
cultural differences/issues 5; in ethical
research 69–70; in interviewing children
175
cultural invention, research as 136–8
curriculum, early childhood 13, 14, 23, 57,
59

Dahlberg, G. *et al* 194
Dallape, F. 9
data/information analysis xvi, 13, 27–8,
131, 158–60; computer software for 94,
159; conceptual/theoretical framework
27–8; in quantitative research,
see statistical analysis
data/information collection 13, 23, 26–7,
128–31; databases for literature search
15–16, 17–19; observation in 129–31,
230–2; timing 128
David, T. 164
Davie, R. 164
Davies, B. 46
deception in research 66–7
deductive approach/methodology 12, 13,
19, 23, 53, 54; in quantitative research
97–9
deficit model in research 140–2
definitions of terms 19, 76–7, 264–74
Delamont, S. 127
Denzin, N. 120, 121, 124, 247
design, research xvi–xvii, 13, 23–6, Chapter
6; in child-centred education 58–60;
cross-sectional 75, 84–5, 86; defined
76–7, 138; equity in, *see* equity; error in
28; hypotheses 23, 24, 27, 80;
longitudinal 5, 75, 86–7; options/types,
see experimental research, non-
experimental research, qualitative
research, quantitative research, quasi-
experimental research; place/setting for
88–9; poststructural 58–62; prospective
approach 75, 85–6; retrospective
approach 75, 85, 87; topic and focus
77–9, 91; varying 23–4
direct observation, *see* observation

Early Excellence Centre, UK (EEC) 150
education, early childhood, *see* children's

learning; classroom-based research;
ethnographic approach to young
children's learning
Educational Resources Information
Collection (ERIC) 15, 16, 17
Edwards, Anne x, xvi
Elkind, David 65
Epstein, D. 200
equity in research design xvii, 10, Chapter
9; and cultural invention 136–8; and
deficit model 140–2; and Eurocentric
paradigm 141–2; and homogeneity/
essentialism 142–3; the meaning of
138–9; non-exploitation 182–4; and
power relations 139–40, 177; see also
Gender Equity Research Group
(GERG) study; gender in a preschool
classroom
equity/inequity, gender 144–5, 210, 215;
see also Chapter 14
essentialism 142–4
ethical issues xvi, 4, 9, 10, 26, Chapter 5,
82; applications to ethics committee
70–1; and child abuse 66–7, 68; and
children as victims 64–5; and
confidentiality 67–8, 122; and consent
of participants/parents, see consent; and
culture difference 69–70; and indigenous
groups 70; in interviewing children
165–8; and plain language statements
(PLS) 26, 184–6; and the risk/benefit
equation 65, 68–9; and videotaping
66–7, 68, 70–1
ethics committees 70–1
ethnographic approach to young children's
learning Chapter 13; and cultural
assumptions/interpretations 195–8; and
human action ('behaviours-with-
meaning') 194–5; participant
observation 198–200; quantitative
method 205–6; and reflexivity 202–3;
and reliability 203; and replicability
203; and observations 200–1; and
triangulation 203, 204; and validity
203, 204
ethnography 151–2; features of 194–5
ethologists, method of 229, 234
evaluative (nursery) case study Chapter 10;
analysis/interpretation of findings
158–60; interviews and questionnaires
151–5, 157–8; parent involvement 150,
152–3, 154, 157; research questions
149–51; sampling issues 155–8
experimental research design 75, 79–80,
81, 84; with animals 81; variables 81

Farrell, A. x, 4
femininity/masculinity, constructs of 4, 138,
255, 256
feminism/feminist research 56, 59, 123,
139, 182–3, 188; in gender equity
Chapter 14; in social construction of
gender in an urban preschool classroom
Chapter 17
feminist criminological theory 244
Fetterman, D. 195, 201, 205
first-time research Chapter 4; in child-
centred education 57–62; finding a focus
56–7; and poststructuralism 56–8
Flake, C. 6
Flin, R. 164
Foucault, M. 57, 61

Garfinkle, H. 195, 196
Gee, J.P. et al 242–3, 248–9
Geertz, C. 120, 195
gender: 'myths' 215; norms 4, 255
Gender Equity Research Group (GERG)
study Chapter 14; action research
processes 211–12; critical reflection in
212–13; development of 210–12;
documentation tools 213–14; feminist
poststructural theory in 208, 210, 215,
216, 217–18, 219, 220; and fourth
generation action research 209, 214–15;
group members 210–13, 215, 216,
220; maintaining integrity 212–13;
'minimal requirements' 209–10;
organisation/ analysis of findings 215,
216–21; paradigm and research
context, influence of 221–2; research
questions 208–9, 214, 219; sampling
issues 215; validity in interpreting data
217–18
gender equity/inequity 56–7, 144–5, 210,
215; see also Chapter 14
gender in a preschool classroom, social
construction of (study) Chapter 17;
findings and analysis/interpretation
259–60; and heterosexuality 255–6,
259–60; paradigm and research context,
influence of 260–1; participant
observation 256; and researcher–
researched reciprocity 254, 256–9
gendered relations of power 56–7
generalisation 24–5, 127
generality and validity 97
Genishi, C. 58–9
Gerson, K. 188
Glaser, R. 249
Glazer, B. 201

governments and social issues, *see* policy research
Green, A. 202
Green, M. 241
Gregg, R. 188
Grieshaber, S. x, xvi, 4, 5, 123
Gudgeon, E. 200

Hammersley, M. 194, 206, 250
Harrison, L. x–xi, xvi, 4–5
Hatch, J.A. 137, 143
Hayes, A. xi, xvi
Head Start programmes 140–1
Hengst, H. 37, 38, 39
heterosexuality in a preschool classroom Chapter 17
homogeneity 142–3
Huberman, A. 158, 203
Hughes, F. xi, xvi
hypotheses 23, 24, 27, 80

indigenous groups xvii, 70
inductive research approach/methodology 12–13, 19, 24, 53, 54
infant crying, response to 5, 7–8
infants, at-risk 5
inference and deduction 97–9
inferential analysis 109–11
interpretivism 32, 35–9, 54; and knowledge 35–6, 45, 58; methodology 36; in research on children and media (Case Study) 37–9, 51; and validity 36
interviews 131, 151–5, 157–8; with adults, *see* adults, interviewing; with children, *see* children, interviewing; five-point model 154–5; parent involvement 150, 152–3, 154, 157; prompts and probes 152, 153–4, 158, 166–7; structured/unstructured 151–2

James, A. 194, 203
justice, *see* equity

Kemmis, S. 209, 210
Kenway, J. 46, 218
Kessen, W. 136–7
key terms, definitions of 19, 76–7, 264–74
Kuhn, T.S. 32
Kulberg, J.M. 144–5

languages/linguistics 41–2; poststructuralism and 46–7, 54
Lather, P. 121, 125, 139, 140, 217, 256
Lewis, A. 166–7
Lincoln, Y. 120, 121, 124, 247

Lindholm, K.J. 141
literature research/review 13, 15–19; databases for 15–16, 17–19; learning from 22; and summarising 21–2; extent of 19; strategies 16–17
logistic regression 110, 111
longitudinal research 5, 75, 86–7
Lubeck, S. 142
Luke, A. *et al* 249

Mac Naughton, G. xi, 59, 60, 120, 125, 215, 217
McNay, I. 243
Manion, L. 166
Marginson, S. 242, 246
masculinity/femininity, constructs of 4, 138, 255, 256
May, T. 158
Mayall, B. *et al* 137, 139, 140
measurement in quantitative research 99–111, *see also* statistical analysis; interval and ratio measures 99, 100; nominal measures and numbers/codes 99; ordinal measures 99, 100; types 101
media, children and the (Case Studies), using major paradigms Chapter 3
Merriam, S. 251
methodologies, research xvii, 12–13, 32; *see also* deductive research; inductive research, interpretivism, positivism, poststructuralism, structuralism
metric/non-metric scales/measures 99, 101
Miles, M. 158, 203
mothers of young children 4; *see also* infant crying, women in prison (policy research)
multiple regression 109

National Health and Medical Research Council 70
Nicolson, S. 228
non-experimental research design 75, 79–80, 82–3; correlational study 82–3
Nuremberg Code 65

Oakley, A. 137–8, 143
Obiakor, F.E. 141
objectivity in quantitative research 94–5
observation 129–31
observation, direct (studies with preschool children) Chapter 15; behaviour categories for research questions 234–5; ethologists' methods 229, 234; findings and analysis 236–7; high quality data, achieving 230–2; observer,

characteristics of 231; paradigm and research context, influence of 237; play environment/context 225–6; reliability rating 233; research questions 225–6, 234–5; sampling issues 233–6; setting/context for 235–6; Strange Situation method 235; techniques of 224–5, 227–9; topic areas using 230; training for 231–2; videotape records 232, 237
observation, participant 198–200, 207
Ochs, E. 196, 200
Ochsner, M.B. xi–xii, 4
Ozga, J. 243

Padilla, A. 141
paradigms 3, Chapter 3; defined 31–2; Eurocentric 141–2; as frames 31–2; links with methods and results 51–2; major 32–52, see also interpretivism, positivism, poststructuralism; structuralism
parent questionnaires/interviews 152–4; see also adults, interviewing
Parten, M.B. 229
participants, research 4, 5; in action research 8, 59, 139; adult, see adults, interviewing; children as, see children, interviewing; consent of 26–7, 65–6, 122, 166, 184–6, 199; and deception 66–7; and ethical considerations 26, Chapter 5; and homogeneity 142–3; numbers of 89; observation of 198–200, 207; selecting 24–5, 89–90, see also sampling
Penn, H. 203–4
Piaget, J. 5, 202, 206
Pinnell, G.S. 204
place/setting, importance of 88–9
plain language statements (PLS) 26, 184–6
play and social behaviour of preschool children (observational studies) Chapter 15
Plummer, K. 249
policy research (Prison Study) 4, Chapter 16; data management strategy 249–50; and early childhood 245; findings 248–50; forms of 246; interviews with key policy players 250–1; methods 247–8; paradigm and research context, influence of 251–2; participant observations 251; policy contexts 244–5; policy defined 241–3; policy document analysis 248–50; process 247; rationale for 246–7; research questions 240–1, 247; sampling issues 248;

theoretical approaches 244
positivism 12, 32–5, 36, 54, 76; and knowledge 32–3, 45, 58; methodology of 33; in research on children and media (Case Study) 33–5, 51; and validity 33, 42
postmodernism 12–13, 45, 46, 58; see also poststructuralism
poststructuralism 32, 45–51, 54; in child-centred education Chapter 4; feminist Chapter 14, 244, Chapter 17; and knowledge 45–6; and languages 46–7, 54; methodology of 47–8; in research on children and media (Case Study) 48–51, 52; and validity 48
power relations 139–40, 177; see also researcher, position of
preschool children: play and social behaviour research Chapter 15; study in social construction of gender Chapter 17
presentation style of research 29
principles of research 9–11
process, research 3, Chapter 2; data analysis xvi, 13, 28–9; data collection 26–7; topic choice 13–15; and writing reports 28–9
prompts and probes in interviewing 152, 153–4, 158, 166–7
prospective research 75, 85–6
Prout, A. 194, 203

qualitative research xvi, 4, 52, 53, 54, 58, Chapter 8; and case studies 126–31; common features in 134; data analysis 27, 131–3; data collection 128–31; design 24, 83, 84, 118; equity in 138; feasibility of 122; history of 119–21; key issues 122–8; modernist phase 119–20, 124; rationale for/purposes of 120–1; and reflexivity 122–4; triangulation in 125–6; validity in 124–6
quantitative research xvi, 4–5, 52–3, 54, 58, 205–6; assumptions of 94–7; characteristics 94; in child-care studies Chapter 7; in design 24, 83, 84; detecting bias in 144–5; equity in 138; and ethics committee applications 71; and statistical analysis, see statistical analysis; strengths and weaknesses 113
quasi-experimental research design 75, 82
questionnaires xvii, 26; five-point model 154–5; parent 152–4
questions, interview: closed/open-ended 179–80; follow-up 180–1
questions, research 13–14, 18, 19, 23–6, 28, 91, 97–8, 118, 169–70, 173, 178–9,

208–9; choice of 149–51;
refining/changing the 20–1
Quina, K. 144–5

racist perspective, anti- 139
random sampling 75, 89–90; cluster 90
rating scales 26, 228
reciprocity of researcher and researched
253, 256–9
reductionism 95–6
references, research 29
reflexivity, self- 144, 145
reflexivity/reflexive research 122–4, 202–3;
and detecting bias 144–5; and the
researcher's position 123–4, 139, 140
reliability 24; of children's interview
evidence 168; in direct observation 233;
in ethnographic research 203; in
quantitative research 96; see also
validity
report, research 13
research: action, see action research; case
study, see case study research; as a
cultural invention 136–8; design, see
design; equity in, see equity; for the first
time, see first-time research; good/bad 9;
learning to do 6–7, 8; principles 9–11;
problems/error 27–8; process, see
process; scepticism in 7–8; surprises 8–9,
28; as a tool Chapter 1; questions, see
questions: wrong 5–6
researcher, position of the 123–4, 139–40,
183–4; and reciprocity 254, 256–9
retrospective research 75, 85, 87
Rich, A. 255
rights, children's 66, 163–4
risk/benefit equation 64–65, 68–9
Robson, C. 154–5
Rolfe, S.A. xii, 226, 229, 233, 234, 235
Ryan, S. xii, xvi, Chapter 4, 210
Ryle, G. 195

Sameroff, A. 85
sampling: for adult interviews 186–7; for
child interviews 170, 173–4; non-
probability 156; probability 155–6;
random 75, 90, 155–6, 157; response
rate 156–7; strategies 24–5, 75, 88–9,
155–6, 215; time and event 228–9
sampling populations 24–6; generalising
from 24–5; size of 156, 157
Saran, R. 248
Schieffelin, B. 196, 200
Sharp, R. 202
Shipstead, S.G. 228

Siraj–Blatchford, Iram xii, 151, 205
Siraj–Blatchford, John xii–xiii
Smithmier, A. 139
social behaviour of preschool children
Chapter 15 and 17
social issues/social justice 4, 14, 56–7
Spencer, J. 164
Stake, R. 127
statistical analysis xvi; controls in 95;
software for 94, 159
statistical analysis in quantitative research
27, 100–11; analysis of variance
(ANOVA) 108; logistic regression 110,
111; multiple regression 110; non-
parametric 101, 104–5, 108–9;
parametric 101–4, 108;
techniques/methods 101–9
Statistical Package for the Social Sciences
(SPSS) software 94, 159
Stewart, I. 139
Strauss, A. 201, 249, 250, 251
structuralism 32, 39–45, 54; defined 40–1;
and knowledge 39–41, 45; and
linguistics/languages 41, 47;
methodology 41–2; in research on
children and media (Case Study) 42–5,
51–2; and validity 42
style, presentation 29
surveys, see interviews/interviewing;
questionnaires
Sydney Family Development Project 5
Sylva, K. 206
Szarkjowicz, D.L. 33, 34, 35

Taylor, S. 246
time dimension xvi, 75; and age groups
84–5; in cross-sectional design 84–5, 86;
in longitudinal research 86–7; in
prospective research 85–6; in
retrospective research 85, 87; variables
84–5
title, research 29
topic, choice of 13–15, 20, 77–9, 91
triangulation 13, 36, 151, 159–60, 199,
203, 204–5, 217; main types of
125–6

UK Effective Provision of Pre-School
Education project 194
United National Convention on the Rights
of the Child 66, 164
Utley, C.A. 141

vaccination choices 69–70
validity 24; ethnographic research 203, 204;

external 97; internal 96; interpretivist 36–9; positivist 133–5; poststructuralist 48–51, 217–18; in qualititative research 124–6; structuralist 42–5
variability, sample 97
variables: control 95; dependent 99, 105–9; design 81, 82, 83, 85; independent 99, 101–5, 106–7; relevant 99, 103; in selection of participants 89, *see also* sampling; statistical measurement of 99–109
victims, children as 64–5
videotaping/audiotaping 59–60, 70–1, 213, 218, 232, 250; and child abuse 66–7, 8

Wadsworth, Y. 6, 18, 249

Walkerdine, V. 200
Waterhouse, S. 202
Weber, E. 137
Weedon, C. 293
Wiersma, W. 27
Williams, S. 139
Willis, S. 46, 218
Wittig, M. 255
women xvii; (with children) in prison, *see* policy research; Women Without Children (research) Chapter 12
Woods, P. 206

Young, I.M. 243–4

Zanker, R. 48, 49–50, 51